D1625805

This book is to be returned on or before
the last date stamped below

LITERARY DETECTION

Literary Detection

How to prove authorship and fraud in literature and documents

DISCARDED
NATIONAL POLICE LIBRARY

A. Q. MORTON, F.R.S.E.

Bowker

Asset No

20165826

NATIONAL POLICE LIBRARY

53 874
3/Q

0009596

Copyright © 1978 Andrew Queen Morton
ISBN 0-85935-062-2

All rights reserved. No part of this publication may be reproduced or transmitted in any form or by any means, electronic or mechanical, including photocopying, recording, xerography, or any information storage and retrieval system, without permission in writing from the publisher.

Published in the United Kingdom by the Bowker Publishing Company and in the United States of America by Charles Scribner's Sons.

Typeset by Preface Ltd., Salisbury, Wilts.

Printed in Great Britain by The Pitman Press, Bath

First impression 1978.

Contents

List of Tables

List of Figures

Preface

Anyone engaged in original research is keenly aware of how much he owes to his colleagues for their advice, suggestions, opposition, corrections and assistance. I hope that all my friends who have helped me, Sir Kenneth Dover, Neil Hamilton-Smith, Sidney Michaelson, James Macleman and James Morton know how much I appreciate what they have done.

But there can be no doubt about who has done most, Dr W. C. Wake. He was first to succeed in this subject and only those who have followed him can know how much he did and, as he did most of it before computers came to assist, how difficult it was to do it. All that one need wish for W. C. Wake is that he receives the credit which is his due.

A. Q. Morton,
Culross,
Scotland

Section I

The Theory of Stylometry

1 The Problems of Identification and Recognition

Some years ago the author was sitting in a coffee shop in the city of Glasgow. Diagonally across the room sat two old ladies, one of whom subjected him to a continuous and critical examination. As they rose and made to leave she came over to him and asked if his name was Morton and had his father been Alexander Morton of Tollcross? It is and he had. 'Then', she said, 'you will be Andrew Morton. I last saw you forty years ago in your baby carriage.' This woman had left Scotland for Canada, spent thirty-seven years there and returned for a holiday.

Some people find that story incredible; some can believe it. In either case it illustrates the mystery of recognition. If you can accept the story, it shows that for all the changes that come with growth, maturity and experience, something identifiable remains unaltered. One simple explanation for her recognition might be that I then looked much as my father had done forty years before when she had last seen him. This might be true, but I look in some ways more like my mother than my father and if it was some general characteristic of the family that she was recalling, what could it have been? Our family have no proud proboscis to pass down the generations.

We all recognise people in the literal meaning of the word; we recognise them; we know them again. To do so we must have information stored ready for use in such comparisons, and fresh information with which to compare it. We do recognise people when we meet them after an interval of many years. Their appearance is often vastly changed but underneath the ravages of time something remains and we say, 'Yes, it is so-and-so'. We have recognised them.

On the other hand if you found the story incredible, then it will illustrate for you another aspect of this fascinating question of recognition. This woman had some information in her memory and something about me stirred that information and matched her recollection. She may have been quite wrong and may have made a hobby of going around asking everyone she met if they were Andrew Morton and by chance alone, in his native city, struck lucky. If this had been the case, it shows that she had some information stored before the identification was attempted. She remembered an individual who was male and about forty years old.

The difficulties in this act and process of recognition has been shown rather more dramatically in Britain in 1976 by a criminal case in which Peter Hain, a public and political figure, was charged with going into a

3

bank, picking up £500 from the counter and running off with it. The conflict of evidence on identification was complete. Some witnesses swore that he was the robber and others that he was not. All had seen much the same thing but used it to make quite different decisions. How difficult this can be, and how unreliable visual identifications often are, was shown by BBC Television who staged a robbery for the purpose. The BBC hired a coach and took a party of ladies to a mansion house telling them that they would be there to supply background for a film. After a relaxing lunch when the ladies were getting ready to hear their instructions, an actor rushed towards them carrying a rolled up painting in his hand and followed by cries of 'Stop thief!' As he approached the group he appeared to panic, turned back, grappled with a colleague, ran across in front of the group and then jumped a wall and made his escape. A few days later the ladies were asked to appear at a simulated police identity parade to pick out the man whom they had seen under quite favourable conditions. The results were revealing. Almost every man in the line up was positively identified by someone as the man they had seen. It was stated emphatically that the accused was not present and equally emphatically that he was. The most sceptical criticism of identity parades was completely justified. Innocent people were positively identified by witnesses whose good faith could not be questioned and who had seen the alleged criminal under favourable conditions.

But this experiment, if it did show how vulnerable the casual witness can be, was less than fair. It neglects the fact that we can all correctly identify a person of whom we know a great deal, given very little information indeed. We might only catch a glimpse of them on a dark and rainy night but we know at once and quite certainly whom we have seen. It is this power to reconstruct a character from a few scraps of information which enables the impersonator to entertain us. He appears in his own character and then by putting on a hat, sticking a pipe or cigarette in his mouth, repeating a few key phrases in a familiar tone of voice and affecting a few striking mannerisms, he becomes the celebrity being imitated. The good impersonator tries to provide some information for every aspect of the character, movements and gestures, tones of voice and habits of speech, mental attitudes and social idiosyncrasies. He supplies the eye, the ear and the mind with familiar information. The audience, who know the personality being imitated, recognise the subject at once. But a visitor from another place or another planet with no knowledge of the prototype, would find no point in the performance. He has nothing with which to compare the impersonation. The reality of an impersonation is created by appealing in the simplest way to the stored information we have all acquired about public figures.

Yet we never accept an imitation as being the real thing. At one time Sir Harold Wilson had a very good impersonator. This man was given a script of one of Wilson's speeches and invited to read it to the accompaniment of a film of Wilson making the speech. When he was quite ready he read the speech in the manner of Wilson, using the film as a guide. When the recording of his reading was played back to a test audience, not one of them thought it was Sir Harold Wilson who was speaking. The imitator could remind everyone of Sir Harold but he could not convince anyone that he was Sir Harold.

It is clear that any act of recognition involves the comparison of fresh information with information already stored, but the mechanism is little understood and the procedure full of uncertainties. Identification in many respects is still in the position that many descriptive sciences were in before methods were developed which provided them with a firm foundation. If you argue that identification is an unscientific mess, then some evidence can be produced, fingerprints for example, which suggest that this is not so. If you argue that it is a proper scientific discipline, evidence of serious miscarriages of justice brought about by mistaken identity can confound the claim.

Identification is accomplished at the moment in many fields by a combination of instinct, experience and trained observation, the complexity of which is only revealed by patient investigation. In face of this complexity many investigations founder. If they had started from the first principle that recognition is achieved by the comparison of fresh information with stored information, a parallel system in which scientific precision of definition is applied to descriptive information and comparisons would have provided a simpler and more reliable procedure.

The great difficulty which confronts anyone who wants to introduce a scientific system of identification is not in devising a descriptive classification, but in persuading those who will have to use it that any such system can be more reliable than their native intelligence and experience. History affords a number of instances in which scientific systems were strongly resisted and some cases in which the man who first brought a system into use fought against its replacement by an obviously superior one.

The best known instances of these problems comes from the Paris police of the nineteenth century. The great Vidocq had founded their record office and had begun the systematic classification of criminals. Each one was photographed and his description recorded. Unfortunately only striking features were noted, scars, tattoos and birthmarks; height was taken simply as tall, medium or small. After a few years the records were extensive – over 80,000 photographs – but useless. Each record was filed under the name of the criminal. Since they were unsporting enough to resort to aliases, no record of these could be used until all the records of the same man had been identified and brought together. This was the state of affairs in 1879 when the department took on a clerk whose past performances – expulsion from schools and failure as a bank clerk – promised little. The only notable fact about Alphonse Bertillon, was that his father was vice-president of the Anthropological Society of Paris.

Bertillon quickly saw that the system was hopeless. He asked permission to measure some physical dimensions of the criminals as they were registered. He took their height, the length and circumference of their heads, the length of their arms, fingers and feet. He submitted a report suggesting that his system might be useful in identification, and when it was ignored he put in a second. In this he claimed that each measurement had a resolving power of four; it would pick out one person among four. Thus ten measurements would pick one person out of one million, twelve measurements one person among sixteen million. The result of the second submission was a stern warning to confine himself to the duties proper to his station as a clerk. But a new prefect turned to him in despair and gave him three months in which to identify one recidivist among the existing files. With only eight days left, he did so. This led to the adoption of his system and the great triumph followed when, in 1892, Bertillon could show that the bomber who attempted to kill the President-Judge and later the State Prosecutor was not a political idealist but a habitual criminal already wanted for more than one brutal murder.

But Bertillon's career ended under a cloud. In 1857 Sir William Herschel had advocated the use of fingerprints in identification, but their use was not practical until a system of classification of the prints had been devised by Sir Francis Galton and modified by Edward Henry, Inspector of the Bengal Police. This system was adopted throughout India in 1897 and by Scotland Yard in 1901. In 1905 fingerprints were admitted as evidence for the first time by a British court. Just as fingerprints were coming into use the Bertillon system was being challenged. In 1903 the United States had produced two convicts from the prison in Leavenworth, Kansas, with identical Bertillon measurements. Not unnaturally they looked alike, but they also used the same name of Will West. This prompted an investigation which showed that however efficient the Bertillon system might be in theory, the actual taking of measurements by clerks in police stations left much to be desired and the margin of error was too great for a reliable routine system. Fingerprints were simpler and better.

This advance Bertillon could not bring himself to accept. He argued with power and passion against fingerprints, bringing out all the common sense objections to their use. How can one argue for an identity in the patterns on the ends of a baby's fingers with those on the gnarled hands of an aged man? How can skin burnt off in an accident reform itself as if equipped with a permanent and infallible memory? How can a trade or profession not alter the shape of hands, fingers and skin?

The feud was resolved by the theft in 1911 of the Mona Lisa from the Louvre Museum. It was recovered two years later in Italy from a thief who had left clear fingerprints on the glass case, and who had a record in

Paris which actually included his fingerprints but only as special marks under the Bertillon system. If the Paris police had used the new system, the crime must have been solved in a few days and not two years. It was the end for Bertillon and his system. When he died in 1914 his place in history was secure but his personal feelings were of failure.

This episode has not just intrinsic interest; it encapsulates the evolution of all systems of identification. They arise only from a pressing need which exposes the inadequacy of common sense conventions. They depend on the creation of a store of information which is simply classified and is suitable for comparisons. Each system has a resolving power which must be enough to enable a unique identification to be made from among the possible candidates. And, as it lies not in the powers of men to be perfect, it must have limitations which are understood to enable precautions to be taken against misleading results.

The main subject of this book is one special aspect of identification, the determination of the authorship of texts. Since the development of photography it has been a simple matter to determine who wrote or who typed out a text. It is even possible to demonstrate which instrument was used in the writing or typing. But such physical comparisons do not indicate who composed the text or altered it from its original form. To enable this to be done a descriptive science known as stylometry is needed. Stylometry is the science which describes and measures the personal elements in literary or extempore utterances, so that it can be said that one particular person is responsible for the composition rather than any other person who might have been speaking or writing at that time on the same subject for similar reasons. Stylometry deals not with the meaning of what is said or written but how it is being said or written. Stylometry does not deal with the evidential value of statements. It does not asked whether this or that particular statement is true or reasonable, but applies itself to the question, 'In whose words are these sentiments expressed?'

When the aim of stylometry and the range of its subject matter are set down as simply and in such a summary form, a reader might be forgiven for assuming that it must be an arcane subject concerned with a few matters of specialist interest. This is far from being true. Disputed authorship to the general reader will seem to concern a few celebrated legal quarrels or a few instances of forgery, real or alleged, such as the attempt to influence an English general election with the spurious Zinoviev letter, or how far the Casket Letters of Mary Queen of Scots might implicate her in a conspiracy. What he will find it difficult to accept is that in this subject the condition which he assumes to be the exception is the rule and the rule is the exception.

To show how far this statement is true it is convenient to look at the

problem of authorship in two forms, forms which correspond to the
ancient and modern methods of book production. In the ancient world
books were written and reproduced by hand, the rights of authors were
minimal and the money earned by publication and distribution largely
stayed with the copyists and booksellers. The author's asset was the
power and influence of his name, his 'authority', the prestige which
derived from the fact that he was the person who expressed such-and-
such opinions.

As a result, taking ancient Greece as an example, the names of authors
were used with a freedom which seems to us, used as we are to a more
commercial convention, not just irresponsible but criminally deceptive.
Anyone who wanted attention for his views, views which would remain
unread under his own name, would borrow any illustrious name which
would serve to get him read. Alternatively, anyone who wanted to say
something but at the same time escape responsibility for having said it,
would borrow a name suited to his purpose.

So general was this practice that the son of the famous orator Isocrates
complains that after his father's death the booksellers of Athens are using
his father's name to clear off their laggard stocks by sticking it on almost
anything. The special interest of this complaint is that not only was the
son not sure what his father had written, he was quite wrong about one
group of orations. Isocrates had started humbly and written some
speeches for people to use in the law courts. When he became famous he
found it politic to disown them and his son loyally accepted his father's
denial of authorship.

The Isocrates case illustrates another complication of authorship. He
wrote speeches for other people to use. His did his best to stand in the
shoes and circumstances of his clients and no matter how much better his
arguments were than any they could advance, the speech would have
failed if it had appeared to the jury anything but the plea of the accused.
The speech became the property of the man who had paid for it and he
could treat it as he liked.

Another reason why the authorship of ancient texts is anything but
clear is one that has not yet passed from the western world. It is the habit
of issuing from a school in the name of the titular head the work done
under his supervision or control. Hippocrates, the great physician, was
the head of a medical school which began by issuing his own works, went
on to put out some in which he had collaborated, then some produced by
his followers and finally, after his death, those compiled by the school he
had founded.

Yet further complications arise from the method of teaching pupils to
write. The usual Greek practice was to ask them to write a piece in the
manner of some respected author. Such a school exercise is unlikely to
confuse a contemporary, but when a scholar comes across it a millenium
later it is not so easy to detect the imposture, especially as the masters

who taught the principles of writing had a knowledge of and a feeling for Greek that no modern scholar can hope to have. In addition the very principles they sought to inculcate were based upon the study of the features of composition which were noticed by and appealed to the critics, the very features used by them to discriminate between authors. Success for a student was to turn out a piece which his instructor could not distinguish from the exemplar. This habit of education by imitation was until recently part of the curriculum of the older universities in Britain and its consequences are still with us. When critics read the features which they associate with a particular author they decide that they are reading his composition. Nothing will persuade such a critic that he is being deceived, least of all deceived by someone trained exactly as he was to supply the kind of information which critics have come to associate with identity.

The last two complications of authorship in Greek texts are most simply dealt with by referring to the motives which inspire them. In the Hellenistic period it was fashionable to have a library, and the newly rich bought a library ready stocked. The complete sets of works needed for this purpose were rarely lacking and many forgeries date from that period and were created for this purpose. Similarly an interest in antiquity and in famous people led to demands for texts written by the illustrious sons of prospering cities. Where the demand for antiquities exists, the supply is never far behind.

A parallel industry was devoted to keeping the memory of a beloved master fresh by adjusting his works to the changing times. One of the most striking examples of this can be found in the works of the Apostle Paul. After Paul had been dead for some years the Gnostic heresy began to trouble the church. Paul had never written against this and so a third letter to the Corinthians was written in his name to provide just such ammunition. The writer of the spurious letter later confessed his forgery and repented of his imposition, but the letter was so useful that one party in the church refused to accept the denial and argued that the letter was authentic.

A reference to Paul might reasonably introduce the last item in this summary catalogue, for many productions attributed to famous people are due to no more sinister reason than the incurable optimism of the human race. Just as the picture in the potting shed must be an Old Master, so the letter in the church cupboard must be Paul's until proved otherwise.

The result of these practices, and others literally too numerous to mention here, is that the authorship of any ancient text must be subjected to a critical study and accepted only after such an examination. There is no corpus exempt from this examination, nor any author too elevated, nor any text too sacred. Nothing can be asserted about one text by taking an uncritical extract from another. Everything must be looked at.

Even when this is done problems yet remain. When Thucydides tells what an Athenian commander said to his troops, was he present and recording a summary of what was said, or is he composing what he felt would have been appropriate for such a man to say at such a time? When the book of the Acts of the Apostles tells what Paul said or Peter said, do the speeches contain anything of Paul or of Peter or are they both what the anonymous writer of the book thought they might well have said? Or should have said? It is not just the authorship of text which is at stake; it is the integrity of texts. This is a most difficult subject in the ancient world where it was customary to lift from any author a passage which better suited your argument than one you could compose yourself. A splendid example of this is to be seen in the Jewish historian Josephus, writing in the first century AD. He is not good at battles and when he comes to one (he is writing a history of the Jewish war around AD 65–70) he cribs the scene from Thucydides who was good at battles.

It is little to be wondered at that Greek and Latin were so long the foundations of education. Not only had one to read literature but one had to question it at every turn. There can have been few more intensive courses in human behaviour, and in the construing of motives, than regular reading of the Classics provided. Nor is it coincidental that with the decline of classical studies the intelligent detective story has been replaced by the 'realistic' gum-shoe style, nor that leaders have been able to keep their subjects in a state where fact and fiction are inseparable, where lies are a political commonplace and the routine product of the speech writer taken to come from the character who reads it in public.

It may seem that to turn from the uncertainties of the ancient past to modern times, from hand-written documents to printing, from imposition to copyright, is to come out into the open air from the darkness and rankness of a tunnel. The comparison may well be valid. The dubieties of one kind have gone. But it is only too true that those of another order have arrived. In the beginning the printer took his text where he could find it and remained subject to all the temptations of his predecessor the bookseller.

It took a long time for authorship to become a profession, trade or vocation. To read Boswell's life of Johnson is to discover how the bookseller employed the writer either by commissioning a work or offering him a fee for what he had already written.

One important difference between the common law of England and of Rome was that, while in Rome anything written on a piece of paper belonged to the owner of the paper, in England the copyright of unpublished works, including letters, belonged to the person who had written them. Thus the rights of authors were potentially secure but it took a long time for them to acquire any value. In the first centuries of the existence of the printed book, the money accrued to the printer-book-seller. He could receive a Royal Warrant, a most valuable property if it covered bibles or prayer books, or he could join with his colleagues in a stationers' company. The Stationers' Company of London incorporated in 1557 protected the rights of its members to print particular books by imposing sanctions and fines upon offenders. The Company gave no protection to authors. It was a company of publishers concerned with their rights and privileges.

In 1709 the first act of Parliament gave English authors the sole right to publish their works for a term of fourteen years, a term which could be renewed for another fourteen years if the author were alive to claim it. But the rights of authors were slow to acquire any monetary value. Milton got £5 for *Paradise Lost*, Goldsmith got a few guineas for *The Vicar of Wakefield*. The only way to make money by writing was either to become a Grub Street hack filling whatever space a bookseller wanted to have filled or, and this was where the rich rewards lay, to put your pen at the service of a political party. It is instructive to see how Johnson reacted to the offer of a handsome government pension for his services to literature and to learning. It was only when he was fully assured that he would not be obliged to put himself at the service of the party that he accepted the pension with suitable expressions of gratitude. But if Johnson was reassured on the point, his enemies were not and accused him of having sold his pen for a pension.

It is the mid-nineteenth century before anything like the modern best-seller appears. The steam presses now poured out books, magazines and all kinds of periodicals. As soon as a feature took the popular fancy there was an instant and clamant desire for more. In the beginning the serial stories had been written to order by any person delegated to write that month's, or week's, or day's ration. But quality began to be valued and so one author would be responsible for a series and he would not be readily imitated. Charles Dickens was the first really popular novelist and journalist and all his life he had to fight with imitations of his works in Britain and pirated editions produced in the U.S.A. After Dickens we find Conan Doyle, who came to regret the wild success of his creation, Sherlock Holmes, a creation which made a fortune not just for Doyle but for his publisher.

In the twentieth century it might seem that all uncertainty has gone, that copyright is almost universal and the flow of royalties is only impeded in the socialist countries of the Russian bloc. This is completely deceptive. It is true that the legal position of an author is much improved and his rights are generally secure, though sometimes prohibitively expensive to assert. But new problems have arisen. A best-seller may now take a million pounds to launch; it has to be marketed and sold as a film before a copy is placed in the hands of a reader. This means that a script has often to be altered either to include material thought to be essential for a successful sale, or truncated to suit the limits of the reader's mind or experience. If these editorial revisions are beyond the powers of the author, the publisher will supply such services and in the end the book as published may be a very different animal from the first draft accepted by the publisher.

Publishers are not specially favoured by providence and so they run the risk of finding themselves with a best-seller in the production line and the author may be inconsiderate enough to die untimely. In such cases there are publishers who will have the book completed and issued and may even perform a modern miracle by producing some works written by an author after his death! These will not be attributed to the editorial assistants but sold as works completed before the demise. A parallel practice is that of launching as later works, the early works of an author which he wrote before producing the success which made the publishing of his work profitable.

Add to these the other complications, that no leader of any nation now reads a speech which he has prepared from his own resources; he reads the product of a team of advisers. It is many years since the author was asked to advise the Russian department of the London School of Economics and Political Science who were then anxious to discover who had written the annual budget review of the Soviet Union rather than accept the suggestion that the man who read it in public had fathered it. It is also now the custom for war leaders to write their memoirs, and for anyone who served under them the reading of the memoirs can be perplexing. It must be concluded either that the leaders had literary gifts which they had been remarkably successful in concealing from their comrades, or that someone else is writing in their name.

The ghost writer is always a problem for the student of history. An example of this was the publication in 1976 of the memoirs of a personal servant of Lady Astor. It seems reasonable to suppose that a personal servant is a good source of personal information. But reviewing the volume in *The Observer* newspaper, the editor, David Astor, pointed out that the family had been shown the manuscript and had offered to provide some editorial assistance to improve it, but that their offer had been refused in favour of a successful ghost writer who took over the script and made a number of alterations intended to make it a more saleable book. He had heightened some things to make them more dramatic, which might seem acceptable, but in doing so he had gone beyond his own knowledge and so imported some errors of fact and interpretation which made the book much less valuable as a source of information than its origin would indicate it to be. What also emerged, and quite incidentally, was that a popular writer credited with some very successful books about 'life below stairs' had not written any of them; all had been produced by this ghost writer.

The introduction of the term 'ghost writer' leads on to one of the more bizarre problems of authorship. Some time ago the author was asked by a branch of the Christian Science Church to authenticate a third volume of the works of Mary Baker Eddy. It was said that this document had been dictated to a medium and its claim to be authentic must be tested. Not all the organisations willing to use such services are otherworldly. The author was asked by a man claiming to represent the American Central Intelligence Agency to prove that two chapters in a recent work of Bertrand Russell had not been written by him but by his secretary. To the question, 'What would happen if Bertrand Russell were to say that though he had not written the chapters he would endorse every word in them?' there was no reply.

The position can be summarised like this. People who read for pleasure can continue to do so without troubling themselves with arguments about authorship, or what is the precise relationship between the name on the spine of the book and the composition of the contents. People will continue to use the twenty-third psalm without caring if it was or was not written by King David or even if the author of it knew about sheep and shepherding. To them the value of the psalm lies in the use they make of it and the associations it has gathered.

But for anyone whose interests go beyond immediate enjoyment, questions of authorship arise. At one level they can be completely satisfied by the publisher's assurance and the name on the title page. It may be that the reader wants to refer to a particular text and the name of the titular author will be entirely adequate for this purpose. But at any deeper level an attribution of authorship can only be acceptable after a critical examination has justified it. How to conduct such an examination is the main subject of this book.

There are circumstances in which to know the author of a text is, literally, of vital importance. In many countries, England, the United States, Canada and Australia among them, many criminal cases are decided on the evidence of confessions recorded by police officers These confessions are often repudiated at the trial, but it must be a matter for concern that half the cases in the crown courts in London are settled on the bitterly contested evidence of two policemen who read out admissions made by the accused which he strenuously denies ever having made. From such cases important issues arise which not only affect the relation of criminal trials to the ideals of justice; there are the practical questions of how much bullying a prisoner can stand before he will agree to anything his captors say just to escape from the relentless pressure, and whether, when he capitulates, he will do so in his own habitual forms of expression or assume those of his tormentors. Another question is how far a police force which achieves as much of its results by confessions likely to pursue other evidence with less thoroughness.

This comes to a head in cases of kidnapping. If a young girl is brutally treated until she comes to accept the mode of life of her captors, will she come to speak, think and write as they do or will she preserve her own identity beneath the veneer of gangsterism? This line of thought can be followed a step further. Some diseases and degenerative conditions affect speech and thought. Would it be possible to diagnose a disorder of the vocabulary before the condition led to the appearance of gross symptoms?

In a celebrated murder trial in the city of Glasgow at the time of World War I, Oscar Slater was wrongly convicted, narrowly escaped being hanged and was pardoned after serving most of a life sentence. The evidence was hopelessly confused by police stupidity, possibly even police corruption. But at the scene of the crime a large, clear, bloody handprint had been left by the assassin. By the time the techniques came into use by which the owner of the handprint could have been positively identified, the evidence had perished. It is the singular feature of literary detection that, on the whole, the evidence is still with us. The next few years will see the resolution of countless dilemmas, the unravelling of age-old mysteries. Many uncritical assumptions will finally be exploded, many impostures exposed. The various kinds of deception which may have passed as genuine, even the loving distortions of discipleship by which one writer has sought to keep the work of another relevant to the changed circumstances of a later generation, will find the going much harder.

To read in the scientific literature of the nineteenth century is to breathe the air of excitement and discovery which led men to think that the application of their discoveries would transform society. It was the time when the word 'research' did not cover the consulting of a list of books in the school library to complete a ten-page typescript which would be called a thesis, a time when the benefits of science did not mean that faster and cheaper mass murder was available to an ever enlarging circle of nations. This air of excitement and discovery, now conspicuously absent from professional science, yet surrounds this branch of science. The useful applications and extensions of knowledge range from the oldest and best known works of literature, the poems of Homer, to criminal trials now in progress.

The simple optimism of the nineteenth century scientist is appropriate to this subject. It cannot kill or maim; it cannot pollute an atmosphere or lay waste a countryside. It can only bring truth from where it has been hidden and reveal human behaviour for what it was. The banker should be honest and the auditor either certifies that he has been or starts the investigations that lead to his removal. So the writer, the historian and the policeman deserve to be rewarded when they are true to their art or craft, and exposed when they are not.

Techniques which enable this to be done are always useful. No doubt the days will come when professional practitioners of this science will disagree for suitably large fees. No doubt, in some instances, the financial consequences of the dispute will be so great that it will once again be shown that experts can be offered irresistible temptations. But at the moment everyone who studies and practises this science does so only to expand knowledge. Let us take care to keep it so.

People study words for different reasons and this is reflected in the different techniques used in the studies. Each different approach is valid within its own discipline but each must resist the temptation to inform the practitioners of other disciplines that there is but one true prophet. In this book words are looked at in a new way. What we seek is the reply to a new and narrow type of question. Is this an occurrence of word A? Does it occur in position P? Is it followed by another word B? We are not at all concerned with the meaning of words. Whether or not it is *le mot juste* is of no concern, nor do we enquire if some other word might have been better than the one which does occur.

Having said that, some exceptions must be noted. If we are counting occurrences of the negative *no* and come to the phrase, 'Telephone No 1234', we recognise that the form of the word in which we are interested is also the form of a contraction of a different word: 'number'. If we count verbs and come to *saw* we must confirm that it is part of the verb 'to see' and not an instrument for cutting wood or a proverbial saying. We must decide if a 'bench' is a garden seat or a reference to a court of law. If we read that someone said 'I do-do-do-do not know', and realise that this is put in the mouth of a character inclined to stammer under pressure, then we will do well to count the occurrence but keep a note that this succession of four occurrences comes in such a situation. It must always be kept in mind that we are recording human actions and when the figures have been collected and analysed it is to this record that we must return. All enquiries start and end with the text.

The question which now arises naturally is, If it is not the grammatical, linguistic or philological role of words which is being investigated, what is it that is being studied? To this reasonable request the only reasonable reply is that we do not know. This state is not without parallels and at least one of them is very relevant. When it was first suggested that finger-prints might be a useful form of identification, counsel had great fun making speeches full of common sense objections to this apparently ridiculous proposal. If it was accepted, it would imply that when the skin of your fingers was blistered or burnt off, some other part of your anatomy remembered the precise pattern which had been there and replicated it. This was indeed the case, but why it should be the case was not really understood for more than a century, until the molecular biologists unravelled the mystery of the double helix pattern of inheritance.

What the patterns of occurrence of words, as distinct from the words themselves which make up the patterns, are likely to illustrate is the way in which the brain stores and retrieves words. From a complete knowledge of the patterns it might be possible to make a wiring diagram of the brain. By way of illustration take the shopper who strolls down Piccadilly and enters the famous store of Fortnum and Mason. The first thing to catch his eye is bottles of champagne and the kinds of delicacies which make fitting companions to champagne. If he continues down Oxford Street and enters Marks and Spencer, the home of many of the best buys in Britain, he will see men's shirts and ladies' tights. What he will have seen exemplifies the different kinds of customers the stores expect and the similarity of the two stores. Both have at hand the goods which appeal to their customers and which are frequently asked for and easily removed. In both stores if you want something which is not often asked for or is not readily portable you will be directed to a part of the building remote from the front door and the rarer the request and the larger the object the further from the door you will find yourself.

In exactly the same way the brain organises and stores its information. What is always being used is held ready for use. What is rarely needed is stored in a less accessible region and a request for it takes appreciably longer to meet. If all the patterns of connection within the brain could be traced we could make a model of the brain. This model would resemble the models of molecules made from table tennis balls. These resemble the molecule only in respect of the connections between adjacent atoms. Such models are like wiring diagrams or railway signalling charts or radar displays. They show only one type of information but they show enough of that to enable them to be useful.

It seems that the brain stores words just as the department store keeps its merchandise. Kept ready for use are frequent words and phrases employed on all subjects and in all situations. Near to these are kept the other words which naturally go with them. In more remote places are the words rarely used. That this is the case can be confirmed by timing the intervals between words in speech. The intervals which precede frequent words are less than those which precede a rare word. The difference is measured in thousandths of a second but it is measurable.

Another indication of the arrangement within the brain comes from common patterns of behaviour. Some words are so frequently used that they literally cannot be suppressed. At one time a radio show asked competitors to answer a series of rapid questions. Contestants might use any circumlocutions or synonyms, but two words which must not be uttered were 'yes' and 'no'. In spite of the forewarning and of opportunities to practise, few competitors could go for thirty seconds without allowing one or other of these words to emerge. It is a comparable mechanism that the psychologist or psychiatrist uses in word association. He wants to explore the deep motives rather than the surface ones and so he asks the brain which words it habitually couples together.

A variation of this coupling is found when two words lose the precise meaning they generally have. The phrase 'penal taxation' has a precise historical meaning. It is used when a tax is imposed at a high rate on some commodity or service to discourage its consumption or use. Whisky in Britain is taxed penally. The excise duty far exceeds the cost of production and is the largest element in the price. There is a sound reason why this should be so. When whisky has been cheap, drunkenness has become a grave social and industrial problem. But in recent years the two words are used to describe something quite different, namely the level of taxation required to support an increasing range of government activities. Taxation may be high without being penal, but the word 'taxation' is used by many people invariably with the accompanying qualification of its being 'penal' and they use it of imposts like death duties which could only be penal if imposed to dissuade people from dying.

However, it is only fair to say that no word is private property and it may be that the new use of this phrase meets some need, even if only that of making a mindless political slogan out of a useful descriptive phrase. No one can say that words will mean only what he chooses them to mean; no one can say why particular words are used. To ask why a word was used is to expect a range of 'right' answers. It was the right word to use. It was the word which precisely conveyed my meaning. It was a word which exactly expressed our theological tradition. It was essential to have a verbal modifier at that point. And so on and on and on.

This state of not knowing precisely what we are talking about when words are under review is the normal one. In his book, *Greek Word Order*,[1] K. J. Dover takes a two word sentence, '*Protagoras is here*', and then gives a list of ten reasons why one word might come before the other. His list covers phonological reasons, longer words come first; morphological reasons, nouns before verbs; syntactic reasons, subject before predicate; semantic, motion comes at the end; lexical (the most usual order in Greek); logical, someone is expected so the emphatic word, indicating who arrives, is put first. These are his first six reasons, but, as Dover says, the list is not in any way comprehensive. All he hopes to do is discover what is the normal order in Greek writers and what effects and consequences flow from variation of the pattern. Dover recognises that language is one aspect of human behaviour, and that as soon as any convention is established there is a potential emotional gain to be had by violating this convention. So, as no one can read the mind of an author and discover if any author actually knows why a word was placed in his text, we shall not concern ourselves with the reasons why things happen but simply record the happening itself.

It will, of course be objected when we count an occurrence of *and* that this word is used sometimes to join sentences, sometimes to join

[1] Cambridge 1960.

nouns, at other times to separate them; it is used to couple the natural pairs, eggs and bacon, and to disjoin unnatural pairs, sardines and cream. All these points are fairly made in other contexts but not in this one. All we are doing is using words as markers in a stream of information. It is as if we were counting letters in the words and saying that this author used x number of 't's, y number of 'k's, etc. Such information is difficult if not impossible to justify for a grammarian or linguist, but in information theory each element has a role, even if the elements are largely outside the choice of the selector. Whether all or any of that information matters depends on who is looking at the word and for what purpose.

2 The First Steps

The raw material of this study is words. Words are, simultaneously, the most common and the most mysterious feature of our life. Words are mere cyphers, marks upon a printed page or sounds that share the air with noise. Yet words have won battles and lost empires; words turn men to rage or women to tears or children from obedience to rebellion. The pen is mightier than the sword because one produces wounds and the other words. Words have the power to carry something from one human being to another. For all their quantity and the unbelievable range of their qualities, they remain mysterious. The backward child can still use words in ways that the cleverest man cannot explain.

Words can be studied in many aspects for different purposes. The grammarian teaches the principles of order and arrangement so that you can say precisely what you mean to say. He struggles to resolve dilemmas. When the book of Acts refers to 'the former book', the Gospel of Luke, does it mean the first of a pair or the first of a series? When Clement refers to 'the letter' Paul wrote to Corinth, does that mean he knew of only one letter or is it a way of saying 'in that letter which Paul wrote to Corinth'? The philologist studies the use and history of words and seeks by comparisons to bring out just what might have been meant in any instance. The historian of language looks to see how words were invented, how their meaning and their use change and shows how languages live by change and growth.

The structural linguist begins by pointing out, very reasonably, that no one learns to speak or write as the models of the grammarians suggest they might. Children begin not at the beginning but somewhere in the middle. So the linguist studies structures; he tries to discover how these are created and then assembled together.

There are other interests which lead to the study of words. The poet and the artist study sounds and shapes. But no subject, nor its practitioners, own the words we use. Yet many scholars seem to acquire proprietorial rights in words and try to erect fences with the signs – 'Keep off! Private property'. They take offence at any use or study of which they do not approve. They make of words a battleground, hurling heavy missiles made of jargon through the unfeeling air.

To determine authorship of texts it is necessary to look at words in a new way. However reasonable the claims of the grammarian, the philologist and the linguist may be, they have not exhausted the possibilities of words or language and they own no exclusive rights over them. The grammarian and the philologist take the meaning of words to be their main value. If you want to convey information with ease and accuracy, they will instruct you in the rules and conventions which will, they assure you, lead to these desirable ends. But in life you will find words more unruly. At the longest road bridge in Scotland the signs say: 'Beware High Winds'. One wonders how many high winds read the injunction. In the Highlands of Scotland the signs say: 'Beware of Lambs'. The plastic bottle tells you: 'Pierce with pin and push off'. Where to? Another plastic bottle says: 'Cut here', but a long arrow points somewhere else. Does one cut at the words or at the end of the arrow? If at the end of the arrow why not: 'Cut there'?

The same difficulties beset the definitions in all the subjects that study words. What is a noun? Is it really what the first book said in school, the name of a person, place or thing? Or is it something which behaves like a noun? Is a Guinness a member of the wealthy family or a glass of stout? Every descriptive classification is an attempt to simplify a natural biological product and by doing so render a mass of information manageable. But biological material knows nothing of classifications and mocks them. There are sponges which sometimes behave like animals. They take in complex foods and break them down. At other times they behave like plants. They build up simple substances to live. This is infuriating for the zoologist but it does not mean that the conceptions of plants and animals are useless; it merely reminds us that to every system of classification there are exceptions. If the classification is useful, the number of exceptions is small in comparison with the whole number; if the classification is not successful, the number of exceptions is large enough to make generalisations based upon the classification unsound.

Words can be classified in as many different ways as there are purposes to be served by the classifications. The only criteria to be used are the rules of classification. These are two in number and very simple to state, if not quite as simple to use. The first principle is that any particular word will always be put in the same class. The second rule is that it will not be put into more than one class. If the subject of study is smokers and these are to be classed as right- or left-handed, then either you put smokers into one group and divide that group into two, those who smoke but are right-handed and those who are left-handed, or you divide people into those who are right-handed and those who are left-handed and take the groups and divide them into two, those who smoke and those who do not. It all looks simple and clear, but what is a smoker? Is a person who tried one cigarette some years ago a smoker? Is a person who gave it up last year a smoker? How many ambidextrous people are there and how should any such person be dealt with?

Successful classification means that one is answering a simple question to which there are only two mutually exclusive answers – Is this word A or is it *not* – A? Is it the first word of a sentence? Or is it a word in any other position? Is it the word *and* or is it any other word? The reasons for classifying words and the rules by which entry into, or exclusion from any class, are determined entirely on the aims and interest of the study. No one holds the patent rights on words and language. You may use them as you will. The risk you run is that if you are too idiosyncratic or adroit no one will understand you or be able to reply.

But whatever rules we make, language will confound them. Question: 'You are not saying that you did not refuse to buy a pound of butter, are you?' Answer: 'I am not.' You are not what? No, I am not saying anything at all, or, I am saying that I did not refuse, or that my unwillingness to buy the butter was couched in terms of such sweetness that it could not be described as a refusal? No wonder literature provides such opportunities for critical discussion and sacred texts admit of as many interpretations. This illustrates the strength of the linguists' case. In many instances the meaning of words depends principally on the context in which they were uttered. Context in this case must include the habits and characters of the speakers. The simplest illustration of this situation is that often a public speaker will say exactly the opposite of what he means and yet the audience will take him to be saying the opposite of what the forms of words he used normally does convey. 'A high level of unemployment is not acceptable to my government.' What is that phrase supposed to mean? If a high level of unemployment is delivered at the door from a van, he will not take it in? He has it and cannot escape from it, so he says it is not acceptable. The reader of these words knows that the government have got a high level of unemployment and can do nothing about it. If they could do anything they would be announcing the measures instead of prattling about it. Not being able to do anything but accept it, they show their concern for the unemployed by asserting that that which they have come to accept is not acceptable.

So it is with some advertisers. The new silent model is a little less noisy than the old one. The giant economy size may hold less and cost more than the one it replaces. The new improved wash powder may contain less of the more expensive ingredients than the one it renders obsolete.

So although this is another book about words it is quite unlike all the other books about words for it only seeks to identify words and to count them. The counting is done for a number of reasons. One is that by counting we can describe in a summary way a mass of information too great to be easily absorbed by the mind. A second reason is that we can use these summary descriptions to decide whether two texts or authors are like or unlike on a scale that reduces uncertainty to a minimum. Just like physical descriptions of human beings, these numerical descriptions can be taken as individuals or grouped into classes. You can record a description of a man or go on to class him as a tall Chinaman by looking at the same information in a different way.

Many people are fearful of figures, largely because they are unfamiliar with them but also because they have never been shown that figures are just another way of looking at things; they are not a way which makes the habitual way nonsense or out of date, simply a way which supplements the familiar descriptions of common sense. For some purposes the new way is better, for others it is useless.

Until recently, historically speaking, mankind was literate but innumerate and the common means of comparison were adjectival. One city was *smaller* or *bigger* than another, an army was *huge* and *fierce*, a fortune was *immense* or even *beyond the dreams of avarice*. The development of science and technology took place when such relative terms were replaced by numbers. There is a world of difference between similar statements made in these two modes.

Literate Statement	*Numerate Equivalent*
There was an encouraging attendance.	Two hundred and four people were present.
His salary is rather less than mine.	I get £10,000 per annum, he gets £9,800.
To save the president we need a company of men both true and steadfast.	To avoid impeachment we need 34 votes.
The host of Midian.	An army of 12,500 infantry.

These alternatives may refer to the same situations but they are not at all similar statements and, whatever the loss to literature, the gain in precision is impressive.

The first point to be grasped is both simple and fundamental; stylometry is a technical and scientific subject and can deal only with data which can be numerically expressed. There is no possible doubt that many of the most important values in art and literature cannot be numerically expressed. *A primrose by the river's brim* is not an ecological statement. But for the narrow and pedantic purposes of literary and historical criticism the features which can be numerically expressed must suffice.

Having made that point as one of primary importance, it is equally necessary to remind the reader that figures, to be useful in stylometry, must describe something. It may seem difficult to create a set of figures which contain no information but it is much easier to do so than most people suspect. There are papers full of figures which describe nothing more substantial than the legendary and invisible snark. Like the assets of bogus companies, figures are used to conceal a vacuum; they literally describe nothing at all.

For example one writer on the epistles of the New Testament begins a chapter on Colossians with the remark that this letter contains no fewer than 80 'non-Pauline' words. But what is a non-Pauline word? Very few of the words in *The Oxford English Dictionary* were used by the Apostle Paul but one hardly imagines that the writer of the paper meant to include them in his count. At no time does he define a Pauline word or a non-Pauline word and though he continues to cite figures for various categories it is impossible to discover from the paper what the subject of the paper is supposed to be. One can guess that what he meant was that there are 80 words in this letter which do not occur in the other letters which he regards as having been written by Paul. But does this mean anything? If he changed his definition of Paul, would the figure change much? If Colossians had contained 60 or 160 non-Pauline words would this prove anything?

Another example of how figures can mislead rather than inform comes from the sales director of a Canadian company. He had acquired a reputation as the wizard of forecasting, for at the end of every year his sales forecasts were accurate to within a few per cent. But what he did was this: he began in January with an estimate – suppose it is 100 units. At the end of the month he made his forecast for sales to the end of February. Suppose his January estimate was badly out, actual sales being only 50 units. At the end of January his estimate is 100, the actual sales were 50 so his error is 50 out of an estimate of 100 – 50% and not very good. But his February estimate is: first, his sales in January, 50 units, plus his estimate for February, again at 100 units and again wrong by 50. At the end of February he now has a record of – actual sales in January 50, plus supposed sales in February 100, total 150. At the end of this month his actual total sales for two months is 100. He is again out by 50 units but it is now 50 out of 150 and so his error drops to 30%. If he kept up this terrible record until the end of December his year-end estimate would be actual sales for 11 months of 50 units, 550 units plus another wrong estimate for December of 100 units, total 650 units. He would be out by 50 units as usual but now it is 50 units in 650, an error of only 7.5%. What he is doing is taking the actual figures for 11/12ths of the year and then dividing his error for the last month by a factor of twelve. No wonder that he was able to claim a slight margin of error for his final estimate.

It may be argued that, however clearly these examples might illustrate a principle, they are too extreme to represent anything but a tiny proportion of the actual instances of the misuse of figures in literary arguments. Unfortunately this is far from being the case. The final example is drawn from a paper which has been published in a reputable journal furnished with referees highly qualified in the arts of literary criticism.

The paper dealt with the problem of the authorship of the *Erotikos* of Plato. This is a short work included with the orations of Lysias and may be either a genuine work of Plato or a pastiche of Plato by Isocrates. The discriminator which was proposed as likely to solve this dilemma was the rate of using the phrase *kai de kai*. This is rare in both writers, about one occurrence in ten pages for one writer and one in about six pages for the other. It occurs a number of times in the few pages of the disputed work and this was taken to indicate the author must be the writer with the higher rate. The number of assumptions made in this proposal is quite frightening. First, neither of the works used as the basis of comparison was tested for homogeneity and nothing is said of the minimum sample size. Secondly, if an event is expected to happen rarely, about one sixth or one tenth occurrence per page, and half-a-dozen occurrences are rapidly recorded, this is not evidence to suggest that the higher rate is the right one; it is evidence that a third and higher rate has appeared which has no connection with the other two. For example, when paper tapes are being read into computers, the reader pulls the tape over a set of lights and every hole in the tape lets the light through to fall on a cell which converts it into a pulse of electricity. In normal use the paper tape has slight imperfections and it also tends to vibrate as it is pulled along. The result is one or two errors in every hundred thousand characters being read. Different readers will have slightly different rates and the rate tends to creep up until cleaning and maintenance are advisable. But any time a reader starts to produce errors at a rate five or ten times normal, the cause has been found to be some quite different mechanism. One difficult case turned out to be a reader with a hair-line crack in its glass cover. The crack reflected light through certain combinations of characters and gave consistent mis-readings which were very puzzling until the cause was detected and confirmed.

So what this critic was confronting was not what he supposed, two groups with different rates of occurrence and a third count which would go with one or other; he had records from three distinct groups. It is always wise to question any result that seems to be too good; a very large difference is often due to the introduction of new factors rather than an extreme case of what has been already measured. So the first point to be made is that figures must be an accurate description of events. What is being counted must be clearly defined and the observations must reflect the actual pattern of occurrences. The next point to grasp is that the events must be fairly frequent in their occurrence.

For this second point and principle there are two reasons, the first of which can be simply illustrated. Suppose that the authorship of a text of 100 pages is in dispute. Further, suppose that all the evidence which is presumed to resolve the dispute is first tabulated and then marked off in the text with red ink. What is wanted is a text every page of which looks red or pink. What is not wanted is stretches of white pages interspersed with a few scarlet pages. It is still surprising to see how often some claim is made that the authorship of a text has been resolved, or the existence of some manuscript has been demonstrated, by evidence which has been drawn from a small portion of the text or manuscript involved. For instance an encounter with the words *'Oh that this too too solid flesh would melt'* can be taken to imply a knowledge of Shakespeare in general or *Hamlet* in particular; or a school study of some parts of the play; or a knowledge of *The Oxford Dictionary of Quotations*; or a penchant for tags. To justify any claim that it is a reference to the text of *Hamlet* rather than one of these alternatives would need further references spaced through the text of the play, unless some other information was added to the reference which resolved any ambiguities about its origin.

The other aspect of the rate of occurrence which requires it to be fairly high is that no prediction can be made about the recurrence of repeated events until a number of occurrences have been recorded. To ensure that prediction is possible, a minimum of five occurrences have to be recorded, or expected, and in practical cases this number is increased because a comparison of different rates is usually involved and the difference between two rates is usually less than either.

The need for a minimum of five occurrences is not an assumption of faith; it is a deduction from a mathematical theorem, the 'central limit theorem'. Again, the principle involved is a common sense one. Suppose that someone complained that London airport had shut down and gave as his reason that he had sat there for four hours and no plane had arrived or left. It would be pointed out that the hours might be early morning hours when noise control limits arrivals and departures, or hours of a holiday, or during a strike, or November hours when fog is likely. To make a substantial complaint the observations would have to cover a period when arrivals and departures would normally take place. A normal pattern would have to embrace night and day, work days and holidays, weekdays and Sundays, summer and winter, strikes and upsets. The point is that observations must be looked for in an interval in which experience has shown that they are likely to occur and occur at least five times.

The necessity of recording events in a suitable interval can be further illustrated by supposing that a number of boys chose to attend a football match rather than school one afternoon. An inspection of the annual figures of attendance at school would reveal little nor would the quarterly or monthly reports, nor even the weekly ones. But if daily records were available, especially divided into morning and afternoon, then the absence is likely to show up. On the other hand, counting the attendance at the match, possibly running to a hundred thousand, will tell nothing about the arrival of twenty schoolboys. Events must be looked for in intervals neither too small nor too large: in one case they are too erratic in their occurrence, in the other they appear too regular.

The next point to be made in connection with the frequent occurrence of events is one already mentioned, the fact that most writers have much more in common with each other than they have peculiar to themselves.

The bias of literary criticism has been to concentrate on events which are comparatively rare. For this there are two reasons. The first is that it is in rare events, such as the use of particular words or patterns of words, that the skill and excellence of the writer is shown. The rare elements of a text show the range of the writer's interests and the breadth of his education; they convey the graces and refinements that have aesthetic appeal. But all these words and patterns are supported by a skeletal structure of frequent words and frequent patterns, a structure which may best serve its purpose when totally unnoticed by the reader. If the questions to be put to the test are not judgments of value but concern critical or historical fact, then the exposure and study of the skeleton is often the quickest and simplest way to resolve the problem.

How far the training of scholars has led them to neglect the frequent words in a text is readily shown. Of all literary texts in Western civilisation, the New Testament has long been the most extensively studied. Numerous helps to its study have been produced and the number of books written upon it is so large that more than one volume has been written on the Apostle Paul for every word that he wrote in the original texts. But it was only in 1961 that a complete concordance of the text was made, a concordance which included every word in its context. When copies of this are offered to traditional scholars, they at once ask for something simpler and nearer to their accustomed tools. The request is always to omit the frequent words. As more than one-third of all Greek texts ever written is composed of the repetitions of half-a-dozen words, scholars have a rather partial view of the contents of a Greek text. It is true that they cannot handle the information concealed in these frequent words. Given half-a-dozen occurrences of rare words, they can classify them and discuss them, but faced with several thousand repetitions of a word, their training suggests no comparable operation or analysis.

Just how deep this bias goes can be surprising. For example, the Apostle Paul writes on average just about one-half occurrence of *and* per sentence. His imitator in Ephesians writes just over one-and-a-half per sentence. To get I Corinthians or Romans up to this level, there would have to be added to the text between five and six hundred occurrences of *and* and yet in all the centuries of New Testament study this difference has gone unnoticed. Conditioned by the tools available, scholars had never been able to see it.

Equipped with the information derived from recording events, the student of stylometry will turn to the comparison of his counts. The comparison of different rates, rates which themselves are variable, is very much the province of statistics and a main reason why statistical techniques were developed. Such comparisons are the subject of later parts of this book where they will be dealt with in sufficient detail.

However, the last point to make in an introduction is that information having been correctly gathered and reasonably interpreted must be used for some purpose. In other words, the whole pattern of stylometry is to have a testable hypothesis to confirm or refute by the evidence. Scientific arguments are always about something; they are never purely descriptive. In recent years it has been shown that rainfall over a large part of the earth's surface varies in a cycle of just over eleven years, so keeping in step with the cycle of sunspots. At the moment no one can supply any reason why rain falling on the earth should be connected with magnetic behaviour in the sun 93 million miles away but no one doubts that some connection can eventually be established. Had the results shown that there was a cycle of fifteen years no one would then suppose a connection with sunspots but the scientist would again suppose some cause and search for it. Scientists collect and interpret data to show agreement or disagreement with some hypothesis. Papers are written which point to regularities or anomalies and require, explicitly or implicitly, some hypothesis to explain the pattern of observations.

It is sometimes difficult to escape the conclusion that any student whose training has been literary and not scientific feels that it is the recording of facts that is important rather than the extraction of information from the facts. Stylometry is essentially a subject in which comparisons are made, comparisons designed to enable a decision to be made that two patterns of data are alike or are different, that they agree with some hypothesis or do not. Stylometry is a science of interpretation and exists only where there is a testable hypothesis; it is, in the words of the title of a popular and useful textbook of statistics, deriving 'facts from figures'.[1]

The rise of stylometry with its testable and verifiable hypotheses has greatly increased the difficulty of evading its conclusions by framing hypotheses neither testable nor verifiable. One example of this is drawn from Plato's Seventh Epistle. The central section of this work has repeatedly been shown to differ from the start and finish of the work. A defender of its integrity has therefore advocated the hypothesis that Plato wrote the first part of the letter, decided to show that he could write in a quite different style (the motives for this display of virtuosity being obscure), and finally, to show that he could revert to his former and natural state, he returned to his first set of habits. This might be a true account of the genesis of the letter but it is difficult to imagine a test, short of exhumation and resurrection, which could confirm or refute it.

Science deals in general principles of the widest application. The more scientific the hypothesis, the more easily it may be refuted if evidence exists to support the refutation. Nature deals with individuals. No doubt every person is unique and in some respects does differ from all others

---

[1] Moroney, M. J., *Facts from Figures*, Harmondsworth, 1956.

but science can only deal with what is common to all. What Plato shared with no one stylometry cannot measure; what he shared with his colleagues it certainly can.

The next sections of this book cover this ground in detail, first to show how data can be expressed and summarised, then how such statistics can be used to make comparisons of sets of data and then what precautions must be observed when dealing with language. Language has characteristics of its own and these must be respected.

3 Statistics and Stylometry

To write a textbook of stylometry is to face two considerable difficulties. The first arises from the range of possible applications. There are problems in poetry, in prose and in police statements; the material can be written or spoken; it can be in ancient Greek or in modern slang; in any one of the several hundred languages of mankind; it may involve masses of material or a few fragments. No one can write a textbook of stylometry in the way that it would be possible to write a cookery book for those of limited intelligence, a book of examples which have only to be followed exactly to ensure success. All that one can do is illustrate the fruitful principles of stylometry and leave the reader to adapt them to his own case.

The second difficulty is no less taxing. Readers of this book must fall into one of two classes: those to whom statistics are familiar and friendly, and those to whom statistics are strange and forbidding. In the nature of stylometry both classes of reader will need an exposition of the principles of stylometry before they can attempt a useful application of them. But whereas those who have some statistical background could absorb a full exposition without difficulty, those who lack it will need something much simpler to enable them to follow the principles as they are illustrated by the applications. For a reader in the first class the ideal sequence of exposition is an introduction, a section on the principles of stylometry and then some chapters on the applications. But for a reader in the other class it is better to have the sequence run thus: introduction, a simple outline of the fundamental principles of stylometry, the applications which can be understood from this outline, then the principles of stylometry explained in detail so that individual applications can be made by using them. That is why this chapter is, in one sense, repeated in later chapters of this book. This chapter deals with the principles of stylometry in the simplest outline. All the necessary statistical details will be found in the last chapters of this section.

It has already been said that the subject matter of stylometry is words. This is a simplification, for the subject matter is really habits which are expressed in words, habits in the choice and placing of words. A useful stylometric test is based upon a habit which is consistent within all the works of a writer, or speaker, or at least within all his works of the same kind – his prose, or his verse, for example. To be useful for comparisons this habit must vary from one writer to another, so that they can be separated by their different rate of using the same habit.

Stylometric comparison is exactly the same as all other systems of comparison in that it is only differences which offer any positive proof. If you have a police card index and are looking for a man six foot tall, with a slight limp and blue eyes, you can prove that a man who is six foot tall and has a limp but has brown eyes is not the suspect. If your man matches the description in all particulars, this only means that there is no obstacle to prevent you proceeding to the next stage of your investigation as the man could be the guilty party. But your comparisons have not proved that he is the guilty party.

It is often claimed that this argument can be reversed at some point because the specification is so precise that it can describe only the accused and no other human being. This is reminiscent of C. Northcote Parkinson's perfect advertisement for an employee: it should be so specific that only one person could apply and he would match the situation precisely. There may well be such situations but they are much less common than is generally supposed. The people who argue for this perfect matching of the individual and the description are rarely aware how often a number of different influences – diet, disease, environment, heredity, and others – can combine to produce similar physical effects and even reinforce each other to increase the likeness.

The author's favourite case of unique description is of Aristotle as the author of his zoological works. These works include the claim that they are by Aristotle and they contain details, particularly of fishes, which it was not possible to confirm as true until after the invention of the micro-scope. The zoological works attributed to Aristotle had been written by someone who has the degree of acuity in sight that enables its possessor to resolve the moons of Jupiter. This acuity has been found in less than one person in five million and, even if some allowance is to be made for a loss of this power with the advance of civilisation, the number of writers on marine biology in ancient Greece in the Aristotelian era can hardly have been large enough to support any suggestion that more than one of them had this power.

It is useful to carry the comparison of physical description and stylometric description one stage further. Physical descriptions usually include two kinds of measurement: quantitative measurements such as height or weight, and qualitative measurements such as eye colour or hair colour. Height is a continuous variable. If it is measured with sufficient precision, it may be that no two people are ever precisely the same height. But such precision of measurement is impossible and height is measured in convenient units of inches or centimetres. This means that any statement that a person is six foot one inch tall is an approximation, and really means that he is around that height. There are two causes of uncertainty: one is the variable nature of human height (we rise in hot weather and sink in cold), the other is the uncertainty of the system of measurement. One way of indicating the height and the uncertainty of it would be to say that if you measure his height you can expect the measurements to average six foot one inch, and to lie between six foot and six foot two inches. As soon as you do this you have begun to argue statistically. You have said of a quantity, the height of a human being, that you have made an estimate of it and attached to the estimate some indication of its variability or uncertainty.

If you continue to the next kind of description, the situation becomes even more complex. Colours are described subjectively, and people may describe the same head of hair in quite different terms. In the author's family runs a shade of brownish copper-red hair. It is much admired in the daughter who has it. She has long ago grown accustomed to requests for the combination of dyes needed to produce such an original shade but still finds it amusing to hear people describe it. It is not red or copper or brown but it is a brownish coppery-red. She has not yet had to be described by a police catalogue, but it might be interesting to read what that would say.

In other words, to the uncertainty of the measurement and of the system has been added a new uncertainty, that of classification. This is often the case with supposed stylistic arguments. The first step has been to classify features of a text and then to count them. But it does not follow that anyone other than the scholar concerned would classify the material in the same way. That is why it is best to avoid the uncertainty of classification where at all possible and, instead of counting something like nouns or adverbs, to count the occurrence of words which are listed and not classified further. An occurrence of *and* is always an occurrence of *and*. But it will not always be accepted as a conjunction. So, for example, rather than deal in prepositions, it is simpler to give a list of the prepositions which have been recorded and simply say that what has been recorded is the occurrence of any of the words on the list. It might seem rather ridiculous to follow this routine, but suppose we are counting occurrences of prepositions and come across an occurrence of *after*. Is this a preposition? Surely it is. 'I feel like the morning after.' Do we count an occurrence of a preposition? You might, and argue that the latter phrase is really a partially suppressed 'the morning *after* the night before'. But you might find yourself in an argument about when the suppression of the succeeding words reduces a preposition to an absurd appendix hardly deserving of the name. On the other hand, if you have merely said that you are recording occurrences of *after* no one can object to your counting. They may object to other things but there can be no dubiety about the inclusion or exclusion of this occurrence. As long as you adopt the brutally simple method of classifying words by their form and not their function, you have reduced the uncertainty of measurement by one degree. The question in its simplest form is always, 'Is this an occurrence of the word X or is it an occurrence of any word other than X?'

Taken in isolation the number of occurrences of any word means nothing. To say that there are 650 occurrences of *and* in a chapter of Dickens' novels may be true, but nothing can be safely deduced from it. Clearly if it was a large chapter it would be expected to contain more occurrences than a small chapter. In writing and in speaking no one ever exactly repeats himself, so that to say that the number of occurrences is X conveys no information beyond the bald statement of that fact. To be helpful this kind of statement must be converted into a more general one, for example, that on the average in a chapter you will find 650 occurrences of *and*. Even that is not much, for chapters will vary and even if all the chapters were exactly the same, the number of occurrences would still vary. To enable any useful predictions to be made the information will have to be in the form that the average rate of occurrence of *and* is 650 occurrences in some specified amount of text which may be defined as a number of pages, a number of words, a number of sentences or even a number of occurrences of conjunctions. Occurrences must be counted in a unit and the average rate of occurrence per unit used as the measure. Then the variations around this average must be calculated or measured.

The most familiar form of average to most people is the percentage. If they read that 5% of a chapter of a novel by Dickens is made up of repetitions of the word *and*, they will correctly conclude that one word in twenty in the chapter has been *and* and if the chapter had been twice as large, or half as large, this need not affect the percentage. Percentages can be misleading – every form of information can be misleading in certain circumstances – and so statisticians tend to use the figures not as percentages but as proportions. Rather than say that 50 words in 1,000 means a rate of 5%, they will be content to say the proportion of occurrences is 50 in 1,000, that is 0.05.

One reason for using proportions in calculations is that it fits in with the definition of probability used in stylometry. Everyone has a common sense idea of probability. It is some measure of how often an event has occurred or can be expected to occur, but the most useful form in stylometry is to define probability as the observed number of occurrences divided by the number of possible occurrences. If a sample has one thousand words in it and 50 of these are occurrences of *the*, then the probability of finding an occurrence of *the* in the sample is $50/1,000 = 0.05$. On this scale, if every word in a text had four letters the probability of finding a four letter word will be 1; if no word had four letters, it would be 0; if half of them had four letter words it would be 0.5.

If therefore we count the proportion or percentage of a habit in a sample, this has the advantages of being independent of the sample size and also simply related to calculations about probability.

A more important reason than these for calculating proportions is that they are the key to the method by which samples are compared and a decision made about whether or not they are alike. Think of two samples. Each has one thousand cards in it. We take the first sample and on 50 of the cards we make a mark or write some word. In the second sample we mark 80 of the cards. Now suppose we start an argument about whether or not these samples differ from each other. If we confine ourselves to arithmetic and common sense, no decision can be reached. The two samples are certainly different, but does the difference matter? It could, for one sample has 80 marked cards and the other only 50, a difference of 30, 60% of the lower rate. But if we divide the samples into halves and compare them we might find that one half of each sample showed the same count. You can go on and on arguing but never reach a resolution.

The statistical method of making this decision is simple. You put both samples together to make a larger group, called, for historical reasons, a population. This will have 2,000 cards in it and of these 130 will be marked, an average of 65 per thousand, a proportion of 0.065. Now suppose we shuffle these cards and deal them out in groups of one thousand. We would expect to get 65 marked cards in any sample of one thousand cards. Common sense tells us that we might get exactly 65 not very often, but numbers near to 65 quite often, and numbers far above or far below 65 quite rarely. About all that can be said with complete certainty is that we cannot get more than 130 cards marked cards or fewer than none. What can be done is that a table can be made up to show, regarding every possible number of cards from none to 130, how often it will occur by the chance mechanism of shuffling and dealing the cards. This enables any difference to be measured by the probability that it will occur by chance. For small differences around 65 marked cards, it will be once in two or three trials (probabilities of $1/2$ or $1/3$); for 1 or 2 marked cards it will be once in many thousand trials (probabilities of $1/1000$ or $1/5000$). So for our two samples we can now say that the difference between them is one that would occur by chance variation once in a certain number of trials. If the number of trials is small, then the differences will be negligible. For such differences no other explanation need be given, or can be given, than the natural chance variations which are a feature of life. Anyone who argued that a difference which was frequently to be generated by chance meant something, would be told that the difference is like finding six heads in a sequence of ten tosses of a coin or getting a hand at bridge which had no ace in it.

On the other hand the difference between the samples might turn out to be one which is very unlikely to be due to chance variation between the samples. This confronts us with a choice. The differences might be due to chance, but this is not likely, or it is due to some other cause. As our interest lies in being able to say of two samples that they are like each other or are unlike each other, this scale gives us just what we need. If the differences between the samples are attributable to chance variation, we can accept them as alike; they can have come from the same population and the differences explained by the chance variations which are to be expected between samples from the same population. If the differences are very unlikely to be due to chance, we conclude that the samples do not come from the same population.

This enables a test of authorship to be defined. It is some habit which can be numerically expressed and for which the rate in samples taken from different parts of a work, or from different works, written by an author will show only chance variations of the kind to be expected between samples taken from a single population. It is also to be hoped that samples taken from the writings of other authors will show the same habit used at a rate which will prohibit any assumption that they could be samples from the population representing the first author.

Using this pattern of argument has a number of important consequences. The first is that the traditional procedure, of making a list of all the differences between two writers or of the habits which are found in one and absent from the other, is of limited value. To be converted into a useful stylometric argument this has to be taken as a special case of general argument, one in which habits used consistently by all writers appear in one author at some specific rate, and in the other at a rate so low that it cannot be distinguished from zero. Only then will the argument have a scientific foundation.

The pattern of argument also has some errors built into it. At some point a line must be drawn between the variations acceptable as due to sampling, and those which are too great to be explicable as sampling variations. These points of decision are called *levels of significance* so that any difference which will occur more often by chance is known as a *random sampling variation*, but any difference which is larger and would occur more rarely by the action of chance is called a *statistically significant difference*. The significance levels in common use are the 5% level, indicating that the action of chance in the equivalent sampling situation would produce such difference less than one trial in twenty, or the 1% level where the difference would occur by chance only once in one hundred trials of the equivalent experiment.

This means that, if you have twenty samples you can expect to find in one of them a difference such as chance will generate once in twenty trials, but if you are using the 5% level of significance you will regard this as a difference too great to be explicable by chance. The existence of this error makes compensation for it a routine matter. There are two courses open to the experimenter; one is to use, for large numbers of samples, the higher levels of significance and accept as a difference not explicable by chance one that will occur by chance, not once in twenty or a hundred trials but one likely to occur only once in one thousand trials.

The second course open to the experimenter anxious to avoid being misled by chance variation is to combine a number of tests. First the tests must be shown to be independent of each other. If this is the case, then two such tests will combine to mislead not once in twenty trials but once in twenty times twenty trials, i.e. once in four hundred trials. Six independent tests will mislead, at the 5% level, once in 64 million trials.

There are two other sources of error which, however regrettable their existence may be, have no practical consequence. The first is that samples from different populations can resemble each other closely. The average Homeric sentence is just over 13 words, so is the average sentence written by the Apostle Paul; but this no more means that Paul wrote Homer than would the discovery that an ancient Chinese writer had written the same average length of sentence as you do would mean that you are the reincarnation of an ancient Chinaman.

The second error is present when a comparison is made of samples from two populations which are distinct but the samples are such that the populations cannot be distinguished. An author who writes something at a low rate would be represented by a high sample from his works, and his colleague who writes rather more of the habit would be represented by a low sample. This is a pity, but no harm will come from it, for as has just been said only differences count in stylometry, and all that will happen is that more labour will be required to separate the two authors with the required degree of precision.

The next point to be grasped is one of the most important in stylometry. It arises from the fact that basic statistical methods all treat of events occurring at random while language is not at all random in fine detail. Language can be treated as random but only under certain conditions. 'Random' is a word like probability of which a simple common sense definition can be given, but of which it is impossible to give an exhaustive and accurate definition. In stylometry the word 'random' means that the events which are being counted are independent of each other. When a pack of cards is being shuffled and a person invited to select one card, then the card chosen at any time is not affected by the card which was chosen the time before or by the next choice to be made. Of course, if you pick a card and do not put it back into the pack you have created a new situation, and one which will give a non-random choice, for you cannot select a card previously chosen and removed.

Language is not random in fine detail and, if it is to be compared with cards shuffled and selected, then it would have to be with a pack of cards which were sticky and tended to come out in small groups. This means that all the habits used in stylometry must be checked for randomness and if they are not random in occurrence – a very common situation – then they must be treated in a way which neutralises this factor.

Randomness can be checked by comparing two aspects of the occurrence of events. The first is the rate at which they occur, and the second is the sequence in which they occur. If you toss a coin you can expect to find equal proportions of heads and tails. You can also calculate how many times two, three or any number of heads or tails will come in uninterrupted succession. If the coin was biased, then not only would there be unequal numbers of heads and tails but there would be too long sequences of one or the other. Exactly the same is true of stylometric applications. If the events are not random, the proportion will change and the sequence of occurrences will alter. It is common to discover that a word which has not been used by a writer for some time suddenly is used two or three times and is then left aside again. This is not a random pattern and to treat it as such without introducing errors you can take three courses. The first is to take large samples so that the addition or the omission of two or three occurrences will not affect the proportion to any extent. This means that events which occur in clusters of three will need samples about three times as large as the minimum sample for a purely random event.

Another way of dealing with the non-random event is to leave the sample unchanged but to alter the method of counting. The simplest way to do this is to count sequences and not single occurrences. Suppose a writer often started a sentence with *but* and every time he did so tended to repeat the habit within a sentence or two. Instead of counting the sentences which have *but* as their first word, you count sentences which have *but* as their first word ignoring all similar sentences which come within the next five sentences. This means that each little cluster is counted as one event and the pattern is random.

The third alternative is to adopt a statistical method which makes allowance for the non-random nature of the event. The non-random nature of language is a fact of prime importance for all stylometric method, and this is the reason why much of the final chapters of this section are devoted to such matters as minimum sample size and periodic effects.

If the tendency of words to cluster together is the main complication of stylometric methods, there is no doubt what is the comparable difficulty in selecting habits for stylometric analysis. It is the effect of subject matter upon the texts. When Paul writes to the Romans about the law, not only is he likely to use words such as law, commandment, obedience; he is equally unlikely to use a large number of words which are totally irrelevant to this subject. His attitude to law will also condition his choice and arrangement of words; if he approves of it he will speak quite differently from a person who disapproves of it. The most pervasive influence on composition is the subject matter and the writer's relation to it. Given a set of police statements, no one can fail to tell which is by an accused person, which by an accuser. It is a much more difficult matter to tell which officer and which accused. A most amusing example of the influence of society on a writer is taken from a little book about the Americans,[1] in which it is claimed that as American men are dominated

---

[1] Gorer, Geoffrey, *The Americans*, Barrie & Jenkins, 1948.

by their mothers, and conditioned by having had bad behaviour punished by sending them supperless to bed, and good behaviour rewarded by a cookie or a sweetmeat, the male vocabulary of compliments for ladies is drawn straight from the larder and contains such items as Honey, Sugar, Sweetie pie; the climactic compliment is to say to a lady, 'You look good enough to eat.'

The choice and use of words as taught in schools – the nouns, the verbs, the adjective and suchlike – are all greatly influenced by subject matter, by our treatment of the subject, by our social milieu and our historical situation. A change in these will change the choice. What remains? The particles and connectives, the filler words and the function words. These are the skeletal support for all we speak and write and, like our bony frame, they work the better for being completely accepted and entirely concealed. Most people are quite unaware of how often we use these words and how important they are. The Greek orator Isocrates wrote over a period of sixty-five years. In all his surviving works there are only 15 words which occur five times or more in each work, but repetitions of these make up about 40% of everything he ever wrote. That is why stylometry deals with these words and the patterns in which they appear.

There is art in the practice of stylometry; it lies in the selection of those aspects of the material which are most relevant to the problem under investigation, and which offer the simplest and most efficient solution to it. How the art may be exercised can be illustrated from the consideration of the occurrence of a word, say the occurrence of *and* in English. This conjunction makes up around 5% of most English texts, and the texts could be divided into samples as small as one hundred words in succession. About 50 to 60 such samples would be needed to establish the pattern of occurrence and of variation around the average, so a useful amount of text might seem to be around 5–6,000 words. But for the comparison of authors it is not the rate at which they use the habit which matters but the difference between the rates in the authors. The difference between any two rates will generally be smaller than either rate and so the samples used for comparisons will have to be larger. How much larger depends on the difference between the rates in the different authors but they can easily be six or ten times larger than the basic 5,000 or 6,000 words. If the comparison was to be of large texts none of which had any internal problems, the simple rate of occurrence of *and* might be a useful test to employ.

But if only the occurrence of *and* is recorded, most of the information supplied by the writers is being rejected. One might use a single occurrence of *and* in many sentences and use it to introduce the sentence. Another writer might use a single occurrence of *and* in many sentences but always as the conjunction of two adjectives, e.g. wise *and* generous, strong *and* skilful. So it would be useful to record the occurrence of *and* in sentences and not just record how many sentences have no occurrence, how many have one, or two, and so on but also to record how many sentences have *and* as their first words and how many do not. It is also useful to record how many occurrences of *and* are as the first words of sentences and how many come in other positions. Tests based upon these habits can be very useful but if the punctuation of the texts is not to be relied on, or the texts contain a mixture of narrative and direct speech, then these tests will be of limited value. It is then better to count the occurrences in collocations, how many occurrences of *and* are preceded by some words, or are succeeded by certain words. These patterns of occurrence are not affected by the difference in literary form within the text nor by the uneven occurrence of *and*, nor do they involve the punctuation of the texts.

It may be that two writers share almost identical habits in the use of *and* but one differs from the other in the frequent use of *but*. In such circumstances it can be worth recording the occurrence of *but* in the spaces which separate successive occurrences of *and*. The range of possible useful habits is very great and some practice will lead to an appreciation of which of them are suited to particular cases and configurations of texts.

Before any habit can be used to determine the authorship of a text, it must be validated by an examination of the habit in a number of authors and texts. These must be chosen to be a fair but searching test of the hypothesis that writers of the type of text under examination employ the habit in a consistent manner. Some habits are affected by the use of dialogue, others are not. Obviously if a text had dialogue in it, only tests independent of dialogue would be used to test it. Generally the more sensitive a test is, the more likely it is to be affected by a change in literary form. This means that material in different literary forms can only be compared when there are large samples and simple tests.

The fundamental principle of stylometry can be set down thus: the authorship of texts is determined by looking at habits which are common to all writers of the class under examination. The habits are used by each writer at his own rate. The different writers are separated by calculating the differences between their rates.

The conclusions of a stylometric argument will come under one of three heads. The initial assumption is that the texts are by one author and the first conclusion may well be that there is no reason to doubt that this is the case. Or the conclusion may be that it is unlikely that this is the case. Or that the evidence will not really support any conclusion. This last result has so far only appeared when texts have been revised or found to contain passages which may be a rewriting of another source.

When the second conclusion is advanced the reply may take the form of asking how unlikely is unlikely? Suppose we start with samples of 5,000 words and find that two such samples differ at the 5% level. This means that two samples which differ to this extent will be found in around $20 \times 5,000$ words, i.e. 100,000 words, equivalent to one large volume. If another test differs at the 5% level, such samples can be expected to occur only once in 20 volumes. Three tests which differ will require, to be explicable by chance, 400 volumes. Six tests will require 160,000 volumes, more than the content of all but the largest libraries.

Looked at from another aspect, one can think of a writer who each day writes his stint of 1,000 words an hour, for 8 hours a day. He writes 300 days a year and so will produce 2.4 million words. It will take him over 26 years to write enough text to make it likely that two samples will differ by the amount needed to show differences significant at the 5% level in six tests. So one can say with considerable confidence that chance is not an acceptable explanation of the differences, and if the tests are well chosen they will also exclude the passage of time, differences of taste or literary form or any alternative explanation other than a difference of author.

Stylometry is a science and a powerful one. It is true that its conclusions must be stated in statistical terms and many people are hostile to any such measure or statement. But it is better to know the grounds for your conclusion. You may be right but, if your chance of being right is less than one in a million, humility might become you. If you are in a controversy and the odds are a million to one in your favour, you can use your knowledge with a becoming modesty, everything is going your way. If the odds are fifty-fifty, you can agree with your opponents that the toss of a coin is all that divides you.

4 Statistics as Description

The human mind is a remarkable instrument for the recording and interpretation of information. It is at its best when visualising and at its weakest when analysing. The eye can see an almost incredible amount of detail but when asked to transform the scene into a few summary characteristics the mind begins to show its limitations. A main purpose in statistical description is to compensate for this feature of the brain and to present in summary form the useful information about a complex set of events. Without statistics life would be very limited; the description of cities or armies could only be in relative terms, smaller than or larger than, or about equal to. Such comparisons are of little value to those who must levy taxes or raise armies.

Not surprisingly many of the early instances of the use of statistics come from efforts to assess the war potential of nations. One such example is recorded in the first four chapters of the Biblical book of Numbers, the title itself being an interesting example of the need which statistics were developed to meet. In Numbers we are told how the children of Israel were counted and classified. In this example there are to be seen the two stages of numerical description. The first is the simple enumeration, the count of the individuals. As soon as the number of individuals, observations or items has been counted the description can proceed in a variety of ways, each being particularly appropriate to some situation. The first choice to be made is of parameters. Parameters are measurable characteristics relevant to the analysis. In assessing the war potential of the children of Israel the parameters were two, namely sex (men only) and age. The men were grouped by tribes and by age starting at 21 years. Nowadays such descriptions would be much more refined and there are a number of descriptive devices which make them at once simpler to appreciate and more detailed in their descriptive powers.

It is often easier to follow a description from an example, so Table 4.1 and Figure 4.1 show three sets of observations. These sets are called frequency distributions for the good reason that they tell how many times observations of certain values were recorded. The vertical axis of the graphs shows how many individuals were recorded as having a character described by the horizontal axis, which shows the weight in grams of specimens. In Set A there were 2 specimens of 8 grams, 3 specimens weighed 9 grams, 5 weighed 10 grams and so on. Although the eye can see the complete pattern of observations, it is very difficult to describe the pattern without repeating it in its entirety. It is in this task of summarising information that descriptive statistics come into play.

Table 4.1   Simple descriptive statistics, means and variances

	Weight of specimen in grams, W	Number of specimens of weight W, F	Total weight of specimens of weight W, $W \times F$
Set A	8	2	16
	9	3	27
	10	5	50
	11	10	110
	12	5	60
	13	3	39
	14	2	28
	Totals	30	330
	(Mean $\bar{x}$ = 11.00 grams)		
Set B	1	10	10
	2	5	10
	4	5	20
	7	3	21
	11	3	33
	16	2	32
	20	2	40
	Totals	30	166
	(Mean $\bar{x}$ = 5.53 grams)		
Set C	1	10	10
	8	2	16
	11	2	22
	14	3	42
	15	3	45
	19	5	95
	20	5	100
	Totals	30	330
	(Mean $\bar{x}$ = 11.0 grams)		

The simplest descriptive statistic is the mean, a statistic so often used in everyday life that it has a common name, the average. Statisticians use a number of different measures of central tendency and the mean is the arithmetic average. It is calculated by dividing the total value of all the observations by the number of observations.

If the number of observations is n and x stands for each observation in turn then the mean, often written as $\bar{x}$, is $\Sigma x/n$ where the Greek letter sigma (Σ) means the sum of all the different values of x.

The mean for Set A of Table 4.1 is simply worked out. In each instance the number of occurrences of specimens of each weight is given and if these two figures are multiplied together the total weight is the result: there are 2 specimens of 8 grams, making 16 grams; 3 specimens of 9

Figure 4.1   Simple descriptive statistics, means and variances

Three sets of observations:

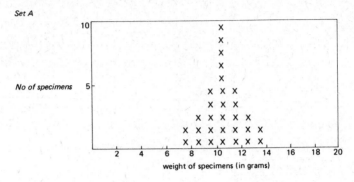

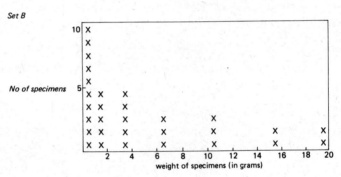

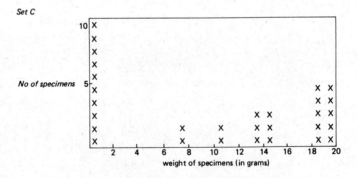

grams, 27 grams, and so up to a total weight for all specimens of 330 grams. As there are 30 specimens the mean weight is 11.0 grams per specimen. In this example the mean is a useful statistic for three reasons. The first is that there are a number of specimens of average weight, in fact 10 out of thirty are average weight. Secondly there are a large number of specimens near to average weight, the mean plus or minus one unit covers 20 out of the thirty observations and, thirdly, there are few specimens which are far from the average weight; in this case all of them lie within three units of the mean of 11 grams.

The second set of observations, Set B, is quite differently arranged, starting with a peak and declining from it as the weight of the specimen increases. The mean of the set, at 5.53 grams, correctly shows this difference from Set A as the mean for Set B is just over half the mean for Set A; but it is also clear that the mean is hardly a representative statistic for this set of observations. There is no specimen of average weight, only three out of thirty lie within one unit of it and most of the specimens lie far from the mean. The range of three units from the mean which covered all the observations in Set A, cover only 8 out of the 30 in Set B.

Set C carries the illustration a stage further, the pattern of the observations is quite different but the mean for this set is the same as the mean for Set A. Set C is like Set B in that the mean is not a very useful descriptive statistic for the observations. Set C has two observations of the mean weight, but only 7 out of 30 lie within three units of the mean.

There are two points to be grasped about the mean. The first is that it is an important and useful statistic, it is one of the most efficient as every observation is employed in the calculation of the mean. The second point is that the mean gives much less than a complete description of a set of observations and it needs to be supplemented with other statistics. In practice the mean is useful for distributions which have a single peak, *uni-modal* is the technical term for them, but it is much less useful for L-shaped or U-shaped distributions and when the distribution has more than one peak the mean ceases to be a simple statistic.

Clearly something more than the mean is needed to describe a set of observations with any accuracy, in particular some measure of dispersion is required to show how the observations gather round the mean, whether they cluster round it or are widely spread from it. There are a number of such measures of dispersion; the most useful are the *variance* and the *standard deviation*. The principle underlying the variance is simple. Each observation is taken in turn and is subtracted from the mean of all the observations, the difference is squared, i.e. multiplied by itself, and the sum of the squares for all observations is then divided by the number of observations to give the variance. In the notation used before, the variance can be written $s^2 = \Sigma(x - \bar{x})/n$. (For a reason to be given and explained later the number $n - 1$ is often used rather then n in the denominator of the calculation of the variance.) The *standard deviation* is just the square root of the variance. One reason for using the standard deviation is that it is in the same units as the mean. In the instance of the three sets of data in Table 4.1, the variance would be in units of the weight in grams squared. (When a number is multiplied by itself it is said to be squared. This is because it had long been known that if three bricks are laid in a line, then three rows of three will make a square.) The standard deviation is in units of grams. The variance is useful; it gives an indication of how the observations are grouped round the mean and so to some extent indicates how useful the mean is as a descriptive statistic. The variance is easily calculated and it is reasonably easy to interpret. The major limitation of the variance is that it is affected by extreme values (this will be shown in a later chapter).

Table 4.1 is continued to show how the variance is calculated; see Table 4.3, p. 48. The first two columns are as before, the weight W in grams of specimens and the number F of specimens of weight W. The next column is headed T and contains values which run up and down from an assumed mean. Anyone asked to find the mean of the numbers 1001, 1002, 1003, 1004 would simply add 1, 2, 3 and 4 and then add 1000 to the answer to get the result 1002.5. In exactly this way the calculation of means and variances is simplified by starting with a convenient guess as to what the mean will be. If the guess is wrong it will only add a little to the complexity of the calculation but it will still be simpler than using the original figures. In Set A the observations gather round 11 grams and this is a fair guess of the mean. So the figures in column 3 are numbered in both directions from the central row of 11; 10 is 11 minus 1 and so 10 becomes —1; 14 is 11 plus 3 so 14 becomes +3 and so on. The next column, 4, is headed FT and is the product of the figures in columns 2 and 3. The entries in this column are exactly those of the third column of the first example except that 11 has been subtracted from each one, the 2 specimens of 8 grams now are registered as 2 specimens of —3 grams. The figures in column four are added separately for the plus and minus signs; these two totals are subtracted and the sign of the larger one is attached to the remainder. In Set A the difference is zero, in Set B the two totals are —100 and +56, the difference is 44 and the sign of the larger total was minus so the result is —44. This difference covers thirty observations so the correction for each is this total divided by 30, for Set B $44/30 = 1.47$. The estimated mean for Set A is correct, the guess was 11 and the positive and negative values cancelled exactly but for Set B the guess was 7 grams and it turned out too high, too high by the amount of $44/30 = 1.47$ grams, so the corrected result is the mean of $7.00 — 1.47 = 5.53$ grams. For Set C the assumed mean is again 11 grams and the two totals are equal so the guess is precisely correct and the answer is 11 grams. It may seem that in such calculations this method hardly saves time or effort but the examples are simple and brief and in practice most distributions are much more extensive and the saving is appreciable.

The variance is calculated by carrying on one step further and multiplying the values in column four by T a second time and so arriving at a set value for FT^2; these are in column five. Two negative numbers are multiplied together and have a positive result so that all entries are positive and add to a single total. To arrive at the variance, the total of column five is taken, and a correction is made. The reason for the correction is that all the values have been measured about the assumed mean and if this is not the true mean the total has to be reduced to compensate. As the variance is at a minimum about the true mean this correction is always to be subtracted regardless of the sign of the partial total at the foot of column four. Naturally if this total is zero, no correction is required. The correction is the square of the difference in the two totals of column four divided by the number of observations, in Sets A and C the corrections is zero, in Set B it is $44 \times 44 / 30 = 64.53$. The last step is to subtract the correction from the total of column five and divide the result by one less than the number of observations, for Set B, $1078 - 64.53 = 1013.47$ divided by 29, result 34.95, which is the variance. The standard deviation is the square root of this variance and so is 5.91 grams.

It is true that the relation of the mean and variance tell something about the nature of the distribution. The ratio of the two shows that for Set A the data cluster closely round the mean but for the others it is much more widely dispersed and so suggests that the mean is not a very good descriptive statistic for these sets.

The mean and variance of a set of observations make a useful summary description of them but they still omit some essential information. For example, neither the mean nor the variance will tell if the observations have one peak or more or whether or not the observations are symmetrically distributed around the mean or have, as for example sentence length distributions generally do, a long tail of higher values. Distributions with a tail running towards the higher values are called *positively skew*, those with a tail extending to the lower values are called *negatively skew*.

The two statistics, the mean and the variance, can sometimes be all the information which is required for complete description. Later will be seen examples of the normal distribution, the familiar bell-shaped curve which covers a wide range of observations from the height of human beings to the weight of the galaxies in the universe. Knowing the mean and variance enables you to calculate every part of such a curve.

But there are other cases where the mean and variance are much less effective. Take, for example, an imaginary office in which twenty people work. It is before the time of women's liberation so in the office we have ten women who get paid 5,000 dollars per year. We have nine men who for the same work get 10,000 dollars per year. We have one man who owns the business and he takes home 200,000 dollars per year. When the time comes for an increase to be paid the boss natually points out that the average salary compares favourably with similar work in other offices, the average is $(10 \times 5,000 + 9 \times 10,000 + 200,000)$ divided by twenty, i.e. 17,000 dollars per annum and on that an increase of ten per cent would be equitable. This means that the salaries would become 5,500, 11,000 and 220,000. He would get the same as the others, ten per cent, but he would get more money than all the others put together.

The trouble is that this kind of average, the mean, is not a good description of the facts. It is better to use another measure of central tendency, as statistical language has it. One such measure is the *median*, the central value of a series. Half the observations will show values above the median, the other half will show values below it. In the above instance the median lies between 5,000 and 10,000 to start with and may be taken to be mid-way between them, at 7,500 dollars. The suggested rise will bring the median up to half way between 5,500 and 11,000, i.e. 8,250. So 750 dollars is a better description of the raise than ten per cent.

The median is useful when the observations contain a small number of extreme values as they will for salaries or written sentences. There are a few rich people whose income and earnings greatly exceed the mean. Sentences range from one word up to a few hundred words. The number with more than sixty or seventy words is small but the presence or absence of a few extreme values will greatly affect the mean.

Descriptive statistics can be legion, each suited to the nature of the observations and the pattern in which they occur, but the needs of literary studies are covered by supplementing the mean, variance and standard deviation with the *mode*, the *median*, the *first* and *third quartiles*, and the *ninth decile*.

It is always easier to appreciate a definition from an example and so Table 4.2 shows the sentence length distribution of the Greek text of the Epistle to the Galatians in the text of Aland, Black, Metzger and Wikgren.[1] According to the definition of a sentence which was used (a set of words ending with a full stop, colon or interrogation mark), this epistle has 166 sentences in its text. Table 4.2 shows that there are two sentences of one word, four sentences of two words and so up to a single sentence of seventy-one words. This pattern of observations can be simplified by grouping, by putting together all the sentences having from one word to five words, those having from six words to ten words and so on. Such groups are called cells, and in this case the cell interval is one of five words as each cell contains sentences within a range of five words.

Grouping has two advantages; it reduces the minor fluctuations in the observations and it enables comparisons to be made between distributions without a lot of calculation which adds nothing to the information obtained by using grouped data. Comparisons are best made using data arranged in from five to fifteen groups, The grouping of the data of Table 4.2 reduces the thirty-seven classes of sentence in the original to seven. It is important when using grouped data to remember that many statistics will be calculated in units of the cell interval and if these are wanted in other units they have to be converted. Table 4.3 shows the mean and variance of the data calculated exactly as before. In this case as the data is grouped when the correction is being made to the

[1] London 1968.

Table 4.2   Sentence length distribution of the epistle to the Galatians

(a)   Ungrouped data

No of words in sentence	Number of sentences	No of words in sentence	Number of sentences
1	2	19	5
2	4	20	4
3	5	21	–
4	5	22	4
5	5	23	2
6	11	24	1
7	7	26	2
8	13	28	1
9	8	30	2
10	15	32	1
11	12	34	1
12	9	39	1
13	7	41	1
14	9	42	1
15	9	44	1
16	7	47	1
17	6	52	1
18	2	71	1

(b)   Grouped data

No of words in sentence	No of sentences
1–5	21
6–10	54
11–15	46
16–20	24
21–25	7
26–30	5
31 or more	9
Total:	166

calculation of the mean, the difference is +15, but this has to be multiplied by 5 if the mean is wanted in words since the unit in the table is a cell of five words.

The *mode* is the most frequent value in a distribution. For the data of Table 4.2 it is 10 words for the upgrouped data, and it is taken to be the central value of the interval between 6 and 10 words, i.e. 8 words, for the grouped data. This example shows how the grouping of data enables the mode to be clarified; in the ungrouped data there are 11 sentences of 6 words, 15 of 10 words and 12 of 11 words. Ten words may be the modal

Table 4.3   Calculation of the constants of the sentence length distribution of the Epistle to the Galatians

1	2	3	4	5
No of words in sentence	No of sentences of X words			
X	f	t	ft	ft^2
1–5	21	−2	−42	84
6–10	54	−1	−54	54
11–15	46			
			−96	
16–20	24	+1	24	24
21–25	7	+2	14	28
26–30	5	+3	15	45
31–35	2	+4	8	32
36–40	1	+5	5	25
41–45	3	+6	18	108
46–50	1	+7	7	49
51–55	1	+8	8	64
71–75	1	+12	12	144
			+111	657
Totals: 166			+15	657

Notes:

(1) $\bar{x} = 13.00 + \dfrac{15 \times 5}{166}$

$= 13.45$

(2) $s^2 = 657.00 - \dfrac{\dfrac{15^2}{166}}{165} = \dfrac{655.64}{165} = 3.998$

$s = 2.00$

value of the ungrouped data, but it is not very clearly so; the grouped data provide a much more realistic mode for the distribution.

The *median* is the value associated with the central member of a series of observations; the median divides the observations into two equal groups. The median of the observations in Table 4.2 will have 83 sentences longer than itself and 83 sentences shorter than itself. Clearly the median lies in the cell 11–15 words for there are 75 sentences with fewer than 11 words. The number required to make up the median from 75 to 83 is 8. The cell contains 46 sentences and is five words wide so that the median is 10 words plus the fraction $(8 \times 5)/46 = 10.87$ words.

The *first and third quartiles* carry the process of division one stage further and divide the observations into four equal parts. Below the 1st quartile lies one quarter of the series of observations, below the 3rd quartile lie three-quarters of the observations. The calculation of the quartiles is exactly parallel to the calculation of the median. For the set of 166 sentences in Table 4.2 the median is at sentence 83, the 1st quartile will be at sentence 41.5 and the 3rd quartile at sentence 124.5. In these descriptive statistics it matters not at all that you cannot record 41.5 sentences; the 1st quartile divides the observations into two groups one of which is three times as large as the other and this division comes between the 41st and 42nd sentences when the sentences are arranged in order of their lengths.

Figure 4.2   Showing how a sentence length distribution is simplified and summarised by using descriptive statistics

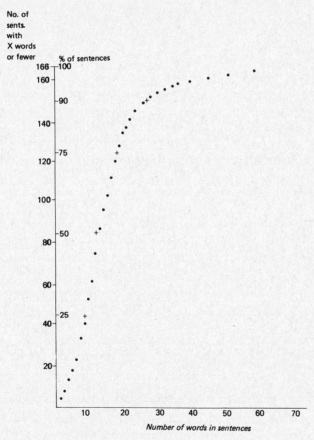

Notes:
x = number of words in sentences
● = points taken from observations
+ =points taken from statistics

The 1st quartile is more than 5 words, for there are 21 sentences of 5 words or less, but is less than 10 words, for there are 75 sentences with 10 words or fewer. The 1st quartile lies in the cell 6–10 words and lies in the cell at the point given by the fraction $[(41.5 - 21) \times 5]/54 = 1.90$ and so the 1st quartile is 6.90 words.

The 3rd quartile lies in the cell 16–20 words and at a point given by $[(124.5 - 121) \times 5]/24 = 0.73$ and so the 3rd quartile is 15.73 words.

The quartiles and median divide the series of observations into quarters but it can be divided into any convenient set of fractions. The *ninth decile* is the point which divides the observations in the ratio 9 : 1, 90% of the observations lie below it, 10% lie above it. The 9th decile is a useful measure of the number of long sentences which avoids the complications which can be produced by isolated very long sentences appearing in a sample. The 9th decile comes at $166 - 16.6$ sentences, 149.4, and so lies in the cell 21–25 words at the point given by $[(149.4 - 145) \times 5]/7 = 3.14$ and so the 9th decile is 23.14 words.

The quartiles show how symmetrical a set of observations is. If the data is completely symmetrical about the mean then the mean will be the median and the 1st and 3rd quartiles will lie at equal distances from the mean and median. If the observations are asymmetrical, as in the great majority of sentence length distributions, the mean and median do not coincide and the 1st and 3rd quartiles are at different distances from the median.

The 9th decile is a useful measure if the observations are positively skew. If they are only slightly skew, then the 3rd quartile and the 9th decile will be close to each other and the 9th decile will not yield new information to supplement that given by the 3rd quartile.

Using this set of descriptive statistics, the complexities of a set of observations can be reduced to a few figures by a description which is at once accurate and summary. The use of these statistics goes much beyond their power of summary description, but before passing on to this further stage the statistics just described are illustrated. Figure 4.2 shows how the quartiles and 9th decile cover a sentence length distribution.

5 The Second Stage in Statistical Description

At this point the reader should be equipped to deal with the first hazard of literary research. When confronted by masses of data he will not be overwhelmed by it but will be able to simplify the data by making a summary description of it. Words are numerous and occur frequently and the normal condition is to have large numbers of observations to grapple with. In that situation literary description falters and some more useful system has to be introduced. That is why the first role of statistics is the accurate summary description of masses of information. In place of large tables and row upon row of figures, there will be a few statistics and these statistics will convey almost all of the useful information which the raw data contained. The next step is to use statistics to make comparisons, to draw up a scale of likeness-to-unlikeness so that it can be said of two sets of data that they are describing things which are identical, or very alike, or alike, or not very similar, or quite different.

But before going on to the analytical role of statistics there is an intermediate stage to be traversed. Just as in certain circumstances the description of individual human beings can be much simplified by using family or ethnic or social classes, so statistics enable some patterns of observations to be classed as belonging to one or other of some common patterns. Being told that a man is a Rothschild, or a Chinaman, or a millionaire, enables some swift and certain conclusions to be drawn. In the same way the information that a set of observations makes a Poisson distribution will simplify the handling of the data. One advantage conferred by fitting observations to a common pattern is that doing so will often tell you something of the nature of the mechanism which has produced them. The pattern of observations produced by recording the heads shown by a tossed coin is binomial. As the name implies it is the result of two mutually exclusive events, one or other of which must occur. The coin must come down and show either a head or a tail. This pattern is quite different from what would be recorded if more than one choice is open, for example if you are recording the colour of human hair. But the colour of hair can be reduced to a binomial event by recording only – is it black? Or is it any other colour at all?

Fitting observations to the standard distributions has other advantages; tables and charts of them are to be found in many text books and so the calculations involved in them are much simplified. It is usual to find that graph papers are available on which the standard distributions can be readily shown. So great are the advantages in using data arranged in these distributions that you will often find that observations will be transformed to suit them. This is a device that critics treat with suspicion, but it is no more culpable than using units of one thousand in a table rather than have three zeros after each figure in the table.

The natural sequence of exposition would be as it is in most text-books of statistics, to start with the simplest mathematical pattern, the binomial, and develop a logical progression to the more complex distributions. Unfortunately this is not at all the natural sequence for students of literature. For them some of the most used and most important statistics come late in the mathematical progression, whereas some of the most commonly used statistical operations are rarely seen in literary applications. So the procedure here is to try to amalgamate the two requirements in a simple and logical sequence with practical illustrative applications.

First comes a series of distributions which are useful for description and comparison of texts. Then follow a number of distributions which are rarely used to describe observations but are often used to describe the statistics based upon sets of observations. For example, one distribution will tell you how the means of observations behave without telling you anything about the underlying observations. Third, there comes a section of useful but miscellaneous distributions. These deal with the choice of samples, with testing to see if observations tend to cluster together, with the choice of scales, and with a number of practical points which are very widely scattered in the usual text-books of statistics.

This whole section should be read through with the aim of acquiring a picture of statistical methods. It is not necessary to attempt to memorise any part of it, for continual reference will be made to the relevant material as applications of it are made. The reader will soon find that he can anticipate the reference as he becomes familiar with the data which is under examination. What he should aim at understanding is the principles which make the application the correct one.

For every distribution a worked example is given, an example drawn from real life. Too often the text-books contain examples which have been simplified and so come out with quite unreal precision. The examples are given so that the student will know what operations have been performed to produce the results. It is now easy to buy pocket calculators to do all the actual figuring and do it in a fraction of a second.

Before going on there are two explanatory notes which should be ingested.

A *frequency distribution*, as the name implies, is a set of observations, or predictions about observations, arranged to show how often certain values have appeared or are expected to appear. A typical distribution will tell how many sentences in a text have no occurrence of *and*, how many have one occurrence, how many have two occurrences, three, four and so on up to the highest recorded value. One type of distribution is called a *length distribution* although it is in fact the frequency distribution of certain lengths. For example, a sentence length distribution tells how many sentences in the text have from one to five words, how many have from six words to ten words, how many have from eleven words to fifteen words and so on. The full title of such distribution is the *frequency distribution of sentence lengths* but this is usually abbreviated to the *sentence length distribution*.

A frequency distribution can either be of observations which have been made or an estimate of what observations would have appeared, given some hypothesis to be true. For example, it will shortly be shown what patterns of occurrences are to be expected if the observations conform to any one of a number of possible distributions. An important aspect of statistical analysis is the comparison of actual observations and the distribution which it has been calculated will describe them.

The second note concerns the idea of *probability* and the use of the word which embodies it. In the context of literary studies there is no need to make heavy weather of the philosophical connotations of the idea of probability. We simply define it as the ratio of the actual occurrences of an event to the possible occurrences of the event. If there are 200 sentences in a sample, there are 200 first words, one for each sentence. If 50 of the first words turn out to be occurrences of *and*, then the probability of finding *and* to be the first word of a sentence in this group is $50 \div 200$, i.e. 0.250. Probability is measured on a scale running from 1.00 for any event certain to happen at every trial down to 0.00 for an event certain not to happen no matter how many trials are made. The mid-point of the scale, 0.5, will be occupied by events which are just as likely to happen or not to happen. A tossed coin must come down and so the probability of getting a result is 1.0; this result can be either head or tail and both are equally likely, so each has a probability of 0.5.

What often causes the beginner to be confused is this. The statistician starts with a record of observations (to resume the example just quoted) of 200 sentences, 50 of which have the conjunction *and* as their first word. Having recorded this fact, the next step may be to refer to the proportion of such sentences in the group of 200. This is $50 \div 200$, again 0.250. But his next reference will be to a probability of 0.250, based upon the same observations, and then he will use this as an estimate of what can be expected to appear in another group. There is only one fact, the occurrence of 50 sentences of one kind in a group of 200. But this can be looked at in a number of ways – the proportion of such sentences in the group, the mean rate of occurrences of such sentences, the probability that such sentences occurred in the group and then the probability that such sentences will occur in a similar group. The root of the difficulty is simply that to spell out in full, each time the figure is used, exactly in what context it is being used, would be tedious. In good writing the actual use should be obvious from the context but this is not always so and the beginner must work it out for himself.

The usual notation when dealing with probabilities is to take the number of actual occurrences of an event as p, the total number of possible occurrences as n, the number of non-occurrences is then $q = n - p$ and the probability of the event occurring will be $p/n = p/(p + q) = (1 - q)/n$. These three forms are interchangeable and are used when one or the other is most convenient to calculate.

Useful Distributions

In the last chapter it was shown that a set of statistics could be used to describe a frequency distribution. The process can often be carried a step further by showing that the observations fit one of the common patterns of distribution. There are two main reasons for taking this step. The first reason is that when the observations have been fitted to a known distribution not only are they easier to handle – tables, charts and special graph papers are available which cover most of the common distributions – but the mechanism which has produced the observations can often be identified and understood. The second reason is that if an analysis is made using two methods, one of which makes no assumption about the distribution of the observations and the other fits them to a known distribution, the second method will generally be found to be the more precise.

Text-books of statistics describe large numbers of distributions but the needs of the literary critic are covered by about half-a-dozen of the simpler distributions. The main difficulty in acquiring a working knowledge of distributions is that they are set out in text-books in the logical and sequential order of their mathematical origins, an order neither natural nor congenial to the student of literature who is most likely to remember the details of a distribution by recalling the practical problems to which it applied.

This chapter in no sense replaces the text-book of statistics; it is meant only to supply a set of examples and references which can be amplified by any text-book of statistics. It does supply a set of illustrations, drawn from literary texts, of the types of distribution most frequently used in the study of such texts.

The Binomial Distribution

As the name implies, the binomial distribution describes the occurrence of an event, such as the tossing of a coin, for which there are two mutually exclusive results. If heads are being recorded then the toss of a coin can have only one of the two results, the occurrence or non-occurrence of a head. This distribution is relevant to such questions as: Does this sentence have the particle *de* as its second word or does it not?

The binomial distribution was the first distribution to be established by Bernoulli, at the end of the seventeenth century; he showed that if the probability of an event is p and the probability of its non-occurrence is $q = 1 - p$, then if a random sample of n trials were observed, the frequencies with which the event occurred 0, 1, 2 . . . times were given by the expansion of the binomial expression

$$(q + p)^n \tag{1}$$

A more convenient form in which to have this expression is the recursion formula where the probability p (0) of no occurrence, the probability p (1) of 1 occurrence and so on is given by:

$$p(x + 1) = \frac{n - x}{x + 1} \cdot \frac{p}{q} \cdot p(x) \tag{2}$$

This recursion starts from the first term of equation (1) which reduces to $p(0) = q^n$,

p(1) is then $\dfrac{n}{1} \cdot \dfrac{p}{q} \cdot p(0)$

p(2) is then $\dfrac{n - 1}{2} \cdot \dfrac{p}{q} \cdot p(1)$

and so on.

The binomial distribution covers events for which the occurrences are independent of each other; a coin which is being tossed is not affected by how often it has been tossed before or what the results of such previous tosses have been. If this were not so there would be a large and lucrative trade in coins which could be relied on to show a bias. This means that tosses of a coin are binomial events. But in literature it is rare for any event to be completely independent of another and the normal situation is that an author who has recently written some word, feature or construction is either more likely or less likely to repeat it quite soon. As a result care must be taken in using the binomial distribution in literature. The necessary precautions are discussed in a later chapter.

The binomial distribution clearly applies to questions which concern the occurrence of some word or phrase or feature where the only answers to the question are the exclusive ones, there is not or there is an occurrence. Corresponding to the binomial distribution there is a multinomial distribution but this is so cumbersome that it is more useful to simplify the data into a series of binomial distributions and treat each in turn.

Table 5.1   An example of a binomial distribution

The occurrence of the conjunction *kai* in blocks of twenty successive words marked off from the start of Book One of Aristotle's *Ethics* (Oxford Classical Text)

No of Occurrences of *kai*	No of Blocks with X occurrences			
x	f	t	ft	ft^2
0	23	−1	−23	23
1	39			
2	26	+1	26	26
3	9	+2	18	36
4	2	+3	6	18
5	1	+4	4	16
Totals:	100		+54	119
			+31	

Notes:

The mean is 1.00 plus $\dfrac{31}{100} = 1.31$

The variance is $\dfrac{119 - \dfrac{(31)^2}{100}}{99} = \dfrac{109.39}{99} = 1.104.$

The standard deviation is the square root of 1.104 which is 1.05.

Instead of asking how many people have blue, grey, brown or green eyes, the questions are framed – How many people have grey eyes and How many do not?

In just this way a complex question 'Does this sentence have the particle *men* among its opening words?' – can be simplified to the form, 'Does this sentence have the particle *men* as its second or third word or does it not?'

The mean of a binomial distribution is *np*. The variance of the binomial distribution is *npq* and, as p and q are less than 1, the variance of a binomial is less than its mean. Not only is this a diagnostic sign that data is binomially distributed, it enables the variance of a set of observations to be reduced when it is desirable for them to have the minimum variance. For example, instead of recording the number of sentences

Table 5.2   The calculation of the expected values for a binomial distribution for the data of Table 5.1

The mean number of occurrences of the conjunction *kai* in blocks of 20 successive words was 1.31.

$$\text{For the binomial, p is then } \frac{1.31}{20} = 0.065$$

$$q \text{ is } 1 - p = 0.935$$

$$n \text{ is } 20.$$

$p(0)$ is 0.935^{20}. This is calculated by looking up the logarithm of 0.935 in tables, which is $\bar{1}.9708$, and multiplying by 20 to get $\bar{1}.416$. The antilog of $\bar{1}.416$, from the tables, is 0.261 and this is $p(0)$. The number of samples with no occurrence in a set of 100 samples is $100 \times 0.261 = 26.1$.

	Expected Number	Observed Number
$p(x)$		
$p(0) = 0.261$	26.1	23
$p(1) = \dfrac{(20-0)}{1} \times 0.070 \times 0.261 = 0.365$	36.5	39
$p(2) = \dfrac{(20-1)}{1+1} \times 0.070 \times 0.365 = 0.243$	24.3	26
$p(3) = \dfrac{(20-2)}{1+2} \times 0.070 \times 0.243 = 0.102$	10.2	9

For more than 3 occurrences, p is 1 less the sum of $p(0)$, $p(1)$, $p(2)$ and $p(3)$ which is $1 - 0.971 = 0.029$ and the expected number is 2.9. For reasons given later this would be included with $p(3)$ to make $p(3$ or more) 0.131, the expected number is 13.1, the observed number is 12.

Chi squared is 0.95 for one degree of freedom.

---

with 0 occurrence of *kai*, with 1 occurrence, with 2 occurrences and so on, the data can be reduced to two classes, sentences with no occurrences and sentences with any number of occurrences.[1]

The binomial distribution is one of the fundamental distributions in stylometry and will be frequently encountered. Charts and graph paper are available for testing the fit of data to binomial distributions.

Fitting data to a binomial distribution, i.e. comparing the observed

---

[1] For a modification of the distribution to allow for a variation in the probability from sample to sample, see Yule and Kendall, *Introduction to the Theory of Statistics*, London 1953, pp. 400–403. For an example of its application to the orations of the Corpus Lysiacum, see Morton, The Authorship of Greek Prose, *Journal of the Royal Statistical Society*, Series A, vol. 128, 1965.

occurrences of some event with the occurrences calculated on the assumption that the data conform to a binomial pattern of distribution, is done by the chi square distribution shortly to be described.

The Poisson Distribution

If a binomial event has a probability of less than about 0.05, then q for the event is 0.95, which is nearly 1 and can be taken to be 1 without introducing appreciable error into the calculation. In those conditions when p is small and n is large, the number of occurrences of the event will be distributed in a Poisson series. (See Table 5.3.) For the Poisson distribution $p = e^{-m}/x!$. In this formula e is the base of natural or Naperian logarithms, the number 2.7183; m is the average number of occurrences of the event in the interval in which occurrences are recorded and x! (factorial x) is the product of all the numbers from 1 up to x. For example, 6! is $1 \times 2 \times 3 \times 4 \times 5 \times 6 = 720$.

The recursion formula for the Poisson distribution is

$$p(x + 1) = \frac{m}{x + 1} \cdot p(x)$$

and p (0) is e^{-m}.*

The mean of a Poisson distribution is m and the variance is also m; the standard deviation is the square root of m.

The sum of two Poisson distributions is itself another Poisson distribution, a result that is not without importance. If, for example, the occurrence of some word were to be classed in four different ways but each of the classifications gave rise to a Poisson distribution, then all the classifications taken together would form another Poisson series and taking them together has not produced any change of distribution.

The Poisson distribution is a form of the binomial distribution for which p is small and n is large and the two distributions give similar results when these conditions apply. For example, if boxes of light bulbs each of which contained one hundred bulbs were known to have, on the average, one defective bulb per box, the proportion of boxes without a defective bulb in them is 36.64% calculated as a binomial distribution and 36.79% calculated as a Poisson distribution. The difference between the two predictions, 0.15%, an amount negligible in practice, would vanish as p gets smaller and n gets larger.

There are two distributions related to the Poisson distribution. The Poisson describes the occurrences of a random event recorded in equal

*The value of e^{-m} is most easily obtained from a pocket calculator or from tables. There is a set in Goodman, *Teach Yourself Statistics*, English Universities Press, London 1966, p. 66.

Table 5.3   An example of a Poisson distribution

(a) The occurrence of *kai* in small samples in the 21st Oration of Demosthenes (Oxford Classical Text)

No of *kais* in sample	No of Samples	Difference from Estimated Mean		
x	f	t	ft	ft^2
0	252	−1	−252	252
1	288	0	0	0
2	161	+1	161	161
3	63	+2	126	252
4	17	+3	51	153
5	6	+4	24	96
Totals:	787		+362	914
			−252	
			+110	

The mean number of *kais* per sample = 1.140.
Variance (s^2) = 1.142.
Standard deviation (s) = 1.069.

(b) Cumulative Totals

Samples with	Number	Proportion
0 *kai*	252	0.3202
1 or fewer	540	0.6861
2 or fewer	701	0.8907
3 or fewer	764	0.9708
4 or fewer	781	0.9924
5 or fewer	787	1.0000

intervals; the *negative binomial* distribution describes the occurrence of a random event in variable intervals, such as sentences, while the negative exponential distribution describes the occurrences by measuring the intervals which separate the successive occurrences, e.g. the number of words which separate successive occurrences of the conjunction *kai*.

The Negative Binomial Distribution

If a word occurs at random and its occurrence is recorded in a fixed interval, say a block of twenty or one hundred successive words, then it

is to be expected that the observed numbers of occurrences will fit a
Poisson series for the expectation of the occurrence does not change
from one interval to another. If the same occurrences were recorded in
sentences which can vary from a single word up to more than two
hundred words, then the expectation does vary from one interval to
another and the observations will fit not a Poisson series but a negative
binomial distribution.

The negative binomial distribution suffers from one serious handicap;
it is derived from one of the mathematical conventions which seem to the
innumerate to be a case of altering the basic rules of the game to suit a
player who has got into a tight corner. In constructing distributions the
first definition was that p is always less than 1, $p + q = 1$ so neither p nor
q could be more than 1 and p multiplied by q never more than 0.25. The
variance of the binomial distribution is *npq* and so is always less than the
mean which is *np*. For the Poisson distribution p was small and 1–q was
taken to be 1, in which case the mean and variance are equal.

But in the negative binomial distribution the variance is greater than
the mean. In the following example from the Greek text of the Fourth
Gospel the mean is 0.679 and the variance is 0.779. Thus the mean np is
0.679, and the variance npq is 0.779. It follows that q is npq/np =
$0.779/0.679 = 1.147$. If p is $1 - q$, then p will be —0.147.

To a purely literary mind the idea of a negative probability seems
absurd, yet this distribution, by using this convention, correctly
describes the occurrence of events in a known situation, where the events
would occur in a Poisson series when recorded in equal intervals they
occur in a negative binomial series when recorded in variable intervals.

(Descriptions of the negative binomial distribution are not found in
many text-books but there is one, with a worked example, in the volume
referred to above, Goodman's *Teach Yourself Statistics*.)

The calculation of the negative binomial distribution continues by
finding n, which is $np/p = 0.679/—0.147 = —4.401$. The recursion
formula for the negative binomial is the same as for the binomial,

$$p(x + 1) = \frac{n + 1}{x + 1} \cdot \frac{p}{q} \cdot p(x)$$

The first term is again $p(0) = q^{-n} = 1.147^{-4.401}$.

The term is calculated by looking up in log tables the log of 1.147, which
is 0.0596, multiplying this by 4.401, the result is 0.2623, subtracting this
from 1.000 to get 0.7367, then looking at the log tables again to get the
antilog of 0.7367, this is 0.5455 and this is the desired result. $p(1)$ is $4.40 \times$
$0.128 \times 0.5455 = 0.3072$, and so on. The last step is to multiply each
probability by the number of sentences in the text 1170, to obtain the
predicted number of sentences for each number of occurrences of *kai*.

In general the negative binomial distribution applies to the occurrence
of words, or other features, which occur at random when the occurrence

Table 5.4   An example of a negative binomial distribution

The occurrence of the conjunction *kai* in the Greek Text of the Fourth
Gospel, British and Foreign Bible Society, London 1964

No of occurrences in Sentence	Number of Sentences	
	In Text	In Neg. Binomial Distribution
0	623	638.2
1	363	359.4
2	138	124.1
3	30	33.8
4	15	4 or more } 14.5
5	1	
Totals:	1170	1170.0

Mean	$0.679 = np$	Chi squared is 2.54.
Variance	$0.779 = npq$	for 2 Degrees of Freedom.
St. Deviation	0.883	p is 0.30.

$$q = \frac{npq}{np} \qquad = \frac{0.779}{0.679} = 1.147$$

$$p = 1 - q \qquad = -0.147$$

$$n = \frac{np}{p} \qquad = \frac{0.679}{0.147} = 4.401$$

$$P(x + 1) \qquad = \frac{4.40 + x}{x + 1} \cdot \frac{0.147}{1.147} \cdot p(x)$$

$$P(0) \qquad = q^n = 1.147^{-4.401} = 0.5455$$

$$P(1) \qquad = \frac{4.40}{1} \times 0.128 \times 0.5455 = 0.3072$$

$$P(2) \qquad = \frac{4.40 + 1}{1 = 1} \times 0.128 \times 0.3072 = 0.1061$$

$$P(3) \qquad = \frac{4.40 + 2}{3} \times 0.128 \times 0.1061 = 0.0290$$

$$P(4 \text{ or more}) \qquad = 1 - P(1 + 2 + 3) = 0.0122$$

is recorded in variable units. The three distributions, the binomial, the
Poisson and the negative binomial form a natural series. If the variance
of a set of observations is less than the mean then they should be tested
for a binomial fit; if the variance is equal to the mean, for a Poisson fit; if
the variance is greater than the mean, for a negative binomial fit. (See
Table 5.4.)

The Negative Exponential Distribution

The negative exponential distribution is related to both the Poisson distribution and to the negative binomial distribution. These applied to the occurrences of a random event recorded in equal or variable intervals, e.g. the occurrences of the conjunction *kai* in blocks of twenty successive words or in sentences. The negative exponential applies to a random event if the occurrence being recorded is the length of intervals between successive occurrences, e.g. the number of words which separate successive occurrences of *kai*.

The negative exponential distribution looks formidable but it is one of the easiest to calculate, it is $E = N (e^{-mt}1 - e^{-mt}2)$. E is the expectation

Table 5.5   An example of a negative exponential distribution

The intervals which separate the first two hundred occurrences of the conjunction *kai* in the *Theogonia* of Hesiod

(a) The observations, their statistics and the expectations of a negative exponential distribution

No of words in Interval	No of such Intervals			
	Observed			Expected
1−10	67			60.4
11−20	46			42.6
21−30	25			29.8
31−40	20			19.8
41−50	13			15.0
51−60	5 ⎫			
61−70	5 ⎬	51−80	17	22.4
71−80	7 ⎭			
81−90	3 ⎫			
91−100	3			
101−110	1			
111−120	—			
121−130	1 ⎬	81−170	12	10.0
131−140	3			
141−150	—			
151−160	—			
161−170	1 ⎭			
	200			200.0

Mean	27.50 words.
Variance	8.32
St. Deviation	2.89

x^2 is 3.19 for 4 Degrees of Freedom.

Table 5.5   (continued)

(b) The calculation of the expected values

The mean is 27.50

The value of m is $\dfrac{1}{27.50}$ = 0.03636.

m x 0 is 0, e^{-0} is 1.000,
m x 10 is 0.36, $e^{-0.36}$ is 0.698,
P(1−10) is 1.000 − 0.698 = 0.302,
m x 20 is 0.73, $e^{-0.73}$ is 0.485
P(11−20) is 0.698 − 0.485 = 0.213
and so on.

The expected values are P(x) x 200.

P(1−10) is 0.302 x 200 = 60.4
P(11−20) is 0.213 x 200 = 42.6
P(21−30) is 0.149 x 200 = 29.8
P(31−40) is 0.099 x 200 = 19.8
P(41−50) is 0.075 x 200 = 15.0
P(51−80) is 0.112 x 200 = 22.4
P(81+   ) is 0.050 x 200 = 10.0
   Notes:

All Values for e^{-x} taken from Goodman, *Op. Cit.*, p. 66.

---

of the intervals, N is the total number of intervals, t_1 and t_2 are the number of words at the upper and lower cell boundaries, m is the reciprocal of the mean interval and e is the base of natural logarithms.

In the first example, the intervals which separate the first two hundred occurrences of the conjunction *kai* from the start of Hesiod's *Theogonia*, the distribution of intervals is set out in Table 5.5. The mean interval is 27.50 words and so m is 1/27.50 = 0.03636. The intervals are grouped in cells which range over ten words; the first cell is of intervals from one to ten words. Actually this interval is from no words to ten words and so t_1 is 0, and the first term becomes e^{-0} (=1) — $e^{-0.03636 \times 10}$= 1.000 − 0.698 = 0.30 and so E (1 − 10) is 0.30 and the expected number of intervals is 200 × 0.30 = 60. The expectation for the next set of intervals is P (10) = 0.70 — P (20) where P (20) is $e^{-0.03636 \times 20}$ = 0.49 and so P (10 − 20) is 0.70 − 0.49 = 0.21.

The second part of the table is a comparison of the observed numbers of intervals with the expected numbers for a negative exponential distribution. This distribution is what is expected for a word occurring in a random fashion in a text, but if the word has a limited mobility in sentences then the distribution will be modified.

Table 5.6 shows the occurrence of the intervals between successive occurrences of the particle *de* in the test of Hesiod's *Aspis*. This particle is

Table 5.6　　An example of how word-spacing is altered by lack of mobility of the word within sentences

The intervals between successive occurrences of the particle *de*.
First two hundred occurrences of the particle in the text of Hesiod's *Aspis*.

No. of Words in Interval	In Text	No. of such Intervals Expected as Negative Exp. Distribution
1–5	29	54.8
6–10	75	39.6
11–15	31	28.2
16–20	19	21.2
21–30	21	26.6
31–40	13	13.8
Longer	12	15.8
Totals:	200	200.0

Mean	15.72
Variance	2.12
St. Deviation	1.06
$m = 0.06361$.	

very frequently the second word in sentences and so the interval between successive occurrences becomes the distance between the second word of one sentence and the second word of the next sentence, the sentence length distribution is reflected in the distribution of intervals. The distribution will not then be negative exponential for there will be too many intervals of about the length of the most frequent sentences and a scarcity of short intervals equivalent to occurrences within sentences.

There are two important points for students of literature which arise from the nature of the Poisson and negative binomial distributions on the one hand, and from the nature of the negative exponential distribution on the other. Both points can be simply illustrated. Suppose a text has 100 pages and an event occurs at random once per page. A Poisson distribution with a mean of 1 will give the expected numbers of pages with no occurrence, with one occurrence and so on. The expected number of pages with no occurrences is $100 \times e^{-1}$ which is 100×0.37 and so 37 pages can be expected to have no occurrence on them. In other words a random event which is expected to occur once per page is absent from no less than 37% of the pages. To have an expectation that less than

5% of the pages would have no occurrence on them requires an average rate of 3 per page. Even this means that for a fairly frequent event, one occurring 300 times in 100 pages, there will be five pages with no occurrence and if these come contiguously they can hardly escape notice and they will suggest to the eye of the layman that this section of the text is quite different from the rest. This is the first point, that random fluctuations are generally much greater than common sense is willing to credit and many claims advanced in literary arguments merely reflect this fact.

The difference between Poisson distributions and negative binomials in this respect is slight so that an event which occurs at random in a variable unit, such as a sentence, will lead to the recording of a number of units having no occurrence and a number with a comparatively large number of occurrences giving an appearance of unevenness is completely deceptive to the untutored eye.

The second point is the inverse of the first. If the spacing of occurrences is recorded, generally a negative exponential distribution will result. For an event which occurs at a consistent rate there will be a surprising number of short intervals and of long intervals in the distribution. Many scholars reading a text are completely deceived by the variability of the spacing of random events. They are in good company for this same distribution represents ruin to many punters who favour racing systems. It is comparatively easy to find a tipster who will select one winner in five; this is not much above the random rate if instead of looking at the horses you pick them by aid of a random number table. It seems simple to make a fortune by backing one winner in five and doubling the stakes to cover the losers. You put one unit on the first horse and if it fails 2 on the next. If this fails you have to put three on the next and then the sum of the previous bets on each successive horse until a winner clears off your arrears. The sum of five terms is only 16 units, the sum of ten terms to cover a losing run of 10 is only 512 units and surely must happen very rarely indeed. Or will it?

The event assumed to be occurring at a random rate has a probability of 0.20, the average interval between successes is 5. But the negative exponential will tell how many intervals there will be of any length. For example, the probability for the number of intervals of between one and five losers will be 1.00 minus $e^{-0.20 \times 5} = e^{-1} = 0.368$ which gives 37% of the runs of losers as 5 or less. The number of losing runs between six and ten in length is $e^{-1} - e^{-0.20 \times 10} = e^{-1} - e^{-2} = (0.368 - 0.135)$ which gives 23.3% of them. So the punter has to cover 13.5% of runs longer than ten losers. He can expect 5% of the runs to be longer than 15 losers and to cover them he nees 16,384 units each time. As the flat racing season runs for about 200 days he will have to cover a run of this length ten times in a season. Not only this, but his average bet is still based on the average run of five and is just over 2 units so his return on capital is very small.

This illustrates the main feature of the negative exponential, that for any rate of occurrence of an event random variations give rise to great differences in the spacing of occurrences. To the unstatistical mind there are a surprising number of both short and long intervals, a feature which often leads, in the study as on the racecourse, to an erroneous conclusion about the pattern of events. The spacing of occurrences is something which takes the eye; the reservations which must be made about their regularity should now be clear.

The three distributions just described and illustrated are often used to summarise large numbers of observations. The next group of distributions are more often used to describe statistics than to describe the observations from which the statistics have been derived. The first of them, the normal distribution, is used to describe some kinds of observation but it is much more often used to describe the behaviour of means, medians, quartiles and statistics like these which are normally distributed. How this is done will be made clear shortly, when we come to the role of statistics in comparisons.

The Normal Distribution

Both the Poisson and the binomial distribution dealt with discrete events and their occurrences. But a variable such as height or weight can take any value, between certain limits, and if we measured height to a sufficient degree of precision, maybe millionths of an inch, we would discover that no two people had ever been exactly the same height.

A distribution which covers a wide range of continuous variables which are symmetrically distributed about their mean is the normal distribution.

The mathematical equation of the normal distribution is complex at a first glance:

$$f(x) = \frac{1}{\sigma\sqrt{2\pi}} \exp\left\{-\frac{1}{2}\left(\frac{x-\mu}{\sigma}\right)^2\right\}$$

But this has been chosen so that when measured in units of the standard deviation s and the mean μ, then simple calculations can be made and applied to a wide range of data. For example, the area under such a normal distribution is one unit and so the distribution can be used as a model for probabilities which also are measured on a scale reaching one unit. The normal distribution can then be used to describe, and to calculate, probabilities. In this scale the probability of an event is the area of the normal distribution, measured in units of the standard deviation,

Figure 5.1 The normal distribution

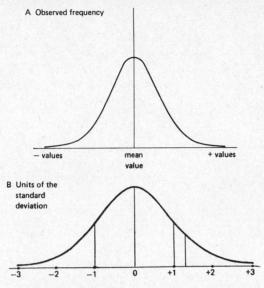

The standard deviation makes a convenient unit in which to measure the area under a normal curve. 68% of the area lies within one standard deviation of the mean, 95% of the area within two standard deviations of the mean and almost all of the area, 99.73% of it, within three standard deviations of the mean.

associated with the occurrence of the event or value of the statistics, divided by the area under the normal distribution as a whole, which is one unit.

The second reason for regarding the normal distribution as of great importance is that many statistics are normally distributed. For example, if we take observations which are quite obviously not normally distributed – say, the series of natural numbers 1, 2, 3 etc. up to 100,000 – and pick out small samples from this series, it will be found that the means of these samples are normally distributed. There is a theorem, the 'central limit theorem', which shows that means are normally distributed irrespective of the form of distribution of the data from which the means have been derived, as long as the variance of the data is finite.[1]

The five distributions which have been described will cover the needs of literature analysis. However, there are two other distributions which are not used to describe data but for testing the hypothesis about data, and these are essential to the investigation of the literary texts.

The first is the *chi squared distribution*, one of the most versatile in

---

[1] For one proof the reader can refer to Paul G. Hoel, *Introduction to Mathematical Statistics*, New York 1963, p. 146.

statistical theory. This distribution is used to test whether the observed frequencies in a distribution differ from those expected according to some assumed hypothesis. For each frequency E, predicted by the hypothesis, there will be a corresponding observed frequency, 0; then the chi squared distribution is :

$$x^2 = \frac{\Sigma(0 - E)^2}{E}$$

That is to say, chi squared is the sum of the squares of the differences between each of the observed and expected frequencies, divided in each case by the expected frequency.

Suppose a coin is tossed, and one hundred tosses yield 45 heads and 55 tails. Someone claims that this is a case of fraud, saying that the expected number of heads and tails should be 50 of each and so there has been manipulation. We can test this hypothesis in the following way. The assumption we are testing is the null hypothesis that our result is not significantly different from the expected result, 50 heads and 50 tails. So we write:

$$X^2 = \frac{(0 - E)^2}{E} + \frac{(0 - E)^2}{E}$$

$$X^2 = \text{For heads} \frac{(45 - 50)^2}{50} + \text{For tails} \frac{(55 - 50)^2}{50}$$

$$= \frac{5^2}{50} + \frac{5^2}{50}$$

$$= \frac{1}{2} + \frac{1}{2} = 1.$$

It should be evident that if theory and practice coincide we should find chi squared 0. To decide whether the value of 1 is enough to cast doubt on the hypothesis that the coin is unbiased, we need to know something else, the number of *degrees of freedom* associated with chi squared. The number of degrees of freedom is the number of free choices which can be made in assembling the data. In this example, there is only a single degree of freedom, for any number of heads at once decided the number of tails. We therefore look up, in any set of statistical tables, the table of chi squared at one degree of freedom; chi squared is 1.1. when p is 0.3. Thus the differences as large as this one, or larger, will occur by chance alone three times in ten trials of the experiment of tossing an unbiased coin. This seems slender evidence to support a charge of deceit.

An example of how chi squared distribution is used to test the fit of a distribution to data is taken from an earlier example, the distribution of *kai* in sentences in the Gospel of John (see Table 5.4). The observed occurrences of *kai* in sentences were as shown; the expected values were calculated by using the mean and variance taken from the observed figures in the recursion formula for a negative binomial distribution.

	Number of *kais* in the Sentences					
	0	1	2	3	4	5
Observed No. of Sentences	623	363	138	30	(15	1)
Expected No. of Sentences	638.2	359.4	124.1	33.8	14.5	

In using the chi squared test there are two conditions to be met. The first is that no expectation should be less than 5. The reason for this is that it is not possible, in most circumstances, to make an accurate prediction of the rate of occurrences of an event until it has occurred at least five times. Thus the two groups, 4 or 5 occurrences of *kai*, are amalgamated to make one group having 4 *kais* or more.

The second condition is not important in this example, but with fewer observations it can be. The chi squared distribution is a continuous one and the expectation could work out that there should be 95.7 sentences with no *kai*. This can only be counted as 95 or 96 sentences. To compensate for this difference between a continuous distribution such as chi squared and an integral distribution such as the distribution of *kai* in sentences, each difference between an observed value and an expected value should have one half – 0.5 – subtracted if it is more than the observation and one half added if it is less than the observation. With numbers as large as these in the example the difference made by the correction is slight, but with small samples the difference is not negligible. This correction is called, after its originator, *Yate's correction*.

To return to the example: chi squared is the sum of all the terms, $(638.2 — 623)^2/638.2$, $(363 — 359.4)^2/359.4$, and so on. The total for chi squared is 2.54. Now there are five groups, and only four choices before the last group is fixed as the remainder of the total less the first four groups, and so there are four degrees of freedom. But two other degrees of freedom have been used, for the figures have been derived by using the mean and variance of the observations to calculate the expectations, and so the expectations have to conform to two further constraints and the number of degrees of freedom is therefore two. Entering the tables of chi squared for two degrees of freedom we find that p is about 0.30; so differences between what we find and what we would expect to find, if the data is described by a negative binomial distribution, will occur by chance alone about once in every three trials.

The chi squared distribution is a most useful one and can be used to test a wide range of hypotheses.

Students' 't' Distribution

If small samples are taken, with less than thirty observations in them, it is wise to use a special test for the difference of two means. As our interests lie in detecting the change in mean level in the smallest possible samples, we shall use a 't' test, based on Students' 't' distribution. The test will be explained in detail in Chapter 7.

The reader should now be in a position to appreciate that large masses of data or groups of observations, too large to be visualised by the human mind, can be summarily described in a few statistics. If the pattern of the observations fits one of the common distributions, then the power of distillations in the statistics can be very great indeed. Even a hundred million observations may be completely described by such simple statements as that the observations fit a Poisson distribution with a mean of m.

Other distributions are used to carry out statistical tests. For example, whether or not the data are adequately described by one of the common forms of distribution can be tested by the chi squared distribution.

6 Like or Unlike? The Statistics of Comparisons

What the previous chapters have described is how a mass of information covering large numbers of observations may be simply summarised into a few statistics, without losing any of the useful information which can be derived from the observations. The simple statement that a set of observations fits a Poisson distribution with a mean of 1.00 can completely describe the pattern of occurrence of literally millions of observations. What has not yet been touched upon is the role of statistics in making comparisons.

The starting point for this exposition is to visualise a large number of observations. If an example is useful to the reader, then they may be thought of as measurements of the heights of human beings. For historical reasons the large group is called a *population*. Now consider a smaller group, called a *sample*, drawn from the population. The sample is drawn according to some rules. Each sample will resemble the population from which it comes, for the very good reason that every element in the sample is also an element of the population. No sample will completely represent the population since not all the elements in the population will be present in any sample. So samples will resemble each other, and the population from which they come, but there will be some variations between samples.

The relations between samples and the population from which they are drawn are controlled by the rules by which the samples are selected. Suppose we use rules directly related to the quantity being measured. One such rule might be: having recorded all the heights on cards, shuffle the cards, pick out sets of five cards, keep the card which records the tallest person and put these aside until you have a sample of one hundred cards. Such a sample will not tell you anything about the smallest person, little about those who are generally short and rather more about those who are generally tall. Such samples are called biased. They have not been chosen by a method which guarantees independence of the choice and the information which results from the choice.

The most common sampling system is to take a random sample. In such a sample every member of the population has an equal chance of being selected for the sample and the usual way to do this would be to number all the cards, shuffle them and draw the required number by lots. As cards are sticky and awkward to handle, it is easier to look up a set of random numbers, in effect tables of numbers which have been shuffled and selected, and use the numbers so obtained to pick out the sample.

71

Having used a suitable set of rules to pick out a sample, the statistics of the sample would be calculated to enable the sample to be summarily described. The statistics might be the mean and variance or a much more elaborate set, but for simplicity in the illustration, suppose that only the sample mean is calculated. If a large number of samples were taken and the mean of all of them calculated, the mean of all the samples would coincide with the population mean as all the different heights in the set which make up the population would also occur in the samples, and the different heights would appear in samples in the same proportion as they occurred in the population. The mean of any sample would be the population mean only by a happy coincidence. In some samples the mean will be higher than the population mean; in others it will be lower than the population mean. It has already been noted that means are normally distributed, so if the means of a large number of samples were recorded then these would fit the well-known bell curve of the normal distribution. The peak of the distribution would lie at the population mean and the means of all the individual samples would cluster round it in the familiar pattern.

The sample means can be used in a further calculation which will give us the standard deviation of the sample means and so enable the normal distribution of the sample means to be fully represented by the two statistics, the mean of all the separate sample means taken together and the standard deviation of these sample means. The mean of all the sample means will be the population mean and the standard deviation of the sample means will tell us how the sample means are grouped around this central value, the population mean. This standard deviation of sample means has been given a special name; it is called the *standard error of the mean*. A traditional pleasantry of the statistician is that the standard error is so called for being neither standard nor an error. But it is an important statistic and its name is derived from the fact that it is a measure of how uncertain an estimate of the population mean the sample mean is. The standard error of the mean is *the standard deviation* $/\sqrt{(N)}$ (where N is the number of observations in the sample). The formula shows that the larger the number of observations in the sample, the more accurate an estimate of the population mean it will provide. It also shows that to halve the standard error, the number of observations had to be quadrupled. It also shows that small samples with few observations must be almost impossible to distinguish from each other.

The importance of the fact that sample means are normally distributed can be seen when samples are being compared. If the sample means are plotted and form a normal distribution, then they can be regarded as belonging to a single population. The plotting of the sample means will show that this is the case; most of them will lie close to the population mean which will be the mode of the normal distribution, few of them will be far from the mode of the normal distribution and they will be symmetrically distributed around the mode.

If there are only two samples, it is hardly practical to construct a normal distribution from them but they can be compared to see whether or not it is reasonable to regard them as coming from a single normal distribution. Another look at Figure 5.1 shows that if two sample means come from a normal distribution, then in nineteen cases out of twenty they will lie within a range of two standard errors of the population mean. So the samples will have means that lie within the range of two standard errors of each other.

Rules can be constructed to fit any situation. The probability that the two samples belong to a single population can be fixed at one in twenty (0.05) or one in a hundred (0.01) or one in a thousand (0.001). It all depends on the balance between the cost of making a decision and the consequences of making a wrong decision. If you were to shut down an oil refinery for three days, and rely on the fact that chance would have produced the evidence on which you acted only once in twenty inspections, you are unlikely to be popular with the company. If you announce that less than one in twenty of your aircraft crash before reaching their destination, you will not be much of a threat to established airlines.

Decisions are made by reference to *levels of significance*. The 5% level of significance is the point at which chance variation will account for the differences between samples only one time in twenty for samples which belong to a single population. The 1% level of significance is the point at which the chance differences will be found in samples from a single population only once in one hundred trials. Differences which are less than those chosen for the levels of significance are called *random sampling differences*. For random sampling differences no other explanation is offered, or can be offered, than natural chance variation such as we are accustomed to see whenever cards are shuffled and dealt or a coin is tossed. Differences which reach the level of significance, or exceed it, are called *statistically significant* and for them some other explanation than chance variation is required. Samples which show, in comparisons, only random sampling differences can be regarded as belonging to the same population. Samples which show statistically significant differences will not be regarded as belonging to the same population.

This pattern of argument contains two built-in errors. Once in twenty trials, two samples from the same population will show variations which chance will produce once in twenty trials but, because of the rule, we will not accept chance as an explanation for the existence of the variations and treat them as statistically significant. This error, being known, can be easily avoided. If two independent comparisons are made of the samples, then the two tests will combine to mislead only once in twenty times twenty trials, once in four hundred trials. The addition of another comparison will reduce the chance effect to once in 8,000 trials and half a dozen comparisons will be adequate to exclude it from almost any situation.

On the other hand two samples can come from different populations, but if one sample is a high estimate of the mean and the other is a low estimate, and each sample tends towards making the populations resemble each other, then it can be accepted that they represent one population, when in fact the correct conclusion would have been that they belong to different populations. This type of error is less important. Not only will it be excluded by any number of comparisons but it will lead to no misjudgement, for statistical argument is always exclusive. It is only differences which are decisive. Two heights may be recorded as five foot eight inches but these do not necessarily refer to the same man. If the two are six foot and five foot then they must refer to different men. Authors are identified not by the habits in which they resemble each other but by the habits in which they differ from one to another, so that the obscuring of any difference, while it is to be regretted, will not lead to any mistaken conclusion.

This argument has been illustrated by considering a single statistic, the mean of samples. But it applies to all the statistics previously described, medians, quartiles, deciles, and so on. All are normally distributed and so can be made the basis of tests of significance which enable samples to be classed as alike, i.e. drawn from a single population, or as unlike, i.e. not drawn from a single population.

It is at this point that a test of authorship can be defined. It is some habit which can be numerically expressed and statistically described for which the works of one author can be regarded as a single population, and all the individual works, or parts of such works, can be treated as samples of that population. This means that the differences within his works, or between his works, in respect of this habit, will be only random sampling differences. If the test is to be an effective one, then the differences between authors in respect of the habit will be large and statistically significant.

7 The Rules of the Game

Statistical method is based on the comparison of samples. A sample is a small group of observations taken from a large group, the population, and the statistics of the sample are useful in so far as they describe the statistics of the population. In literary studies a sample may be a complete text, or it may be some part of a text; the population may be the whole corpus of an author's writings or all the works he wrote in a particular literary form, for example in hexameter verse or continuous prose, or it may be the remainder of a text from which the sample has been extracted.

Populations can be real or hypothetical. One population can be a large collection of the heights of human beings duly recorded. Another population can be the calculated results of tossing a perfect coin. The essential requirement of a population is that it should be homogeneous, that is it should comprise the same material in all parts. It should not be made up merely of similar observations. When bowmen were busy, long bows were much the length of the archers who used them. So a record of bow-lengths and another of the heights of archers would be indistinguishable but this would not make them a single population; the origin of the two kinds of information is quite different. This may seem to be labouring the obvious but the fact that the mean sentence length in Homer, 13.13 words per sentence, is much the same as the mean sentence length for the prose of the Apostle Paul, has been taken by at least one classical scholar to suggest that they have a common source.

A first step is to select the samples. Before doing so it may be well to consider the gulf that separates the two words, *sample* and *example*. An example is an instance chosen to illustrate some point which an author wishes to make and the example is selected with no other purpose in mind. A sample is selected by rules which exist quite independently of the investigator and the sample is used to represent some features of a population. A sample can support a hypothesis only in as much as the statistics of the sample confirm a hypothesis which has been expressed in statistical terms.

There are a number of ways in which samples can be selected and the use of any particular method of sampling is determined by considering the nature of the observations, of the problem being investigated and of the resources which can be economically devoted to the project.

The earliest method of sampling used in literary studies was *random sampling*. In a random sample every member of the population has an equal chance of being chosen for the sample. One way of selecting a random sample is to number all the items in the population, say the words or sentences in a text, and compile the sample by using a set of random number tables to pick out the required number of items. Random sampling is useful for primary mathematical investigations but its limitations in literary studies are obvious and acute. Suppose that the Gospel of John in the Bible is under examination. Two parts of the Gospel of particular interest are the story of the woman taken in adultery (7.53–8.11) and the final chapter, chapter 21. Random samples could be drawn for a very long time without revealing much about either passage, as random samples would be unlikely to include them.

A second sampling method, pioneered by Dr. W. C. Wake, is that of *spread sampling*. As the name implies, spread samples are used to give a summary view of large texts and they are selected by such rules as: 'Take the second sentence on every third page.' Spread sampling has its uses, but many texts, for example those of the New Testament, are so short that spread sampling is of little interest to the student of them.

The third method of selecting samples is to start the sample at any point in a text and to carry on until the sample is large enough to represent the text or author. This method, also due to Dr. Wake, is called *block sampling*. Block samples are not usually random samples; they would only be random samples if every observation after the first one which starts the sample were independent of those before and after it. In literary texts this is not often the case. The reason for this is that language is not random in its fine detail, and can only be treated as random when the sample is large enough to eliminate periodic effects. That language is not random is simply illustrated. On the average, one word in twenty in all Greek writing is a repetition of the conjunction *kai*. If language were random in structure then once in every twenty times twenty words, i.e. once in every four hundred words, two occurrences of *kai* would come together. In fact no such pair of successive occurrences has yet been found in a Greek text.

Dr. Wake established the minimum sample size for sentence length distributions by a method of general application. He started with a text much larger than the minimum sample size and wrote out a set of cards, each of which bore the number of words in a sentence of the text. He then had two populations, one the sentences of a Greek text in their sequence, the other a set of cards each of which represented a single sentence of the text. He then compared the behaviour of the two sets of samples which resulted from dividing the text, and the cards, into smaller and smaller groups. The difference between the sets of samples is that the sentences remained in text sequence but the cards were shuffled and random samples selected from this population. The shuffled cards are a random structure, and sub-division of a random population has entirely predictable results. The means of the samples remain normally distributed and the range of values in the samples remains consistent. But the sub-division of the text showed that Greek writing is not a random structure. Long sentences and short sentences tend to form groups. When the samples are of less than 50 sentences they might contain a large number of long sentences or of short sentences, and so the range of values in the observations contracts and the sample means are no longer normally distributed. A series of experiments of this kind enabled Dr. Wake to fix the minimum sample size for sentence length distributions of Greek writers. The minimum sample size runs from about 50 to 100 sentences. Minimum sample size must be determined by experiment and investigation; it is unwise to make confident statements about this subject on the basis of intuition.

Block sampling is a useful method of selecting samples but it is by no means ideal. For example, if it could be shown that in Paul's second epistle to the Corinthians Chapters 10 to 13 differed from the rest of the epistle (the sample is quite large enough to be representative of the author), such a demonstration would only raise another question. Is the difference spread through the whole passage or is it confined to a few sections of the passage?

The ideal sampling method would be one which made a complete and continuous inspection of the text, an inspection which would isolate any sections of the text which differed by a statistically significant amount from the remainder of the text. Such a method exists but it by no means relieves the scholar of responsibility for his critical judgements. The method is also subject to the usual restraints of all sampling systems. In the first place, the overall requirement of a minimum expectation of five occurrences of the event being recorded remains and usually fixes the minimum sample size of section which can be isolated by a continuous sampling method. A complication arises in the inspection of large texts. For example, if a sequence of 1,000 sentences is being examined for some occurrence, then it must be borne in mind that this sequence could be divided into 100 sequences of 10 sentences, or 20 sequences of 50 sentences, and so it is only to be expected that statistically significant differences will appear by the operation of chance alone.

The real value of continuous sampling methods is the isolation of passages which show statistically significant differences in comparison with the rest of the text and the concentration of critical attention on these. The method has also great negative value in that a scholar who has argued that some part of a text is very markedly different from the rest will find it an embarrassment to discover that the passage does not differ from the body of the text.

An inspection of a text by continuous sampling will present the critic with a list of sections which require study; the evidence is that some feature of the text, of about the length indicated, and near to the position indicated, is significantly different from the text as a whole. The reason for the uncertainty in size and position can be seen when the method of

Figure 7.1   A cumulative sum chart of the data of Tables 7.1 and 7.2

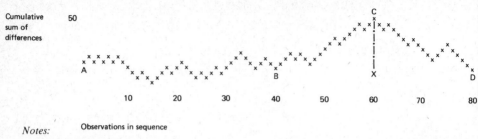

Notes: Observations in sequence

A cumulative sum chart of the observations of Tables 7.1 and 7.2, the 80 observations have a mean of 0.50, variance of 0.25 and standard deviation of 0.50. The vertical scale is in tenths of a unit to avoid fractions.

continuous sampling, the cumulative sum chart – usually abbreviated to cusum chart – is illustrated. The minimum size of sample which can be treated as a random sample is easily seen from the inspection of a cusum chart of the series of observations. An example of this will be shown later (see Figure 7.1).

A cusum chart could hardly be simpler in conception. It is a chart on which is plotted the cumulative sum of the differences between each successive observation and the mean of all the observations. The power of the cusum chart derives from a simple principle. If there is a change in the mean of a part of the series, then the change in each successive observation is added so that the change is more readily apparent. In the other methods of comparison such changes, which are often quite small, are not added and so remain less readily detectable.

A cusum chart of a homogeneous series of observations is like the profile of a range of hills; the line rises and falls but does not depart much from the horizontal and starts and finishes on the horizontal. If there is a section in the series which has a mean higher than the mean for the whole series, then the cusum chart will climb away from the horizontal; if there is a section with a mean lower than that of the series the cusum chart will fall away below the horizontal. All these features are obvious from an example. Table 7.1 and Figure 7.1 show a set of 80 observations. In forty instances an event has occurred and its presence is recorded by 1; in forty instances it has not occurred and its absence is recorded by 0. The sequence of eighty observations has been constructed. The two halves of the series contain equal numbers of 1s and 0s, so the means, variances and standard deviations of both halves are identical. In fact the first forty observations are a random sequence of twenty 1s and twenty 0s, but the second half has been fabricated from 15 1s and 5 0s and then 15 0s and 5 1s. The reason for selecting 15 and 5 is that these numbers represent the smallest difference within the series which is statistically significant. The whole series has equal numbers of 1s and 0s so that a section of twenty observations would be expected to have 10 of each. The observed

Table 7.1   The series of observations

A

1–10	1	1	0	1	0	1	0	1	0	0
11–20	0	0	1	0	0	1	1	1	0	1
21–30	1	0	0	0	1	0	1	1	0	1
31–40	1	1	1	0	0	0	1	1	0	0
41–50	1	1	1	0	1	0	0	1	1	1
51–60	1	1	0	1	1	1	1	0	1	1
61–70	0	0	1	0	0	0	0	1	0	0
71–80	0	1	1	1	0	0	0	0	0	0

B The differences between the observations and the mean of the series, in units of the first decimal

+5	+5	−5	+5	−5	+5	−5	+5	−5	−5
−5	−5	+5	−5	−5	+5	+5	+5	−5	+5
+5	−5	−5	−5	+5	−5	+5	+5	−5	+5
+5	+5	+5	−5	−5	−5	+5	+5	−5	−5
+5	+5	+5	−5	+5	−5	−5	+5	+5	+5
+5	+5	−5	+5	+5	+5	+5	−5	+5	+5
−5	−5	+5	−5	−5	−5	−5	+5	−5	−5
−5	+5	+5	+5	−5	−5	−5	−5	−5	−5

C The cumulative sum of the differences, in units of the first decimal[1]

5	10	5	10	5	10	5	10	5	0
−5	−10	−5	−10	−15	−10	−5	0	−5	0
5	0	−5	−10	−5	−10	−5	0	−5	0
5	10	15	10	5	0	5	10	5	0
5	10	15	10	15	10	5	10	15	20
25	30	25	30	35	40	45	40	45	50
45	40	45	40	35	30	25	30	25	20
15	20	25	30	25	20	15	10	5	0

[1] See Figure 7.1.

numbers of occurrences 15 and 5 give chi squared 4.05 for one degree of freedom with Yate's correction.

If a cumulative sum chart of the data is drawn (see Figure 7.1), it looks obvious that there is some degree of difference between the parts of the series. The chart rises and falls no more than fifteen units until the 40th observation; it then rises to fifty units at the 60th observation, and falls back to zero at the end. To find whether or not the difference illustrated by the chart is statistically significant, a base line has to be established, in this case BD. Then the vertical height or depth of the highest peak or deepest valley on the base line is measured, in this example CX. This vertical height is divided by the standard deviation of the series and the result is read from Table 12a (p. 39 of the Manual referred to)[1]. For this

[1]'Cumulative Sum Charts' *I.C.I. Research Monograph 3.* Oliver & Boyd, Edinburgh, 1964.

example BD is 40 units, CX is 50 units and the standard deviation is 0.5 units; but CX was measured in units of the first decimal and so the result of dividing CX by the standard deviation is ten. Entering the table for a span of 40 units and an amplitude of 10 units, we read that p is about 0.03.

There are a number of difficulties in this procedure. One is that it is not easy to establish a base line. In the example, the last point of the series is clearly enough one point to choose, but the anomalous section might start at observation 47, rather than 40; or observation 36 or, rather less likely, at observation 29. To ensure that the result is the best mathematical estimate of the change which has occurred, all these alternatives must be investigated. This is why a computer is often used for dissecting a cumulative sum chart.

Another difficulty is that the estimates of the meeting point of two series of observations is always uncertain to an extent dependent on the variances of the series. Figure 7.2 shows why this is so. In Figure 7.2 two series of observations, series A and series B, are represented. As the series have different means, the cusum chart will appear as a triangular waveform with random fluctuations superimposed on the waveform. The mean of each series can be shown by a line drawn through the ascending and descending sides of the waveform, and two other lines can be drawn for each series to contain the random variations above and

Figure 7.2   *The uncertainty of cusum charts illustrated*

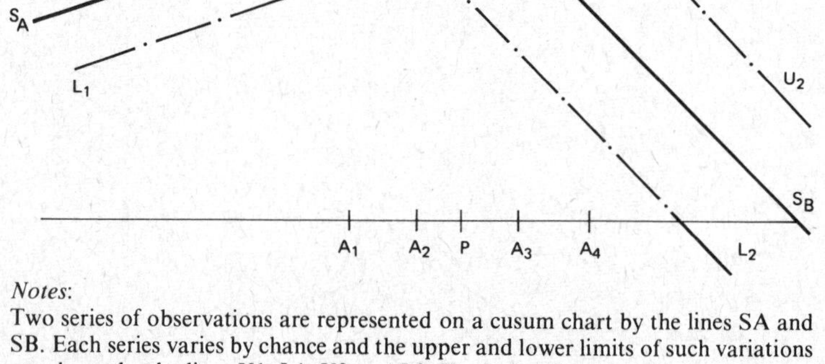

Notes:

Two series of observations are represented on a cusum chart by the lines SA and SB. Each series varies by chance and the upper and lower limits of such variations are shown by the lines U1, L1, U2 and L2. The series should meet at point P but where they actually intersect depends on the variations of the series and can be anywhere from A1 to A4. If the four points A1, A2, A3 and A4 can be detected from the chart the mean of the four points will lie near to P.

below the mean. A pair of lines could be drawn to represent the variance of each series; the variance line would represent the root-mean-square average of the variations above and below the mean line.

Figure 7.2 shows that the uncertainty in a cusum chart can be represented by a quadrilateral defined by the four points at which the upper and lower boundaries of the two sets of observations intersect. Figure 7.3 is an illustration of the occurrence of the four points in a Greek text. The first part of the *Athenaion Politeia* is a historical review of the constitution of Athens and the second part is a critical study of the constitution as it was about 325 BC. From a composite review based on earlier sources and other historians, the writer of *Athenaion Politeia* turns to write in his own free composition his analysis of the constitution. The last sentence of the first part is sentence 454 of the text. Figure 7.3 shows that this transition is not very clearly marked but the average of the four adjacent turning points indicates a position very near to the true turning point.

These figures show that it can be quite advantageous to have a series of observations in a form which has a low variance. As long as no statistically significant difference is obscured by the transformation of the data then the form which has the least variance will be that best suited to examination by cusum chart. For example, Table 7.2 shows two series of one hundred observations. Each series is a Poisson distribution, the first series having a mean of 1.00 and the second a mean of 1.60. The third column in the table, headed chi squared, indicates whether or not the difference between the distributions in that cell is statistically significant or not, Yate's correction having been applied. The chi squared column

Figure 7.3   The uncertainty of a cusum chart illustrated from a Greek text

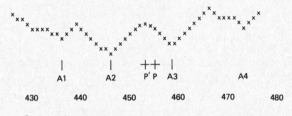

Sequence of sentences in text

Notes:
This is a small section of the cusum chart for the occurrences of the particle *de* as the second word of the sentences of *Athenaion Politeia*. The true division of the text is at sentence 454 which is not well represented in the chart. But the mean of the four minima nearest to this point is between 452 and 453.

Table 7.2   An illustrative comparison of two sets of observations

No of occurrences	Number of observations with X occurrences in				
X	S 1	CS	S 2	CS	$\frac{S1 + S2}{2}$
0	37	4.50	20	2.25	28.5
1	37	0.24	32	0.12	34.5
2	18	1.12	26	0.56	22.0
3 or more	8	5.64	22	2.82	15.0
Totals:	100	11.50	100	5.75	100.0

Notes:

For the table taken as a whole, chi squared is 16.25 for three degrees of freedom so that p is near to 0.001. In the table the columns CS give each element of chi squared calculated as the observed figure for each series compared to the expected value in the final column.

S1 has 6 observations with 3 occurrences and 2 with 4 occurrences; S2 has 14 observations with 3 occurrences, 6 with 4 occurrences and 2 with 5 occurrences.

shows that the differences between the two series concern the first and last classes. If the observations are grouped so that there are only two classes, then in two instances, the first when one group is of no occurrence and the other is of all occurrences, the second when the first group is of two occurrences or fewer and the second group is of three occurrences or more, the differences remain statistically significant. The variance of the data is reduced and the uncertainty in a cusum chart based on the data is also reduced. If, however, the data is divided into two groups, one of no occurrence or one occurrence and the other of two occurrences or more, then the statistically significant differences are obscured and the advantage of the transformation is lost. It is only by inspection of the actual sequence of observations that the most convenient form in which to use them will be apparent.

Cusum charts were developed for industrial use, for monitoring continuous processes. The problem confronting the industrialist is exactly parallel to that facing the student of stylometry; in both cases the aim is to detect any alteration in the mean level of the observations, yet to ignore any random changes in the series. The observations on which the chart is based must be derived from a suitable test of authorship.

Cusum charts are prepared simply by a computer. They can also be dissected by the computer but unless the texts under examination are quite extensive the use of the machine for this purpose has only marginal advantages. The kind of complication that besets the machine can be readily illustrated. Suppose that a computer is asked to read the two Poisson series just described and to analyse a cusum chart of them in sequence. The machine would be instructed, by most cusum programs, to read the whole series and establish a mean for all the observations. In this case the result would be a mean of 1.30 for the 200 observations. The variance for the two hundred observations would not be far from 1.30 and so the standard error of the mean for the whole series, as read by the machine, would be not much under 0.10. So when the machine read the first hundred observations it would decide that they do not differ from a series with a mean of 1.30 and when it read the second hundred it would decide that, with their mean of 1.60, neither did those differ from the overall series. But if the machine had been told to test one part of the series against the other it would have concluded, correctly, that statistically significant differences existed.

The alternative is to instruct the machine to take the observations in sequence until it reaches a turning point and then cut off the text up to the turning point and use this as a test piece. But this procedure has problems too. For example, if a section has a low mean and is followed by a section with a higher mean but one not significantly different from that of the first section, then the machine will not separate this second section. If a third section followed which had a much higher mean, then this section would be isolated and the machine would conclude that a section with a mean of about the middle of the range of values had been followed by another which had a high mean. If it was then asked to read the series backwards, it would start with the high section, carry on with the mid-section and isolate the low section. The correct conclusion is that between two sections with high and low means there is a third section which could belong to either but not to both. This can best be shown by instructing the machine to read the text in both directions and comparing the results of the two searches.

For reasons of this kind it is often just as simple to instruct the machine to make a list of the observations and construct a cusum chart of them. The chart is then inspected and the machine asked to test any section which seems to be of special interest. It can be useful to make a V-mask according to the instructions in the research manual referred to. The mask is laid over the chart and will at once indicate sections which show statistically significant differences.

The reservations about the use of cusum charts having been explained, it might seem that they are cumbersome and not of much practical interest in the study of Greek texts. To show how useful they can be, Figure 7.4 shows a section of the chart of the Fourth Gospel covering the text of the story of the woman taken in adultery. The chart is of the occurrence of the particle *de* as the second word of sentences, a test first described by Morton[1] and amplified by Michaelson and Morton.[2]

[1] Morton, A. Q., 'The Authorship of Greek Prose', *Journal Royal Stat. Soc. 128*, pp. 169–223, 1965.
[2] Michaelson, S. and Morton, A. Q., 'Positional Stylometry', *The Computer in Literary Studies*, Ed. Aitken, Edinburgh University Press, 1972.

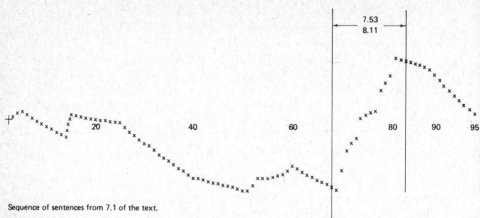

Figure 7.4   An illustration of the use of a cusum chart

Sequence of sentences from 7.1 of the text.

Notes:
The chart is of the occurrences of the particle *de* as the second word in sentences in the text of the Fourth Gospel from 7.1 to 8.20. The story of the woman taken in adultery is clearly anomalous, and calculation confirms that the difference between this story and the rest of the text is statistically significant.

At this point it should be clear that a method exists by which a whole text can be examined, but no mention has yet been made of how much of a text is needed to make a safe sample. Minimum sample size can be determined from a cusum chart. Before dealing with this aspect of their use it may be well to review the general principles which bear on the determination of minimum sample size.

The first requirement is that the sample will contain, or can be expected to contain, five occurrences of the event being observed. If ten percent of the sentences in a text have the particle *de* as their second word, then the minimum sample size for this author would be fifty sentences, the number needed to record five occurrences. If half the sentences had the particle in this position, the minimum sample would come down to ten sentences. In the first instance the minimum interpolation which could be detected, periodic effects being disregarded for the moment, would be six sentences, every one of which had an occurrence of the particle as their second word.

The next requirement of the minimum sample is that within the sample periodic effects should be negligible. The branch of statistical theory which deals with the detection of periodic effects is serial correlation, a technique for looking at the influence of one observation over the next observation. The kind of question investigated by serial correlation is whether or not the writing of a sentence which has the particle *de* as its second word makes it any more likely, or any less likely, that the next sentence will have a similar occurrence. Serial correlation tests will indicate the presence of periodic effects and, if they are present, then they will bear on the minimum sample size.

Figure 7.5   An illustration of the use of a cusum chart

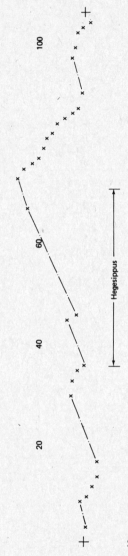

Notes:

A cusum chart of the text of Eusebius from 2.19.3 to 2.23.18 covering his major citation of Hegesippus. The chart is one of sentences which have no occurrence of the conjunction *kai*, and the text of Hegesippus runs from sentence 30 to sentence 70 of the sequence. Calculation confirms that the difference between this section and the adjacent text is statistically significant.

There are two types of serial correlation test which will be found useful in literary studies. The first is the runs test. A runs test is a prediction of how often, in a random sequence of observations, observations of one type will come together to form a run of similar observations. For example, if in a series of 200 sentences there are 50 which have the particle *de* as their second word, then a runs test will tell you how often there will be runs of sentences with the particle in this position in the sequence of 200 sentences.

If, as in this case, there are two classes of observation, an occurrence denoted by *a* and a non-occurrence denoted by *b*, then in a random sequence the expected number of sequences of *as* is:

$$E = \frac{a(b+1)}{a+b}$$

The standard error of this estimate is:

$$\sqrt{\frac{E \cdot b \cdot (a-1)}{(a+b)(a+b+1)}}$$

For the figures quoted *a* is 50, *b* is 150 so the number of sequences of sentences with *de* as their second word is: $E = 50(151)/200 = 37.8$, which must be rounded to the nearest whole number. The standard error of this estimate is:

$$\frac{37.75 \times 150 \times 49}{200 \times 201} = 2.63.$$

The calculation of the standard error of this estimate enables it to be said that chance will be an acceptable explanation for any number of runs which lies within two standard errors of the estimate, i.e. for numbers which lie between 37.8 + or − 5.2. So any number of runs of sentences with *de* as their second word which is more than 32 but less than 43 indicates a sequence which can be regaded as a random one.

In the epistle to the Galatians the number of sentences is 166, the number of sentences longer than the median length of sentence is 87 and the number shorter than the median length is 89. Proceeding as before, *a* is 87, *b* is 89, E is 47.2 and the standard error of E is 3.7. If the sentences of the epistle were a random series, then the number of runs of sentences longer than the median length would be between 39 and 45. The number of such sequences in the epistle is 38, indicating that serial correlation is present but not to any large degree. What a runs test will not show is whether the difference is due to each sequence being a little longer than it would be in a random series or if the result is due to a small number of long runs. An example of this latter effect can be taken from the first 35 sentences of Galatians. For these sentences we have *a* is 27, *b* is 8, E is 7.5 and the standard error of E is 1.1. The upper and lower limits for the number of runs of sentences longer than the median length are 9.7 and 5.5. There are 7 such runs in the text. This seems to indicate that the sequence does not depart from randomness, which is correct, but what it does not show is that of the 28 sentences in 7 runs, an average run length of 4 successive occurrences, two are single occurrences, two double occurrences and one run is of four occurrences, one of five occurrences and one run is of 13 occurrences, i.e. nearly half of the occurrences are in a single sequence.

The second test of serial correlation is one developed for literary use by Dr. W. C. Wake and deals with the variance of a set of observations and the differential variance of the same observations. The differential distribution of a set of observations is the distribution of the differences between successive observations. If there is a set of sentences containing 10, 15, 20, 15 and 10 words, then the differential distribution of the observations will be +5, +5, +5, —5 and —5; in each case the number of words to be added to each observation to get the number of words in the next observation. Wake showed that, if the variance of a distribution is calculated and then the variance for the differential distribution of the same data is calculated, then serial correlation in the data is tested by the relation:

$$\frac{\text{Differential Variance}}{\text{Variance}} = 2(1 - r)$$

where r is the coefficient of serial correlation. The coefficient of correlation varies from +1, which would indicate a complete dependence of one observation on the preceding one, through 0 which would indicate no dependence of an observation on its predecessor, to —1 which would indicate an observation completely controlled by the previous one but on the opposite sense to it. In Greek prose writers, sentence length distributions show positive serial correlation but in Homer the correlation is negative. This is because prose writers tend to follow a long or short sentence with another of the same kind, but in hexameter verse the long sentence will run over a line-ending and so is likely to be followed by a short sentence required to complete the next line. In hexameter verse a short sentence of less than one line, is also likely to be followed by a long sentence which will run on to the next but one line-ending.

When serial correlation has been shown to exist, then the minimum sample size may be determined by this effect rather than the requirement of having five occurrences. One method of determining the minimum sample size is to divide the text into halves, quarters, eighths and so on, until the sub-samples so obtained no longer behave as they would do in a random series of observations. This is a straightforward if rather laborious procedure and all the information can be obtained by looking at a cusum chart. Not only will this show if serial correlation is to be reckoned with, it will also show what the consequences of the correlation are and where they come in the text. In any but a routine investigation both methods would be employed and their results used to check their conclusions. A number of examples will be shown in succeeding chapters.

A cusum chart, more usually a set of several charts, is used to display tests of authorship through the whole of a text. The same operation enables the minimum sample size to be determined and this in turn makes possible comparisons of sections of the text with each other or with other texts. By using such charts, the authorship and integrity of a text can be explored.

The determination of the minimum sample size from a cusum chart could hardly be simpler. A chart should start with the first observation of the block sample and it extends until the ratio of the vertical departure from the horizontal axis (above or below the axis) to the horizontal length of the chart represents a difference which is not statistically significant. An example of this use of the cusum chart will be shown later in connection with sentence length distributions.

Samples are compared by using the statistics of the samples. The statistics described in an earlier chapter included the mean, the variance and standard deviation, the median, the first and third quartiles and the ninth decile. In the comparison of sentence length distributions, all these statistics can be employed, for Wake showed that, in these distributions, all these statistics are independent. That they are likely to be independent in this application can be readily illustrated. Two authors can write sentences of the same mean length but one will range widely from the mean while the other writes nothing much removed from it. These two authors will have the same mean but different variances, quartiles and ninth-decile. Two authors could write sentence length distributions similar in all respects except that one will write long sentences in regular steps of, say ten words, while the other will write a few about the ninth decile and then a smaller group scattered well above it. In other words, writers can resemble each other in all but one of these statistics yet differ in the sole exception.

This independence of statistics is not general; it is, in fact, quite exceptional. For example, if a set of observations fits a Poisson distribution, then all the statistics of the distributions can be calculated from the mean. Similarly, all the statistics of a binomial distribution can be calculated from the mean of the distribution. The statistics of the negative binomial distribution can be calculated from the mean and variance of the distribution. In such cases the comparison of the mean and variance imply all the other comparisons of the statistics.

One of the statistics, the variance, differs from the others in one important respect. The variance is the sum of a set of squares, which means that it is greatly affected by any extreme values in the observations. For example, if a set of one hundred sentences has a mean of ten words and to this set is added another hundred sentences each of twenty words, then 2000 words are being added to the text and the mean rises from ten words per sentence to fifteen words per sentence. The addition to the variance is $100 \times 5 \times 5 = 2,500$ units. If a single sentence of 111 words had been added to the original set, then the mean would have risen to eleven words per sentence, the sample would have been enlarged by 111 words, but the variance would have increased by $1 \times 100 \times 100 = 10,000$ units. For this reason comparisons of variances tend to be much less sensitive than the comparison of other statistics, and are not often made.

Cusum charts are designed to show changes in the mean of a series of observations. This limitation is no great handicap. In the first place, the mean is the most efficient statistic; every observation is used in its calculation; and it is the statistic from which many others can be derived, or the form to which many others can be converted. For example, if the median of a series of observations has been calculated, then the observations can be arranged into those above and those below the median value and the mean of this series used for a cusum chart. An example of this transformation will be seen later.

A further advantage of comparing sample means is that sample means are normally distributed, no matter what the form of the series of observations may be, as long as the series has a finite variance. This is an important feature of the mean. For example, if the series of natural numbers 1, 2, 3 and so on up to 100,000 is taken and samples of even six numbers are taken, the means of the samples will be seen to be normally distributed even though the original series is anything but normal.[1] This is a result of primary importance. It implies that, if the means of a set of samples from a population are calculated and plotted, then these means will fit a normal distribution as shown in Figure 5.1.

Figure 5.1 also shows that sample means which represent the same population mean will lie within a range of two standard errors of each other 19 times in twenty, within a range of three standard errors of each other 297 times out of three hundred. This enables quick comparisons to be made by using the standard errors of the statistics.

[1] For one proof of this theorem, see Hoel, P. G., *Introduction to Mathematical Statistics*, Wiley, New York and London, 1963 (page 145).

Statistic	Standard error of Statistic
Mean	$\dfrac{\text{St. Deviation}}{\sqrt{(N)}}$
Median	$\dfrac{\sqrt{(N)}}{2Y}$
1st and 3rd Quartiles	$\dfrac{\sqrt{(3N)}}{4Y}$
Ninth decile	$\dfrac{3\sqrt{(N)}}{10Y}$

(In all cases N is the number of observations, Y is the number of observations in the cell in which the statistic falls. Examples of the use of these standard errors will be given in later chapters.)

For a more general comparison of sample means, Students' t test is used. It should always be employed if the number of observations in the sample is less than thirty. For two samples of N_1 and N_2 observations, with means of $\bar{x}_1$ and $\bar{x}_2$ then

$$t = \frac{\bar{x}_1 - \bar{x}_2}{s\left\{\dfrac{1}{N_1} + \dfrac{1}{N_2}\right\}}$$

where s^2 is =

$$\frac{1}{N_1 + N_2 - 2}\left\{\Sigma(x_1)^2 - \frac{(\Sigma x_1)^2}{N_1} + \Sigma(x_2)^2 - \frac{(\Sigma x_2)^2}{N_2}\right\}$$

This pair of equations may look complicated but all elements used in their calculation can be taken directly from the calculation of the means and variances of the samples in the pattern which has been illustrated. For example, Table 7.3 shows the two Poisson distributions used in a previous example. The calculation of the mean and variance of each distribution is exactly as before. The term required for the calculation of s^2 in the t test is the corrected total brought out as the last but one step in the calculation of the variance.

The t test is incorporated in most of the computer programs used for cusum charts. A useful addition is to be able to insert a pair of markers in a text, asterisks for example, which will instruct the machine to carry out a t test on the observations between the markers and any other set which

Table 7.3   The effect of re-grouping the observations of Table 7.2 in binomial form

A

No of occurrences	Number of observations with X occurrences in	
	S 1	S 2
0	37	20
1 or more	63	80
Mean	0.63	0.80
St. Error	0.05	0.04
0 or 1	74	52
2 or more	26	48
Mean	0.26	0.48
St. Error	0.04	0.05
0 or 1 or 2	92	78
3 or more	8	22
Mean	0.08	0.22
St. Error	0.03	0.04

B

A 't' test on the series S 1 and S 2

$$s^2 = \frac{1}{100 + 100 - 2} (97.00 + 152.00)$$

$$= \frac{249}{198} = 1.68.$$

$$S = 1.30$$

$$t = \frac{1.60 - 0.99}{1.30 \sqrt{(0.02)}} = \frac{0.61}{0.182} = 3.35$$

For a large number of degrees of freedom t is 3.29 when p is 0.001.

have been selected as a standard for comparison, most often the whole of the series of observations excluding those which lie between the markers.

Almost all statistical theory is based upon the assumption that samples are random. This is often not the case when the samples are block samples drawn from literary texts. To enable such samples to be treated as random samples there are three alternative methods of proceeding safely. The first is to use samples which are above the minimum size needed to include any periodic structures and so are large enough to behave as if they were random samples. The second resource is to use another form of distribution to describe the observations, one which makes allowance for some variation in the expectations. For example, in a series which one might expect to be binomial, the use of a specified word as the first word of sentences, a block sample may not be random as one occurrence of the word is likely to generate another soon after. In such circumstances the use of a Poisson distribution to describe the observations will provide a good fit simply because the variance of this distribution is rather larger than the variance of a comparable binomial distribution. It must be borne in mind that the distribution has to be an adequate description of the observations, nothing more nor less. The third alternative is to look at the observations in a slightly different way. Instead of recording how many sentences have the key word as the first word, the question can be changed to How many sequences of one or more sentences in succession have the word in this position?

At this point the role of statistics as description has been explained; the use of statistics to compare samples and to classify them as alike, in as much as the differences between them are explicable by chance, or unlike, if the differences between them are too great to be explained by chance, has been described; and the sampling method best suited to the examination of the authorship and integrity of literary texts has been set out. Attention can now be directed to the tests of authorship which will make effective use of these tools.

Section II

The Features of Language which are of particular interest in Stylometry

8 The Writer in his Works

An examination of any literary text, written or spoken, poetry or prose, Greek or English, will show how similar is the pattern of composition. The bulk of the text will be made up by the frequent repetition of a few word-forms but by far the largest group of words, when they are classified by counting, will be that of the words which appear once in the text. Upon this simple observation has been based most critical analyses of texts. The largest group of words in the text is the rare words and these are not only rare but full of interest. It is the rare words which separate the man of education and of judgement from the dull hack; it is the rare words which reflect his background, his experience, and which show his powers of mind; it is the rare words which show his skill and convey delicate shades of meaning; it is the rare words which show the subtleties of excellence. Little wonder that students of literature have concentrated their attention on the rare words, especially as the frequent words tend to be connectives, particles, pronouns and articles, words whose meaning and use are much more prescribed and conventional than is the case with rare words. To most students of texts the centre of interest has been the rare words. The choice of words which creates vocabulary is best seen in the range of rare words employed by a writer.

However useful and attractive the rare words may be, the study of them has not been fruitful. For stylometry their number and variability make them difficult to handle and when statistics are enlisted to help with vocabulary, they tend to bring out even more clearly the difficulties of the study. The curve of vocabulary is a long sloping one, rather like a rope hanging out from a flagpole. At the ends of the curve are two large groups; at one end is the large number of words used once, at the other the few words very often repeated, and so the mean is not a useful descriptive statistic and the variance is large. If asked to illustrate the kind of distribution which makes it difficult to separate samples from similar but different populations, it would be hard to better the long tailed curve of vocabulary.

Not only is vocabulary difficult to measure but the attempts to measure it have often seemed to question the idea that there is any single quantity which can be called vocabulary. What is represented as the result of a writer's choice of word is not one quantity but several separate quantities. There are more than a million species of insect known and named. So a writer of a text-book of entomology must either be credited with a vocabulary of more than a million words, which is absurd, or it must be admitted that the vocabulary belongs to the subject matter rather than the writer. The aim of every scientist is to produce papers which are absolutely impersonal and for that end a special language of science has been developed with a vocabulary appropriate to every subject.

There are situations in which vocabulary will provide no foundation for any argument about the authorship of the text. It was once argued, at the end of the nineteenth century, that the Gospel of Luke had been written by the man whose name headed it and, as tradition had him a doctor, then his profession and authorship of his book could be demonstrated by his medical vocabulary. Hobart counted 400 medical terms in this text of just over 19,000 words. The most frequent noun in the text is not at all surprisingly the name 'Jesus' but it occurs less than half as often as the alleged medical terms. It is difficult to conceive a more ridiculous hypothesis. Cadbury spent some time in showing that most of the medical terms were used in the Greek Old Testament in non-medical contexts and that most of them were used by Josephus who did not practise that profession. Finally it was pointed out that if Luke had been a doctor and produced the Gospel he must have changed professions by the time of writing the Book of Acts, for the same pattern of argument demands that the latter chapters of Acts be written by a seaman with some experience of shipwrecks. Of course the fact that both the Gospels of Luke and the Book of Acts are compilations in which 'Luke', whoever he may have been, only acted as editor was ignored in the eagerness to show that Luke could be identified from his vocabulary.

There are circumstances in which vocabulary is of value in determining the author of a text. Dr. W. C. Wake showed [1] that the works of Hippocrates which were statistically consistent dealt with joints and fractures of the limbs of the type met with in athletics and sporting contests. Presumably this is where Hippocrates began to practise his art; he did not hang up his shingle in a prosperous suburb.

This simple approach to literary texts, the inspection of them and examination of their most striking features, will not take the subject of stylometry very far. It is better to begin from the other end, to look at tests of authorship and see how they may be developed and applied to what the texts contain.

As it has already been said, to be useful in the determination of authorship, a habit must comply with three conditions: first, it must be a habit apparent in a choice which frequently confronts all authors; second, it must be a habit which can be numerically expressed; and third, it must be a habit which can be shown to be unaffected by changes in subject matter, by the passing of periods of time, by reasonable differences in literary form and all other possible influences which might affect the habit. Each of these conditions implies a limitation of choice and they

[1] *The Corpus Hippocraticum*, Ph.D. Thesis of University of London. 1951.

are best considered in isolation though, in reality, they all operate together.

It has been pointed out that we are all instinctively aware of revealing ourselves when we write. It is a common experience for us to be able to hear the words of a personal letter being spoken by our friend. From experiences of this kind we go on to argue that it must be possible to reconstruct from an author's writings his mind, circumstances and character. The difficulty in making a distinction between the genuine and spurious works of an author lies in the fact that we adapt our writings to different situations and to different factors. We write differently on chemistry or cookery or love. We write differently to the Lord Chief Justice on a legal matter and to a friend on a personal one. So we deduce that these factors will mould our writing. We change with the years and so deduce that we write differently on the same subject to the same person in similar circumstances if enough time has separated our compositions.

All these deductions may well be correct, at least in part, but only when they have been measured can we say how much they do affect our writing. Listing these possible influences serves to direct attention to the kind of choice which is likely to tell us what we want to know. An indicator of authorship will be based on some habit not affected by the factors and influences just named. Of course every habit can be transformed by extremes of any one of these influences; setting down a chemical formula, compiling a railway timetable, writing a matrix, or composing a sonnet, are such different activities that any habit not affected by them is likely to be unaffected even by a difference of authorship. But such dramatic differences in literary form do not concern us in this book, only such differences as are to be found in historical problems or current disputes, and these have a range which, compared to that employed either by modern prose writers or by the Greek orators, is narrow. Similarly our concern is not to compare the first scribbles of an infant with those of a centenarian, but only to cover the intervals, all lying between the end of adolescence and the onset of senility, which are relevant to the study of these problems.

Even this provisional specification of a suitable indicator of authorship will direct attention to some possible choices and away from others which would be unsuitable choices. For example, it is clear from the work of Dr. W. C. Wake[1] that the most frequently used nouns in a piece of Greek prose indicate the subject matter of the prose but tell you little about the identity of the author. If a piece of continuous prose is divided into sections, it is found that the number of nouns in the separate sections varies so much that counting the proportion of nouns used in a text is also, in this simple form of argument at least, irrelevant to the question of

---

[1] Wake, W. C., Doctoral Thesis, University of London (1951).

authorship. Any habit which is bound up with nouns, tied as they are to subject matter, is unlikely to make a good indicator of authorship.

The second point to be made about any habit which would be useful in a determination of authorship is that it must be one which can be numerically expressed. This, it must at once be admitted, is a great restriction in the range of study but it would be out of place in an exposition of a quantitative method to waste time expressing regrets that much literary material is not suited to examination by this method. It is better to accept this constraint and look at indicators which comply with it.

An illustration of the point may be helpful. There is no doubt that some New Testament writers show, in their writing, Semitic influences. It is easy to illustrate a Semitic habit in Greek prose writing, for example, the substitution of a pair of 'and-clauses' for the combination of a participial and a main clause. But when you try to count the number of Semitisms in, say, the Book of Acts as estimated by different scholars, the differences in classification are so large that no consistent count is possible. So Semitisms are unlikely to play any part in the primary determination of authorship by quantitative methods.

What can most readily be expressed quantitatively is the size or frequency of specified events. It is easy to count the number of words in a sentence, or the number of ten-word sentences, or how often a word-form occurs in a text. It is therefore with this kind of habit that numerical methods must deal.

The third point about any habit which is to be useful in the determination of authorship is that it must be frequent. If you look through a microscope at objects smaller than the light waves which are supposed to illuminate them, the objects do not disturb the waves and simply, because of their size, remain invisible. In the same way, an industrial historian who wants to confirm a report of a one-day strike will not read the records of annual or quarterly output; he will look at daily or hourly totals or daily deliveries, events which occur daily.

Thus to detect a change of authorship in a section of text you must look at some habit which you will normally expect to occur in the section of text. To make any useful contribution to the determination of the authorship of the Pauline epistles in the New Testament, you must be able to say something useful about 1,500 words of Greek prose. To test any hypothesis statistically using, for example, the chi squared test you need an absolute minimum of five occurrences, and it would be better to have ten. So any habits useful in the kind of comparison which is relevant must occur about ten times in any 1,500 words of Greek prose. If you want to test sections smaller than this, say half this size, then you must have habits with twice the rate of occurrence and look at those which occur on the average once in every 75 words of Greek prose.

To approach the problem from a rather different angle: there are likely to be, in 1,500 words of Greek prose, written by a representative author, about one hundred sentences. The mean sentence length of Greek prose writers ranges from less than ten words to over thirty words per sentence. Thus the sentence is a unit common enough to be valuable in analysis. It follows that a habit, such as the use of a conjunction, which is related to the sentence, will also be useful if it occurs in a reasonable proportion of sentences, say in more than one sentence in ten.

It has been objected that the sentence is not at all a suitable unit to use for analysis, for two reasons. No definition of a sentence has gained general acceptance and, even if such a definition were formulated, we have no way of knowing what sentence markings were made by the writers of Greek prose themselves, as the punctuation of ancient copies of the texts is rudimentary and erratic and the punctuation of the modern critical texts is mainly editorial.

Now it is true that structural linguistics has demonstrated the difficulty of formulating a completely satisfactory definition of 'sentence'. Whatever definition may be offered, exceptional and ambiguous sentences can be produced to challenge the definition. But this is the common situation in all descriptive sciences. Animals exist and are classified, but nature, being indifferent to and ignorant of our systems of classification and interpretation, has produced creatures which seem to be an irrational mixture of plant and animal, and these cannot be included in the definition of one or the other. This does not mean that definition is impossible or useless. It only illustrates that whenever a boundary is drawn, there is so much common to the territories which lie beside the boundary, and so little in common to these territories and the remote central areas which demand that the boundary be defined, that any boundary looks foolish if attention is narrowed to its immediate surroundings.

The sentence is generally used and widely recognised. The human race daily writes several millions of them. Any one of a number of definitions will cover all but a small number of exceptional instances.

In statistical work on Greek prose a sentence is defined to be the group of words marked by a modern editor by a full stop, a colon, or an interrogation mark. To the structural linguist this is a very crude definition indeed, but the only question which need concern us here is whether or not the number and proportion of exceptions and ambiguities to this definition are large enough to give rise to statistically significant differences.

The answer to this question is bound up with the answer to the second objection. It must be admitted that we have no way of knowing how the original authors of Greek prose would now mark their texts if asked to do so in the conventions of modern punctuation. What has happened is that a number of individual scholars, and of committees of scholars, have studied Greek texts and imposed punctuation upon them. When the definition above has been used, it has been found, in a number of trials, that the differences in sentence markings between the texts produced by the different scholars, or committees, are negligible compared to the expected differences of random sampling.

In fact the only large difference between texts and editors concerns the use of the full stop and the colon. If these two marks are accepted as interchangeable then the differences are no longer statistically significant.

The question which concerns us is not, 'Are there differences between textual traditions and editors in the conception of a sentence or the use of punctuation?' but 'Do statistically significant differences arise from editorial differences which would lead to the drawing of erroneous conclusions from the data?' This question has been answered in the negative for Greek prose writers. There may well be complications in dialogue and oratory – it is usual for structural linguists to illustrate the difficulties of sentence length definition from dialogue or recorded speech – but these are irrelevant to general studies of prose writings.

A more important difficulty associated with the sentence as a unit of measurement is its variability. In Greek texts there are sentences of one word and some nearly two hundred times as long. The probability of a word occurring in one must be about two hundred times as large as it is for the other. The simplest way out of this difficulty is to chop the text into equal blocks of successive words. The text could be cut into sections each as long as the average sentence in the text. This will give a unit constant within each text, and varying little from one work to another for the same author, but the unit will vary from author to author.

The most convenient unit is the reciprocal of the rate of occurrence of the most frequent habit which has been shown to be useful in determining authorship. The conjunction *kai* (English = *and*) makes up about 5% of all Greek prose and so an efficient unit is a block in which the expectation of *kai* occurring is $20 \times 0.05 = 1$, i.e. of a block of twenty successive words. It is a simple matter to have a computer divide a text in this way.

Having fixed on a natural unit, the variable sentence, and an artificial unit, the fixed block of twenty words, attention can be given to what habits are common enough to be useful and how they might best be examined.

Sentences have been examined for length using the word as the unit of measurement. If has been suggested that there might be advantages in using the syllable rather than the word as the unit of measurement. This is not likely to be generally true. The length of a sentence measured in syllables will be the length in words multiplied by the average number of syllables in the words. The variance of the measurement will have a component derived from different numbers of words in the sentences and another component derived from differing numbers of syllables in the words. The efficiency of the habit as a discriminator between authors is determined by the relation of the mean and variance and this is not going to be much improved by counting in syllables.

Sentence length distributions are commonly grouped for statistical purposes in cells of five words and this leads to authors of Greek prose having about ten to fifteen cells in their distribution, a favourable number. Too many cells make for extended calculations and too few mean a loss of sensitivity.

If sentences are classified by the number of clauses they contain then there will be too few cells to make a sensitive indicator. If they are classified by structural types of clauses then there will be too many groups to deal with.

By and large, sentence length distributions counted in cells of five words are both efficient and effective in Greek prose. An uninflected language – English, for example – makes sentence length distributions much less useful for the reasons just explained; the mean length is greater but the variance even more so.

Turning to habits which are concerned with the occurrence of words, the first inclination is to look at classes of words rather than individual words, and look at such questions as 'How many nouns does this author use?' and 'How often does he use them?' That nouns depend too much on subject matter to contribute to a determination of authorship has been demonstrated by W. C. Wake.[1] This is also true of verbs, though something can be made, as will be seen in a later chapter, of a classification by voice or mood. Proper names, for both people and places, occur irregularly and are of little consequence in authorship studies by quantitative methods. Questions and quotations do seem to be habits personal to authors but they are in relation to the phenomena discussed here, very rare. In few authors can you expect to find a quotation or a question in every one thousand five hundred words of text, though the Apostle Paul does have an average of over twenty questions in every one thousand five hundred words.

There are only two classes of word likely to repay investigation. Adjectives and adverbs, though used a variable number of times by different authors, seem to be drawn by each author from a constant stock and so to be typical of an author. This accords with common sense. One author will write 'The man sat down in the chair', and another will write 'The bent old man sat down slowly in the red chair'. One has made the simple statement, the other has added to it his personal observations. Adjectives and adverbs often have psychological connotations and are best treated in detail both lexically and statistically.

The most favoured class of words in classical studies has long been the *hapax legomena*, the once-occurring words. For this concentration of interest there are two reasons. First, the fact that in any piece of text many words occur once. In the New Testament as a whole there are 1,934 *hapex legomena*, in the Gospels and Acts 670, 634, 971, 375 and 943 respectively. The second reason is the general feeling that these words are

[1] *The Corpus Hippocraticum*, Ph.D. Thesis of University of London, 1951.

representative of the range of an author's interests and indicative of his literary skill or pretensions. Dr. W. C. Wake showed, in the thesis referred to above, by a complex mathematical treatment known as a modified probit analysis of noun distributions, that there is undoubtedly something in this impression, but he also showed the formidable difficulties in treating this class of word.

The high rates of occurrences of *hapax legomena* are attractive but deceptive. The proportion of *hapax legomena* varies with text length and included in the one class of *hapax legomena* are all parts of speech, each of which might well need separate treatment. It should also be noted that if there are 1,934 *hapax legomena* in the New Testament, there are six word-forms each of which gives a higher total. All the parts of the verb *to be* aggregate 2,450 occurrences, instances of the preposition *en* (in) total 2,713, the particle *de* occurs 2,771 times, the pronoun *autos* (he, she or it) 5,534, the conjunction *kai* (and) 8,947 times and the definite article 19,734 times. In all, these six words account for 36,613 occurrences, nearly twenty times as many as the *hapax legomena*.

From these figures it would appear that these common words would make good indicators of authorship if it could be shown that an author used them at a constant rate and individual authors differed in their rates of use. The difficulty in using them as a test of authorship is that their occurrence is too readily influenced by the literary form of the work being studied. For example, Table 8.1 (a) shows the occurrence of the definite article in the epistle of Isocrates. The nine epistles span from the sixty-eighth to the ninety-eighth years of the writer's life but are written on much the same subject, politics, and in the same literary form. The chi squared test reveals no obstacle to the hypothesis that all were written using the same proportion, 13.32%, of the definite article.

But Table 8.1(b) shows the occurrence of the definite article in the first two hundred sentences of each book of the History of Herodotus. For the data of Table 8.1(b) chi squared is 75.8 for eight degrees of freedom, as there are nine books, and so p is very much less than 0.001. The variation in the rate of use seems to be connected with the changes in the literary form of the text such as the change from speech to narrative.

A test based on the simple rate of occurrence of the definite article would therefore always confront the analyst with a choice of explaining a significant difference as due either to a change in literary form or to a difference of authorship. Major differences in literary form are easy to see, but literary form cannot be clearly defined in detail and the result of tests based on the definite article could be endless debate about the classification of literary forms.

So far it may seem to the reader that stylometry is not an efficient discipline. Starting with vocabulary studies which seek to encompass the writer's choice of word, it looks as if this choice is not of much practical consequence, partly because vocabulary is a variable quantity and partly

Table 8.1   The occurrence of the definite article

(a) In the Epistles of Isocrates

Epistle	Occurrences of the article in the epistle	Occurrences of all words in epistle
1	73	585
2	168	1,278
3	53	420
4	108	824
5	39	281
6	118	888
7	105	780
8	87	664
9	162	1,134
Totals:	913	6,854

Notes:

For these epistles chi squared is 5.56 for 8 degrees of freedom, p = 0.70.

(b) In the History of Herodotus

Book	Occurrence of the definite article	Occurrence of all words
1	444	3,458
2	589	4,346
3	516	3,896
4	488	3,721
5	456	3,605
6	582	4,078
7	424	3,830
8	513	3,740
9	440	3,466
Totals:	4,452	34,140

Notes:

Each sample is the first two hundred sentences of the Oxford Text.

For all nine samples chi squared is 75.8 for eight degrees of freedom.

because it is not amenable to statistical description and analysis. If the wide range of rare words is excluded and attention concentrated on the frequent words, it might seem that things are not much better. It is true that all languages and texts have a number of frequent words which make up a surprising proportion of any text, and the rates at which these words occur can be used as tests of authorship, but it is in the exceptional situation that they are most effective.

A well-known pioneer investigation of the disputed authorship of the *Federalist* papers by Mosteller and Wallace illustrates this point.[1] Mosteller and Wallace looked at three sets of words which were possible discriminators between the rival candidates for authorship. The first was a set recommended by their colleagues on literary and historical grounds; the second was a set chosen by them for mathematical reasons; the third was the set formed by the most frequent words in the texts. One of the conclusions of the enquiry was that this third set turned out to be the most effective.

However, Mosteller and Wallace had two advantages in their investigation. The first was an ample supply of text to sample. They could take thirty or fifty samples of a couple of thousand words in block samples and record the distribution of the frequent words in these sets of samples. The distribution was generally negative binomial, suggesting that the words were not equally likely to occur in all samples of the same size.

The second advantage which they enjoyed was that their problem was one of matching. Essentially, they were allocating the papers to the author of three most likely to have provided a sample with given characteristics. If, for example, they recorded five occurrences of *and* in a sample, then they limited themselves to answering the question, Which author is most likely to have written this number of occurrences in this size of sample? Not surprisingly they made much use of likelihood ratios. If Peter writes a thirty-word sentence once in fifty sentences but Paul writes a thirty-word sentence only once in five hundred sentences, then a thirty-word sentence is more likely to have been written by Peter in the ratio of $(1/50)/(1/500) = 10:1$.

For problems of this pattern, a plenitude of samples and a limited choice of authors, the rate of occurrence of frequent words offers ample material for decision. But if these two factors are lacking, there is much less scope. That is why the third aspect of the act of composition is much more rewarding for analysis. Not only does a writer select words and repeat them; he places them in position. Placing words in position is obviously more variable than merely selecting them and using them. A sample may contain fifty occurrences of *and* in one thousand words of a block sample but some of these occurrences might introduce sentences, some might separate nouns, and others separate adjectives; some will join together natural pairs, ham and eggs, others will disjoin unnatural pairs, strawberries and vinegar. In other words, the simple rate of occurrence of *and* in the sample will contain little of the information which is to be extracted from the whole pattern of occurrence if placing is included.

---

[1] *Inference and Disputed Authorship: The Federalist*, F. Mosteller and D. L. Wallace, Reading, Mass., 1964.

In stylometric studies the placing of words has two connotations. It can have a positional reference; the occurrence is the first, or second, or last but one, or the last word, in a sentence. Or it can have a contextual reference; the occurrence is preceded by word X or is followed by word Y. Both aspects of placing words can be examined in any text or language but the study of placing does reflect the fundamental difference between the two types of language, the inflected and uninflected languages. This is because in the inflected language the words have a great freedom of movement conferred upon them by the fact that the role of the words is shown by their inflection. In the uninflected languages, such as English, word order is restricted by the necessity of conveying the role of the words by their sequence. It is immediate context which is more indicative of the author in the uninflected language. In English 'The man shot the dog' is not at all the same sentiment as 'The dog shot the man'. In Greek the role of each word would be shown by its inflection and so the word order would be more flexible. If the statement is transformed to 'The dog was shot by the man', then the creation of a collocation is illustrated, and occurrence of *the* is now preceded by an occurrence of *by*.

It is for this reason that the exposition divides in two. The description of word movement and mobility in the natural unit of the sentence is illustrated from an inflected language, Greek, while the study of immediate context, particularly the study of collocations formed by the successive occurrence of two frequent words, is done in English texts and authors. The principles of each system are applicable to both but the efficiency of one system is so much greater in the inflected than in the uninflected language, that it seems only reasonable to take them separately.

The study of word mobility and word position in sentences is erected on the foundation of sentence length distributions so that examples of sentence length distributions are an essential preliminary to such studies and so are included with them. Then follows a chapter on collocations which are the better used on, and illustrated from, English texts and authors.

A third chapter illustrates and discusses some word pairings which operate in a way which must support the claim made earlier in this book that the subject under investigation is the storage mechanism of the human brain. The connection between the words which occur as pairs is not grammatical, nor philological. The first reference to such word-pairs, now called *proportional pairs*, was in the work of Ellegard.[1] In an examination of the disputed letters of Junius, he noted that there were a number of word pairs – *and/also, since/because, scarcely/hardly*. All that Ellegard claimed was that the different authors to be considered relevant to the problem habitually used one member of the pair at a

[1]*A Statistical Method for Determining Authorship*, Alvar Ellegard, Gothenburg 1962.

higher rate than the other, and that the habit of doing so varied from one author to another. Ellegard did suggest that there might be some element common to both words but explained that it was not a simple preference for one of two forms grammatically or semantically alternative.

The author came to word pairs by a very different route. He started to look at adjectives in Greek. These make up only about two percent of Greek text but seem to differ markedly from one writer to another. But a count of adjectives showed that the pattern of occurrence was that the majority of occurrences were of the adjective *pas* (all) followed at some distance by occurrences of *polus* (many) and the remainder were few in number and variable in selection. So the effective difference between writers came down to the comparison of the occurrences of these two adjectives, *pas* and *polus*.

The pairing has been shown to be characteristic of Greek writers in general. Now there are circumstances in which it can be claimed that the use of *all* is a psychological characteristic of one type of author where another type would prefer to say *many*, but this kind of explanation will not cover any more than a small proportion of the occurrences. All that is certain in word pairs is that, if one word is used as a marker to count the other, then the proportion in which they occur is a characteristic of the writer. It has since been shown that what is true of *pas* and *polus* in Greek is also true of *all* and *any* in English. So it is with the alternative forms in English of *no* and *not*, and with the three alternative negatives in Greek – *ou, ouk* and *oux*.

Common to both investigations of Ellegard and of the author was the discovery of word-pairs in which the use of one word as a marker by which to record the occurrences of the other illustrates a stable habit of the writer without any necessary connection between any occurrences of the words.

Ellegard came to this conclusion by looking at a set of texts and selecting the words which maximised the differences between them. The author came to his conclusion as a result of a general survey of the role of adjectives in Greek. But the simplest illustration of how word-pairs behave and so reveal themselves is to be found in a paper on the use of the genitive forms of the personal pronouns in Greek.[1] The author and a colleague were watching a line printer producing a concordance to a set of Greek texts. It was then printing out the entries which covered the personal pronoun. At one moment it would tick over a few occurrences, at another it would be ripping out some hundreds of entries. But the proportion of the occurrences which were in the genitive case looked constant. That they might well be so was first tested by laying a measure down the print out and counting the occurrences in inches of print. Word-pairs are detected by observation. It may be possible to give a rational explanation of why some pairs are linked, the pair *and* and *also* for example, but there are others for which no such simple explanation can be put forward and the point to be grasped is that the observation of such pairs is not dependent on the reason for their presence being known.

In sum, the writer's choice of words is not an effective discriminator when it is taken in total as his vocabulary. His choice and rate of using frequent words is much more effective, especially when there are large amounts of text to sample and few contenders for the authorship of it. But by far the most effective discriminator between one writer and another is the placing of words. The placing can be looked at as the position within a sentence, the most effective method for inflected languages, or in immediate context, which is the method most effective in uninflected languages. Proportional pairs of words come somewhere between the frequent words and the placing of them in effectiveness; they have the great advantages of being independent of punctuation and simple both to record and analyse.

9 The Inflected Language

All developed languages have sentence structures. Sentences have their place in the succession from single words to words gathered to make phrases, to a sequence of phrases intimately connected to make a sentence, to a group of sentences which form a paragraph and a number of paragraphs which comprise a chapter and chapters which make books. The classification varies but the elements can be identified. The sentence is one link in the progression making it possible to develop long utterances which will be both logical and pleasing.

Languages are divided into two groups, the inflected language in which the role of a word is indicated by a change in its form, and the uninflected in which the role of the word is shown by its position in a sequence of words. Clearly this fundamental difference will be reflected in the sentence structure of the two types of language. In an inflected language, such as Greek, sentence length distributions are an effective indicator of authorship. Sentences will range from one word up to a couple of hundred, the mean for representative writers will be around ten to fifteen words. In an uninflected language, like English, the range of sentence length is much greater, and sentences of four, five or even six hundred words are not very rare. This can be readily explained and illustrated; to say 'I shall have been rescued', takes five words of English, only one in Greek. 'I went into the house' is another five words of English, whereas in Greek it would take three.

In the uninflected languages the difference in form between recorded speech, direct or indirect, and simple narrative is exaggerated in comparison with the inflected language. This difference is often enhanced in the case of Greek by the fact that in classical times there was no distinction between the spoken and a written style. Reading was voiced and not silent; writing was a kind of personal dictation in which the text was spoken as it was being written. In Greek texts there is often complete confusion between the words for speaking and writing. The Gospel of John has the story of the woman taken in adultery and brought before Jesus. He stooped down and wrote with his finger in the sand. The narrative continues with the words, 'When they heard what he had written'. This is not because some obliging spectator read the words for those not able to see them; it records the usual practice of saying aloud what you were writing down. Another incident concerns the arrival of an imperial letter for a man attending a lecture. He was faced with the demand that the letter should be read at once. But having to read it aloud would disrupt the lecture and divulge the contents publicly. He tactfully slipped into another room and read over his letter aloud. Silent reading and writing come in with the Middle Ages.

(i) *Positional Measurements and Word Mobility*

When W. C. Wake's paper was published in 1957,[1] the present author was engaged, with the late G. H. C. Macgregor, in an attempt to produce a scientific stylometry useful in the study of the New Testament. The first reaction to Wake's analysis of the Pauline epistles was to repeat his work on other texts. Wake had used an 1881 version of the *Textus Receptus*, and it was soon shown that the use of either Souter's *Novum Testamentum Graece*,[2] or the 23rd edition of the Nestle text, affected neither the analysis nor the conclusions. The opportunity was also taken to extend the investigation to a number of Greek writers not examined by Wake.

The next step was to launch a research project whose aim was to provide a set of samples which would constitute a fair but searching test for any hypothesis supposed to apply to writers of Greek prose. Naturally it was not possible to include samples of all Greek writers but the principles on which the selection was made were obvious. It might seem that a writer's composition changed with subject matter, or with the passing years, or with a change in literary form. The samples therefore would include sets designed to isolate these effects by cross comparison and enable them to be measured. Included in the samples would be works written by the same author about the same time but on quite different subjects, and works written by the same author on much the same subject but composed many years apart. The samples comprised works by Herodotus, Thucydides, Plato, Aristotle, Xenophon, Strabo, Diodorus Siculus, Plutarch, Josephus and the complete orations of Lysias, Isocrates and Demosthenes. It was at this stage that a computer came into use; the counting of any feature in such a range of texts was impractical without its aid.

Supplementary to the standard samples was a short blacklist of texts which have been traditionally reproduced as part of a corpus but are universally acknowledged to be spurious, and a grey list of texts over which critical opinion is sharply divided. A useful test of authorship would show only random sampling differences within the works of an author and clearly distinguish them from any black texts associated with his corpus. The kind of light cast on grey texts can be seen in the case of Plato's Seventh Epistle where it was soon clear, and repeatedly demonstrable, that the central section of the epistle differed from the start and the finish. The conclusion about authorship reached by critics of this epistle depended very much on what point of the text they had reached when making up their minds.

[1] Op cit.
[2] Oxford 1947.

For the reasons which have been already summarised, the investigations based on the standard samples left aside the complex problem of low-frequency vocabulary and started with the more manageable problems of high-frequency vocabulary. The boundary of high-frequency vocabulary in Greek is marked by the appearance of the most frequent noun in the text. The next years saw the preparation and publication of a series of papers[1] each outlining tests of authorship which had been proved over the wide range of authors and samples. Most often the subject of these papers was a particle or connective.

It soon became apparent that high-frequency vocabulary in Greek has a marked positional bias. Among the first three or four words of Greek sentences there is a high proportion of high-frequency words, mostly particles and connectives. In the middle of sentences there is a mixed vocabulary which includes a small proportion of the high-frequency vocabulary, but among the last words of sentences high-frequency vocabulary is almost absent. These observations generated two hypotheses which were then investigated. The first was that a classification of the last words of sentences might be a simple and useful test of authorship – and so it turned out to be. The second hypothesis was that, if position was so important an element in vocabulary, then word position and its general description, word mobility, would be equally worth investigating.

Before introducing positional stylometry, it may be helpful to illustrate the point which has just been made, that the vocabulary of the different sections of a Greek sentence is radically different. Table 9.1(a) shows the frequency distribution of the first and last words in the 1171 sentences of the text of the Fourth Gospel in the text of Aland, Black, Metzger and Wikgren.[2] The difference between the two distributions is striking. Of the 1171 sentences, more than two-thirds, 68.7%, have as last word, words which occur five times or fewer. Less than one third, 28.6%, of the first words occur five times or fewer. Of the last words 36.7% occur once but of the first words only 12.4% occur once. Half the sentences have as last words forms which occur once or twice; for the first words the proportion is only 18.0%. The restriction in vocabulary between the last words and the first words is clear; in 1171 sentences there are 601 different last words, only 257 first words. If the table had been extended to show the occurrence of the second words in sentences it would have been even more revealing. As the second word in sentences there are 179 occurrences of the particle *de* and 189 of the particle *oun*.

Table 9.1(b) shows another aspect of the same phenomenon. In its

[1] (a) S. Michaelson, A. Q. Morton and R. E. Osborne, 'Forgar', *Science and Archaeology*, 5, 1971.
(b) S. Michaelson and A. Q. Morton, 'The New Stylometry', *Classical Quarterly*, 1, 1972.
(c) A. Q. Morton, 'The Authorship of Greek Prose', *Journal of the Royal Statistical Society*, A 128, 1965.
[2] Michaelson, S. and Morton, A. Q., 'Last Words', *New Testament Studies*, Vol. 18, pp. 192–208.

columns are classed the 66 first and last words of the epistle to the Colossians and in the middle column are 66 words selected from the text by random number tables. The random sample has a distribution intermediate between those of the first and last words.

Position is a relative measurement and is recorded as a distance from a reference point. In Greek composition the two reference points which immediately suggest themselves are the beginning and end of sentences.

Table 9.1

(a) The contrasting distribution of first and last words of sentences in the same text, the Gospel of John

| No of occurrences of word | Number of words which occur as | | | | |
| | (i) 1st word | | | (ii) Last word | |
N	No	%		No	%
1	145	12.4		430	36.7
2	33	18.0		82	50.7
3	14	21.6		35	59.7
4	13	26.0		15	64.8
5	6	28.6		9	68.7
6	4	30.7		6	71.7
7	8	35.4		4	74.7
8	2	36.8		7	78.9
9	5	40.7		4	82.0
10	1	41.5		—	
11	3	44.3		1	82.9
12	3	47.4			
13	5	52.9			
14	2	55.3		2	85.3
16	2	58.1		1	86.7
20	2	58.1	19	1	88.3
24	1	63.5	24	1	90.3
26	1	65.8	32	1	93.1
27	1	68.1	39	1	96.4
28	1	70.5	42	1	100.0
30	1	73.0			
55	1	77.7			
70	1	83.8			
71	1	89.8			
120	1	100.0			

Notes:

The percentages are cumulative: they specify what percentage of the 1171 sentences are occupied by words occurring N times or less.

Table 9.1   (continued)

(b) A comparison of the distributions of the first and last words of the
sentences of Colossians with a random sample taken from the same sentences

No of occurrences of word	Number of words in sample of		
	(i) 1st words	(ii) Random	(iii) Last words
1	39	46	62
2	3	3	3
3	3	–	–
4	2	1	1
5	1	2	–
9	1	–	–
Totals:	66	66	66

Notes:

The random sample was taken by using random number tables to select one
word from each successive sentence of the text.

In both tables (a) and (b) different cases of nouns and adjectives and
different parts of verbs are all counted separately.

Position is recorded by counting the ordinal position of the occurrence of
the count-word, so that 2 denotes an occurrence as the second word, or
second last word, in a sentence. Two distributions are compiled, one by
counting the positions from the first word of the sentence to the count-
word, the other by counting from the last word back to the position of the
count-word.

In this convention the actual occurrence is counted twice, once in each
distribution, with the result that the sum of the two positions is always
one more than the number of words in the sentence. A sentence which
has no occurrence of the count-word is ignored; a sentence which
contains two occurrences is recorded twice; a sentence with N occurrences is recorded N times, once for each position within the sentence.

As there is such a close connection between the positional
distributions and the sentences in which they have been recorded, it is
advantageous to use the same units for both sets of measurements, to
record positions by counting the number of words from the beginning
and end of sentences, to group the observations into cells five words
wide, and to use the same descriptive statistics in their analysis. There is a
limitation in this last procedure for in texts as short as those of the New
Testament epistles in which the numbers of observations are comparatively small, the ninth decile is rarely useful and the first and third

quartiles are of limited application. This constraint can be turned to advantage for positional distributions are less asymmetrical than sentence length distributions and so can very often be shown to be log normal, in which case the only statistics required for comparisons are the log mean and log standard deviation.

A pair of positional distributions describe the mobility of the word whose positions have been recorded. The mobility of a word can range from the full mobility which allows a word to occupy any position within a sentence from first word to last and shows no preference for any position within this range, through a limited mobility in which a word has a tendency to prefer some positions in the range, to the state of complete immobility in which the word would be found in only one position.

Mobility can be measured in many ways but the most convenient to use in this context is a definition in terms of *isotropy*. Isotropy is the property of having the same characteristics irrespective of the direction in which they are measured. Sentence length distributions are isotropic; it makes no difference whether the number of words in a sentence is counted from the first word to the last or from the last to the first. Isotropy is relevant to positional measurements because a mobile word, one which occupies all possible positions within a sentence, will have an average position at the mid-point of the sentence and the mid-point of a sentence is an isotropic position. It matters not at all if the mid-point of a sentence is counted from the beginning or the end of the sentence.

It is therefore convenient to define a mobile word as one having isotropic positional distributions, that is one for which the differences between the forward and backward positional distributions are only random sampling differences. Words which are not mobile will have anisotropic positional distributions; for these the forward and backward distributions will show statistically significant differences.

It is true that there are other configurations than complete mobility which produce isotropic positional distributions. For example, a word which occurs only as first and last word of sentences, and equally often as either, will also have isotropic positional distributions, but these configurations are not of practical importance in the study of Greek texts. For isotropic distributions the forward and backward distributions are two estimates of the same thing and so they can be added to give the *mean positional distribution*. As the number of observations is also doubled the statistics are not affected.

The differences which appear in anisotropic distributions range from a mild degree of anisotropy, which is not seen until ungrouped data is used for the examination, to the extreme case where all occurrences are in one position. If, for example, all the occurrences of a word were as the first word of sentences, then the forward distribution would have a mean of one and a variance of zero and the backward distribution would replicate the sentence length distribution. The two classes of distribution, isotropic and anisotropic, require separate treatment for a number of reasons, the most important of which is that isotropic distributions are not independent of the sentence length distributions in which the positions are recorded, but many anisotropic distributions can be made independent of the sentence length distributions in which they have been recorded.

(ii) *Isotropic Distributions*

The positional distributions of mobile words have a number of interesting features and a corresponding variety of applications. The main feature of isotropic positional distributions is that when they are recording the positions of a word which occurs in a sentence length distribution which is longer than the minimum sample size, such distributions are tests of authorship though not tests which are independent of sentence length. The reason for this general principle applying to all the mobile words which are recorded in a sentence length distribution is readily seen. For unimodal and roughly symmetrical distributions the variance of the observations depends on the number of observations and on the range of the observations. For a sentence length sample these two factors are the number of sentences in the sample and the difference between the number of words in the longest and shortest sentences in the sample.

For any mobile word whose positions are being recorded in the sample, this number of positions is usually less than the number of sentences in the sample. All but a very small minority of words occur less than once per sentence, and the range of the observations is much the same as it was for the sentence length distribution, since the range of positions is from the first word of any sentence to the last word of the longest sentence. As a result the variance of the positional distribution within a sentence length distribution is, almost without exception, larger than the variance of the sentence length distribution and all the statistics have correspondingly larger standard errors. This in turn means that the differences between samples can be larger without being statistically significant.

The fact that the positional distributions of mobile words are not independent of the sentence length distributions in which they have been recorded does not mean that they yield no information which is not to be had from the parent sentence length distributions. Two writers might have sentence length distributions which are identical but one will use short sentences which are imperative or interrogative while the other writes short sentences which are indicative. The two writers will use different particles and connectives in their writing and the positional distributions of these words would show a clear separation of the authors.

The fact that certain words occur mainly in certain types of sentence gives positional distributions a useful property of selection. By a suitable choice of mobile word, features of the parent sentence length distribution can be enhanced, reduced or even eliminated. Two illustrations of this technique can be given. The first is a reference to Plato's writing. W. C. Wake found difficulty in dealing with Plato because of the mixture of dialogue and continuous prose in his writings. The dialogue exchanges have a high proportion of short sentences, sentences with less than six words, and the proportion of these sentences in any sample reflected the proportion of dialogue and prose within the sample. Excluding the short sentences from the comparison was not completely satisfactory. Truncated distributions are not easy to handle and the samples should contain a small proportion of short sentences and excluding them all is not a happy solution to the problem. If the positional distributions of the conjunction *kai* are recorded, the complication vanishes. The conjunction is not frequent in the short sentences so that most of them are not recorded. The difference in the proportion of short sentences between prose and dialogue disappears and the selection of the sentences for the comparison is made on an unambiguous basis.

Table 9.2 shows the effect produced by the use of the positional distributions. The two samples from Laws 3 and 5 represent the extremes of continuous prose and continuous dialogue exchange. For these the positional distributions show no statistically significant difference. This conversion does not diminish the sensitivity of comparisons for both

Table 9.2   The positional distribution of the occurrences of the conjunction *kai* in samples from Plato's Laws and from the central section of Epistle Seven

Positions of Occurrence in Sentence	Laws Bk. 3	Laws Bk. 5	Epistle 7
1−5	49	28	19
6−10	47	45	41
11−15	30	49	13
16−20	25	28	24
21+	49	50	47
Totals:	200	200	144

Notes:

These are the mean positional distributions, being the sum of the forward and backward distributions.

samples can be distinguished from the relatively short central section of the Seventh Epistle.

The next illustration is taken from the text of Homer. The complication in this case is the bi-modality of the sentence length distributions. The most frequent sentence in Homer is the one-line sentence and the next most common sentence is the two-line sentence. One-line sentences average seven words, two-line sentences average around fourteen words. The result is a bi-modal distribution with peaks near to seven and to fourteen words.

In the text of the *Odyssey* the sentence length distributions show two clear peaks and though the grouped data can be fitted to a log normal distribution, Table 9.3, the closer examination of the ungrouped data in the region of the two modes shows how misleading the fitting procedure is when applied to grouped data whose grouping obscures the essential features of the distribution. If the positional distribution of the conjunction *kai* is recorded within the same sentences, the observations can be fitted to log normal distributions in both grouped and ungrouped

Table 9.3   Homer, *Odyssey* Book 17; the sentence length distributions and the positional distribution of the conjunction *kai* compared

(a) The sentence length distribution

	Grouped Data			Ungrouped Data	
No. of words in sentence	No. of sentences		No. of words in sentence	No. of sentences	
	O	*E*		*O*	*E*
1−5	44	46.9	6	37	27.5
6−10	148	146.7	7	50	30.9
11−15	101	102.2	8	30	30.9
16−20	45	43.0	9	19	28.7
21−25	24	21.1	10	12	28.7
26−30	8	9.8	11	18	23.8
31−35	4		12	28	21.9
36−40	1				
41−45	1	9.4			
46−50	1				
Totals:	377	377.0			

Notes:

The expected figures are from a log normal distribution calculated from the quartiles and median. The group data conceals the double peak at 7 and 12 words and suggests a fit for the distribution which is quite misleading.

Table 9.3   (continued)

(b) The positional distribution

Grouped Data			Ungrouped Data		
Position of Occurrence	No. of occurrences in position		Position of Occurrence	No. of occurrences in position	
	O	E		O	E
1−5	38	37.0	6	8	7.1
6−10	33	33.2	7	11	6.5
11−15	23	20.0	8	6	7.2
16−20	9	13.1	9	5	6.2
21−25	4		10	3	6.2
26−30	4		11		
41−45	1		12	8	10.1
Totals: 112		112.0			

Notes:

1) For the comparison of observed and expected values for grouped data, chi squared is 1.77 for 2 degrees of freedom.

2) For the comparison of the ungrouped data, chi squared is 2.46 for 3 degrees of freedom.

3) The use of the positional distribution removes the difficulty of the bimodal distribution and provides a good fit to a log normal distribution.

states.[1] The reason why this is so is that there are relatively few occurrences of the conjunction in the short sentences and the mode which came at seven word sentences is reduced below the level at which it is statistically significant.

This ability to select certain types of sentence by a choice of count-word means that the positional distributions of mobile words within sentence length distributions might be much easier to use than the parent sentence length distributions in a number of cases involving verse, direct speech, dramatic dialogue or other complicating factors.

Something can be learnt from the distribution of the lengths of the sentences in which the occurrences of a count-word are recorded. The examination is handicapped by a feature of the counting convention if, as in the book of Revelation, one sentence should contain 31 occurrences of the conjunction *kai*, this sentence is recorded 31 times and so produces a pronounced mode in the distribution.

[1] S. Michaelson and A. Q. Morton, 'Positional Stylometry', in *The Computer in Literary Studies*. Ed. Aitken, Edinburgh University Press 1972.

From the definition of mobility which has been adopted, the mean position of a mobile word is at the mid-point of the sentences in which it occurs; conversely, the mean length of sentences in which it occurs is twice the mean position.

A further distinction can usefully be made between types of positional distribution and for this purpose some further definitions are helpful. The sentences picked out from a sample sentence length distribution because they contain some occurrences of a word can be called a *selected sentence length distribution*, abbreviated to *ssld*.

If the occurrence of the count-word was independent of sentence length, then it would occur in a random sample of sentences selected from the parent distribution, the positional distribution would have a mean length half that of the parent sentence length distribution, and necessary allowance being made for the double counting of the occurrences, and the result would be a *random isotropic distribution*, abbreviated *rid*.

If the occurrence of the count-word is not independent of the length of sentence, then it will occur in sentences which are, on the average, longer or shorter than those of the parent sentence length distribution and though the positional distributions will still be isotropic, they will be, on the average, longer or shorter than the average length of sentence in the parent distribution. Such distributions are conveniently called *biased isotropic distributions*, abbreviated *bid*.

This point is much easier to appreciate from an example. In I Timothy the mean sentence length is 16.03 words. The mean length of sentence in which an occurrence of the conjunction *kai* occurs, the *ssld* for the conjunction *kai*, is 24.18 words with a standard error of 1.44 words. The mean positional distribution, the sum of the forward and backward positional distributions added because they show only random sampling differences, has a mean of 13.51 words with a standard error of 1.19 words.

In this instance if either the mean of the positional distribution is doubled or the mean of the *ssld* is halved, the figure so obtained lies within the range of two standard errors of the other estimate and its standard errors. In this Epistle the mean of the positional distribution is not statistically significantly different from half the mean of the *ssld*. It is, however, significantly different from the mean of the whole sentence length distribution, a result which is hardly surprising as the conjunction *kai* plays a role in sentence extension and so occurs more often in longer sentences. This means that the positional distribution of *kai* in I Timothy is a biased isotropic distribution.

Effective use can be made of this bias by calculating the mean length of sentence in which the occurrences of the count-word appear. It will be recalled from an earlier chapter that the mean is independent of the form of distribution as long as the variance is finite and so the multiple

Table 9.4   A comparison of the positional distributions of a word in two
Pauline letters and in Ephesians

	I Corinthians	Galatians	Ephesians
No. of words in text:	6735	2211	1918
No. of sentences in text:	555	166	80
Mean sentence length, words per sentence:	12.23	13.78	30.31
St. Error of mean:	0.34	0.77	3.21
No. of occurrences of *Christos*:	58	38	45
Mean length of sentences with occurrences of *Christos*:	20.59	19.45	61.11
St. Error:	1.78	2.18	6.59

counting of certain sentences will not affect this statistic. An illustration
of this application is shown in Table 9.4. The first step is to record the
positional distribution of the word being examined to ensure that it can
be regarded as mobile. This requires about 30 occurrences. The nominal
adjective *Christos* is mobile and occurs in a number of epistles often
enough to make a test based on its occurrence a useful indicator. From
the table it is clear that though both Paul and the writer of Ephesians use
this word in long sentences, the writer of Ephesians uses it in sentences
proportionately much longer than those written by Paul.

Another feature of isotropic positional distributions is the appearance
within them of periodic effects. Two illustrations are shown in
Figure 9.1. The first is from the occurrence of the conjunction *kai* in
I Corinthians (this will be referred to later in more detail), and the second
is the positional distribution of the neuter article *to* in the Fourth Gospel.
A word of warning is necessary in connection with periodic effects. There
is no subject in which it is more easy to mislead oneself. The reason is that
the human eye can pick out seeming regularities from a very large
number of alternative structures with such ease that it is difficult to
realise from how many configurations the regularities have been
selected. It is remarkably easy to forget, in this connection, that a
periodic structure significant at the 1% level will appear if one hundred
random structures are tested.

These pitfalls can be safely negotiated if two principles are kept firmly
in mind. First, the periodic structure should be clearly marked. This
would be necessary in any case for the number of observations involved
in even the most striking structure is a small proportion of the total and
to be statistically significant the difference created by the periodicity
must be large. A periodicity which needs careful analysis to be revealed is
unlikely to bear on the authorship and integrity of Greek texts.

The second principle to keep in mind is that some literary explanation
of the periodicity is necessary. This can be illustrated in both positive and
negative senses. The positional distribution of the occurrence of *kai* in

Figure 9.1   Two positional distributions

(a) The positional distribution of occurrences of the conjunction *kai* in the sentences of I Corinthians

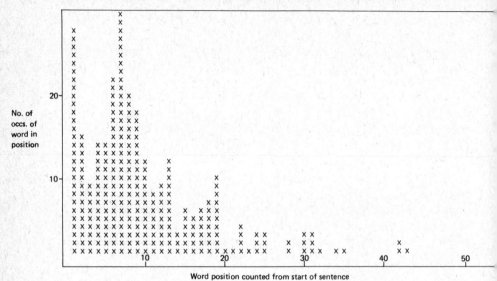

Word position counted from start of sentence

(b) The positional distribution of occurrences of the article *to* in the fourth Gospel

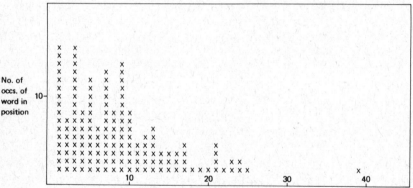

Word position counted from the last word of the sentence

I Corinthians reinforces a conclusion demonstrated some years before that when Paul extends a sentence he uses a group of six words one of which is an occurrence of the conjunction. It is now clear that he tends to begin his sentences and his extensions with the conjunction. The negative illustration comes from early days in the application of computers to the New Testament. Professor Michael Levison looked at sets of letters in Greek texts, at how often any letter appears with any other or any pair appears with a third letter and so on up to sets of six or eight letters. From the matrices so produced it seemed that writers of Greek do have characteristic preferences for some sets of letters in sequence, but it was never possible to provide any literary connotation for these sets.

The last feature of the positional distributions of mobile words to be commented on at this juncture is their role as tests of integrity. This is possible where a text of undoubted integrity exists and the word has been shown to be mobile within that text, the forward and backward positional distributions show no statistically significant difference.

Suppose that into such a text some sentences are inserted from another writer. The occurrences of the count-word will, on the average, be either a little too early or a little too late in comparison with the sentences of the text, unless the two authors are indistinguishable. If the number of occurrences of the count-word is sufficient, then the forward and backward distributions will separate and show statistically significant differences. This hypothesis can be readily confirmed by taking a few sentences from one Greek author and inserting them in a text of another.

To summarise, it can be said that all mobile words form a single class. Included in the class are some words like the conjunction *kai* which have long been studied, and for such words positional distributions extend the range of study and simplify some aspects of their occurrence. Included in the class are words like the preposition *en*, the occurrence of which has been previously studied under the considerable handicap of a large number of occurrences coming together in single sentences. Positional studies remove this handicap. Also included in the class of mobile words are many of the main subject matter nouns and adjectives. Their use as tests of authorship is only possible since the introduction of positional methods.

(iii) *Anisotropic Distributions*

Logically there is no justification for treating anisotropic positional distributions in more than one class, as the mobility of a word can contract from the full range of possible positions to the ultimate rigidity of a single position by an almost infinite series of small steps. In practice there is good reason for taking them in two groups, those which can be illustrated and analysed by cumulative sum charts and those which cannot.

Suppose a sample has 100 sentences; in such a sample it will only be useful to make a cusum chart of an event which occurs in at least 10% of the sentences and even that rate of occurrence is likely to enable only some simple comparison to be made of one half of the text against the other. In other words in samples of this size, around 1500–1800 words of Greek and about the size of Ephesians, Philippians and Colossians, only words which occur rather more than ten times in the major preferred positions can be used in cusum charts. There are few words which meet these conditions but they occur in a surprising number of sentences. In the Fourth Gospel there are only 54 words which occur fifty times or more but these make up one third of the text of the gospel.

The constraints on the use of cusum charts means that the procedure for testing anisotropic distributions is very simple. The text, or sample, is indexed (using a computer this is literally a matter of a few minutes) and all the words which occur more than, say, twenty times in the text have their positional distributions recorded. The positional distributions will be either isotropic or anisotropic. The isotropic distributions will furnish tests of authorship which are useful but not independent of sentence length. The anisotropic distributions will show anything from the mildest degree of anisotropy to almost complete immobility.

As the distributions are being recorded it will become clear which are suitable for use in cusum charts. These words will have positional distributions with two characteristics; first, there will be some major preferred positions and the number of occurrences in these positions will be at least ten percent of the number of sentences in the sample or text. Second, the occurrences of the word in the major preferred positions will have been shown to be independent of sentence length.

Greek particles furnish a number of instances of words which have a strong preference for positions among the first four words of sentences and whose occurrences are independent of sentence length in these positions. The only new information added by positional studies to the previous examinations of individual particles concerns such words as *oun*. This particle occurs infrequently in most writers so that a wide ranging examination of its occurrence is not practicable. But in all the authors in which it occurs often enough to be tested, its occurrence is similar to that of the particle *de*. This suggested a hypothesis which was confirmed, that words which have similar positional distributions allow similar inferences to be drawn about their behaviour.

The clear exception to this rule concerns the occurrence of the introductory verbs, *elegon*, *apokrithe* and *aspasasthe*. These words have highly anisotropic positional distributions but their occurrence is tied to the literary form of the text; they introduce direct speech or address. The rate of occurrence of the verbs within the literary form seems to be indicative of the author but their irregular occurrence in the text makes them of little practical consequence.

The remaining words whose positional distributions are anisotropic but do not occur often enough to be a basis for a cusum chart have to be taken as simple binomial tests. How many occurrences are in position x and how many are in all other positions? For example, a useful test is to ask how many occurrences of *Theos* are final words in sentences, and how many are not? The simplicity of such tests is no barrier to their effectiveness as tests of authorship.

A question of some importance in positional measurements is the separation or aggregation of word-forms. The effects are most clearly seen in the case of the definite article. By most writers on vocabulary and on stylometry, and by almost all concordance and index compilers, all the cases of the article are taken together. In positional studies the underlying assumption which leads to such aggregation seems to be unwarranted. No distinction has yet been made between the singular and plural forms of the article but the mean position of occurrences of the cases differ. In some authors, Aristotle for example, the mean position comes later in the sequence of cases, the nominatives are earlier than the accusatives, which precede the genitives, and last come the datives but this order is not invariable. It is therefore unwise to aggregate cases without reflection.

As words occur less frequently, aggregation of forms becomes less important. With fewer occurrences the standard errors of the positional distributions increase until the mean positions of different cases show no statistically significant differences. It may well be that only in the case of the article or of very large texts is there danger in aggregation.

At first sight the claims of positional stylometry are rather startling. All words which occur more often than a simply determined minimum number of times within a sentence length sample which is satisfactory can be used as tests of authorship. The positional distributions fall into two groups, those which are independent of the sentence length distributions in which they have been recorded, and those which are not independent of sentence length. Most of the positional distributions which are not independent of sentence length afford opportunities for differential comparisons.

In other words, given two samples of Greek text which are known to be larger than the minimum sample size for sentence length distributions for the author, then positional stylometry enables all tests of authorship which comply with the primary statistical conditions to be identified and used. For the first time stylometry has acquired a general theoretical foundation.

The claims made in this book are general and can only be validated by a wide range of evidence which is set out in the various references, but it may be useful and helpful to have a simple example of the techniques at this point. The example embraces the career of the orator Isocrates. Isocrates was born the son of a middle class citizen of Athens in the 68th Olympiad and so was seven years older than Plato. He founded a famous school of oratorical instruction; Demosthenes sought to enter it but could only raise one-fifth of the fee of one thousand drachmas and was rebuffed by the remark that the instruction could no more be cut into parts than could a fine fish. The orations of Isocrates were highly

Table 9.5

(a) Isocrates: sentence length distributions

No. of words in sentence	Number of sentences in oration						
	1	2	3	4	5	6	7
1–5	7	1	3	12	10	2	5
6–10	59	16	18	29	34	15	18
11–15	59	38	33	51	46	34	34
16–20	36	25	32	55	62	48	38
21–25	11	21	22	47	40	44	16
26–30	8	19	16	42	34	18	17
31–35	8	3	12	25	23	17	14
36–40	2	3	7	20	20	13	10
41–45	2	3	3	21	5	8	10
46–50	–	4	5	9	9	3	4
51–55	–	1	2	11	10	2	6
56–60	–	1	–	7	6	7	1
61–65	1	–	1	8	2	1	3
66–70	–	–	–	4	6	2	4
71–75	–	–	–	1	4	2	1
76–80	–	–	2	2	–	2	1
81–85	–	–	–	2	3	2	–
86–90	–	1	1	3	3	–	–
91–95	–	2	–	1	–	1	–
96–100	–	–	–	2	–	1	–
101–105				2	1	–	
106–110				1	–	–	
111–115				1	2	1	
				130 → 2	150 → 1	125 → 1	
				135 → 1			
				190 → 1			
Totals:	193	138	157	360	321	224	182

No. of words in sentence	8	9	10	11	12	13	14
1–5	12	6	3	4	20	–	5
6–10	24	12	13	9	41	4	18
11–15	42	26	17	12	56	8	16
16–20	50	42	16	17	53	9	17
21–25	31	25	18	21	57	6	21
26–30	34	17	22	16	48	5	12
31–35	23	5	9	4	40	3	9
36–40	14	6	10	6	34	4	8
41–45	18	7	5	3	28	3	5
46–50	5	8	6	7	15	–	5
51–55	14	4	1	2	14	2	1
56–60	5	5	1	3	16	–	3
61–65	6	4	1	–	2	–	4

Table 9.5 (continued)

No. of words in sentence	Number of sentences in oration									
66–70		2	1		1	1		9	–	1
71–75		4	–		1	–		8	–	–
76–80		–	1		1	1		7	1	1
81–85		–	2		–			1	–	
86–90		1	–		1			2	–	
91–95		1	2		–			6	1	
96–100		–			1			5		
101–105		2		150	1		110	2		
	130	1		165	1		115	2		
							120	1		
							125	3		
							135	1		
							150	1		
							160	1		
							190	1		
							215	1		
Totals:		289	173		129	106		475	46	126

No. of words in sentence	15	16	17	18	19	20	21
1–5	20	2	11	3	5	1	1
6–10	75	12	19	24	21	3	13
11–15	83	12	30	29	15	7	11
16–20	97	10	28	28	27	6	12
21–25	98	13	11	20	23	10	10
26–30	62	13	16	13	11	5	3
31–35	49	12	8	13	5	5	–
36–40	46	6	14	8	7	2	4
41–45	38	2	3	4	3	–	1
46–50	22	4	3	3	3	3	–
51–55	22	3	1	5	3	1	–
56–60	12	3	2	–	3	–	1
61–65	3	–	2	–	1	1	–
66–70	8	–	–	–		–	–
71–75	1	–	–	–		–	1
76–80	6	2	1	1		–	
81–85	2	–		–		1	
86–90	2	–		1			
91–95	2	1		1			
96–100	4	–		1			
101–105	1	2		1			
121–125	1	1			115 1		
176–180	1						
Totals:	653	98	149	155	128	45	57

Table 9.5 (continued)

(b) The constants of the sentence length distributions of the orations of Isocrates, linear scale

Oration	Mean	S.E.	Median	S.E.	Q1	S.E.	Q3	S.E.	D9	S.
1	14.89	1.71	12.58	0.69	8.50	0.51	17.74	0.84	26.06	2.
2	21.80	1.25	17.80	1.18	12.30	1.59	25.66	1.59	37.00	5.
3	23.31	1.29	18.91	0.95	12.80	0.82	28.28	1.70	39.43	2.
4	30.04	1.23	23.51	1.01	14.80	0.81	37.25	2.05	56.43	4.
5	27.25	0.90	21.06	1.12	13.94	0.84	33.21	1.69	52.95	2.
6	27.00	1.26	21.48	0.85	15.52	0.68	32.06	1.91	49.33	7.
7	25.17	1.17	19.47	0.88	13.31	0.86	33.04	2.09	47.25	5.
8	27.67	1.10	22.66	1.37	14.32	0.88	35.27	2.63	52.54	1.
9	26.53	1.44	20.10	1.32	14.86	1.10	31.75	5.70	52.13	4.
10	28.85	2.20	24.31	1.58	14.78	1.45	34.25	2.73	47.58	2.
11	25.74	1.43	22.62	1.23	15.44	1.31	30.38	5.57	47.43	2.
12	33.42	1.25	26.09	1.13	15.17	0.89	41.29	1.68	66.94	3.
13	26.80	2.58	21.11	2.83	14.67	1.84	34.17	4.90	44.00	3.
14	25.18	1.41	21.67	1.34	12.66	1.52	33.06	2.70	47.40	3.
15	27.46	1.04	22.65	0.46	14.13	0.67	35.82	1.20	49.41	1.
16	29.74	2.22	25.00	1.90	14.38	1.79	34.79	1.79	53.67	4.
17	21.74	1.11	18.13	1.11	11.49	0.90	28.83	1.68	38.75	1.
18	23.23	1.29	18.75	1.11	11.98	0.93	29.42	2.07	40.75	4.
19	22.67	2.74	19.26	1.05	12.00	1.17	27.27	2.23	42.00	5.
20	25.22	1.93	22.75	1.68	15.89	2.08	31.75	2.91	39.38	2.
21	18.44	2.36	16.46	1.57	10.52	1.36	22.88	1.64	36.43	2.

regarded as models of style and argument. One happy result of this was that while his orations were preserved and emulated they never became sacred texts which had to be corrected to meet the changed circumstances of later generations and so are comparatively free from editorial emendation.

Isocrates was a writer of speeches; of the twenty extant orations he himself delivered only one in public, and in many of the others, particularly the forensic orations designed to be used in the courts, he sought to identify himself as far as possible with his clients.

The unique feature of Isocrates' career is its duration. He published his last work, oration 12, in his 98th year and the series covers a period of 65 years. The orations are classified in a variety of forms; one group is defined by the use for which they were written, another, the epideictic orations, is defined by the elevated style in which they were written and the remainder are classed by their subject matter as educational or political. This illustrates one of the difficulties of defining literary form, that while some varieties, hexameter verse or continuous prose, are objectively defined and rarely disputed, many of the sub-divisions are made on personal and subjective grounds to suit some special purpose.

Table 9.5 (continued)

(c) The constants of the sentence length distributions of the orations of Isocrates, log scale

Oration	Log mean	St. Error of log mean
1	1.093	0.017
2	1.250	0.020
3	1.278	0.020
4	1.370	0.016
5	1.329	0.016
6	1.342	0.016
7	1.306	0.022
8	1.353	0.017
9	1.324	0.019*
10	1.365	0.024
11	1.343	0.021
12	1.405	0.011
13	1.340	0.040
14	1.320	0.028
15	1.353	0.017
16	1.368	0.029
17	1.259	0.024
18	1.274	0.023
19	1.268	0.023
20	1.354	0.033
21	1.200	0.033

Notes: *Davies' coefficient + 0.206.

Although Davies' coefficient suggests that, for all the orations except oration 9, a log scale should be used, the orations do not have log normal sentence length distributions. This does not affect the two conclusions to be drawn from the figures: that oration 1 is not Isocrates', and that a difference in form produces a difference in sentence length.

Fortunately, in many instances, and this is one, the matter is not of much consequence. As will be seen, the orations of Isocrates fall into three groups, the forensic, the epideictic and all the others.

The use for which this data was collected was a study of chronological change in Greek writers, a purpose for which Isocrates is uniquely valuable, and the first step in the enquiry was to test the authenticity of the orations and confirm that the tests used to do so were either quite unaffected by the passage of time, or so little altered by it, that they were valid indicators of authorship. The next stage was to discover habits that changed in a linear manner and could be useful in estimating dates of composition. The data is set out in Tables 9.5 and 9.6.

Table 9.5 shows the sentence length distributions for all the orations. Oration 1 is spurious, at least it is certainly not a free composition of

Table 9.6

(a) An illustration of the dependence of vocabulary on position in the orations of Isocrates

Position of word in sentence	Number of different words in the position
1st	768
2nd	405
3rd	1037
4th	1437
5th	1600

Notes:

In orations 2–20 there are 4,018 sentences. Forty sentences have four words or fewer, so that the possible choice of fifth words in sentences is 3,978.

Isocrates though he may have had some connection with its compilation. The sentence length distributions of Isocrates are not log normal; they have too few short sentences and too few long sentences. For all but oration 9 the log mean may be the most useful statistic. The analysis of the sentence length distribution shows that there are statistically significant differences within the corpus. Within a single population can be placed either the forensic orations or the epideictic orations and all the others. But the whole range of literary form cannot be embraced without statistically significant differences appearing. The explanation of this is the difference in the contrast in literary form for an analysis of the data shows no change of the sentence length distributions with time. This confirms a previous conclusion of a similar study.[1]

Tables 9.6(a) and (b) are of frequent words in preferred positions. The reason for collecting this data is simple. Any feature which is to be used in making a judgement about a complete set of orations must not only appear in them all, it must appear frequently in them all. To enable tests of significance to be employed, the features must occur at least five times in every oration. There are only fourteen words which occur in all the orations of Isocrates more than five times. The fourteen are particles and connectives, articles and pronouns. Of the fourteen, the frequent particles which tend to occur among the first words of sentences form the great majority.

An illustration of the positional bias of vocabulary is shown in Table 9.6(a). The restriction of the vocabulary of words which stand second

[1] Morton, A. Q., 'The Authorship of Greek Prose', *Journal of the Royal Statistical Society*, op. cit.

Table 9.6 (continued)

(b) Isocrates: the occurrence of some frequent words in preferred positions

Duration	D2	T	G2	T	M2	T	A1	T	Ou1	T
1	28	108	55	76	30	79	2	31	2	10
2	20	80	26	39	24	64	1	44	1	7
3	33	86	31	40	19	65	2	53	5	23
4	102	339	95	121	39	233	5	110	26	71
5	92	261	86	101	25	156	14	90	8	51
6	76	198	46	66	26	116	6	67	3	22
7	45	126	56	71	19	89	6	58	7	30
8	85	252	72	97	34	165	7	91	14	52
9	48	136	34	51	32	96	7	58	8	28
10	47	127	32	48	19	77	5	41	8	20
11	28	81	27	32	13	61	7	36	5	16
12	134	400	99	151	71	294	20	194	23	98
13	15	39	11	15	5	29	1	15	3	8
14	38	86	34	45	11	61	3	40	4	20
15	193	491	150	195	87	320	24	192	16	83
16	36	114	21	27	8	66	3	24	8	15
17	53	101	21	26	16	59	7	21	3	11
18	65	121	16	26	12	64	2	44	3	26
19	39	86	25	34	13	52	6	81	3	13
20	14	27	10	12	3	17	–	13	1	3
21	13	43	12	17	9	29	1	9	1	5

Totals:
| 1–21 | 1176 | 3194 | 904 | 1214 | 485 | 2113 | 127 | 1231 | 150 | 602 |

Proportion in preferred position:

| | 0.3682 | | 0.7747 | | 0.2295 | | 0.1032 | | 0.2492 | |

Notes:

D2 denotes an occurrence of the particle *de* as the second word of sentences, G2 one of *gar*, M2 one of *men*; A1 an occurrence of *alla* as the first word of sentences; Ou1, an occurrence of the negative *ou* as the first word of sentences.

in sentences is very marked and it is due to the occurrence of a small number of frequent particles in this position.

The results of the analysis are shown in Table 9.6(b). From these it is clear that there are some tests which are completely unaffected by the variety of literary form, some which are affected by a change in literary form and others which are affected by the passing of the years. As long as care is taken in making comparisons of texts which are in contrasting literary forms, tests of authorship are reliable.

10 The Uninflected Language

If we now turn from the inflected language to an uninflected language, it is apparent that sentence length distributions, and measures which are related to them, are likely to be much less efficient in an uninflected language than in an inflected one, also that the variation within writers will be larger and the differences between them lessened. This should not be understood as suggesting that such measures should not be used in uninflected languages, merely that another aspect of word placing will often be more efficient as a test of authorship in uninflected languages.

The feature of word placing which is independent of sentence length, the preference for certain positions at the start and finish of sentences, will not be affected by the change from inflected to uninflected language but the differences in such preferences between the literary forms, e.g. prose, dialogue and verse, will be enhanced.

The feature of word placing which offers most scope for tests of authorship is the creation of collocations, the placing of two or more words in immediate succession. Collocations of frequent words are themselves also frequent, a first requirement of tests, and vary little within authors and largely between authors, two very desirable characteristics of tests of authorship.

The problems with English arise not from the nature of the language but from its history. English has a history of continual change and development running for more than a thousand years. From the end of the Middle Ages there has been a constant expansion of vocabulary parallel to the rise of a complex civilisation. Within the language, science has created another kind of English. The free communications of our times have produced a world-wide exchange of words and forms. Popular culture and the demands of the advertising agency have twisted the natural forms until they scream for help.

It is quite possible to claim that a theory is of general application in Greek. Classical Greek has survived in manageable quantity. To the end of the pre-christian era it amounts to no more than twelve million words. There are poems, narratives, inscriptions and a range of literary forms. But one only has to pose the question, What is a fair sample of English? to realise how vastly different the position is. Does a reasonable sample of English amount to one hundred million words or ten times as much? Will it include sonnets, calendars, railway timetables, chemical formulae, advertising jingles? It can be argued that all these and much more should be included.

However, most of these literary forms do not present historical problems of authorship in the sense in which these words are used in this book. Their origins may be uncertain and bitterly disputed but in every type of problem the disputed material must be compared with similar material, and this book deals only with speech and writing of the kind which has come down from the past and is familiar to students of history. To produce a representative selection of English is an impossible task. Fortunately it does not have to be attempted. This is one great advantage of putting forward a general theory of stylometry rather than looking at the particular features of any individual case. A theory which is advanced to fit any writer in any language need not be tested as intensively in each new language as it would have to be if advanced to cover only that language. If the habit is not affected by time in one nationality of writers, it needs only to be confirmed that this is also the case in a second nationality. If hexameter verse in Greek produces a pattern clearly dependent on the verse form, then a simple experiment will confirm that this is either true in English or is not true.

So the approach to English can begin from the fact that in Greek the two factors that change the kind of habits which are the subject of stylometry are a contrast in literary forms (comparisons within the same form are simple but comparisons between forms must be made with care) and the passing of long periods of time. In Greek the time required to show that changes have taken place is of the order of forty years and the minimum change detectable is about six years. A general theory can then be advanced and tested to see whether or not it behaves in English as it does in Greek, and it is best tested by making an examination of the extreme conditions which have been shown likely to affect stylistic habits.

What was available to the author at the start of his enquiry into English was a set of ten samples of English prose prepared by a Polish professor who came to Edinburgh to study the use of prepositions in English writers. The ten samples are listed in Table 10.1.

The first step was to make a set of concordances of the ten samples. To

Table 10.1   The ten writers used as samples

GREENE, Graham:	*Brighton Rock*, London 1938
HUXLEY, Aldous:	*Point Counter Point*, London 1928
LEWIS, C S:	*That Hideous Strength*, London 1945
MAUGHAM, W Somerset:	*The Moon and Sixpence*, London 1919
MURDOCH, Iris:	*The Severed Head*, London 1961
SNOW, C P:	*The Masters*, London 1951
WAUGH, Evelyn:	*The Loved One*, London 1948
WELLS, H G:	*Tono-Bungay*, London 1909
WOOLF, Virginia:	*Night and Day*, London 1920
WYNDHAM, John:	*The Seeds of Time*, London 1956

enable any testing of the samples to be done, each would have to be sub-divided into as many parts as would still allow the minimum number of occurrences per sample required for tests of significance. The concordance showed which words met these conditions. The number of words which supply information in a sample of 1,000 to 1,100 words of English is not large and Table 10.2 shows which words they are. Only sixteen words occur often enough, on the average, to supply the five occurrences required for most statistical tests. It would seem that comparisons using only the simple rate of occurrence of these words would be of little value.

Attention was then directed to those words which appear in preferred positions, generally words which open sentences or end them. The testing routine was precisely that used in Greek for words which behaved in the same way and which was described in a previous chapter. Then an examination was made of the collocations in which frequent words appear.

In both cases the testing followed the same pattern. The sample of each of the ten authors was divided into as many sub-samples as would leave an expectation of five occurrences per sub-sample. The sets of sub-samples were tested for consistency. In most cases the conclusion was that the occurrence was consistent within the whole sample. But in a number of instances periodic effects were found to be present, and a further investigation of these was undertaken.

Table 10.3 shows the words which occur often enough in preferred positions to enable them to be used as tests of authorship involving samples of a thousand words or more. The next table, Table 10.4, shows a typical example of the occurrence of a word in a preferred position, but it might be helpful to explain at this point the routine of testing which the author followed. The occurrences of each key word in a preferred position, or in collocation with any other word which occurred often enough to form a useful basis for statistical testing, was listed in the ten samples. Only if the occurrence was consistent within the sample and differed between the samples was it accepted as being, prima facie, a test of authorship suitable for further investigation. Before such habits could be accepted as tests of authorship two things had yet to be established. The first is that they were stable under extreme conditions. The second is that they are independent of each other. Neither of these characteristics could be demonstrated on ten samples of English prose.

The first characteristic, stability under extreme conditions, was investigated by a three part experiment. Samples were prepared which showed the maximum of internal change within an author, which showed the maximum external change of his circumstances likely to bear upon his writing, and then an examination was made of three works written by an author who prides himself in being able to write quite differently in different genres.

Table 10.2   The occurrence of some frequent words in ten writers of English

WORD	WRITER										TOTALS
	GREENE	HUXLEY	LEWIS	MAUGHAM	MURDOCH	SNOW	WAUGH	WELLS	WOOLF	WYNDHAM	
A	33	32	31	24	23	24	28	27	19	33	274
ALL	7	3	5	4	3	3	11	7	6	4	53
ALSO	–	1	–	–	–	1	1	–	–	–	2
AND	22	25	37	24	41	21	24	52	26	22	294
ANY	1	–	3	–	–	–	3	1	4	2	14
AS	8	13	5	2	10	10	1	8	8	4	69
AT	12	12	6	5	3	5	4	2	11	10	70
BEEN	1	3	1	3	5	10	2	4	1	3	33
BUT	5	10	2	7	9	2	2	7	4	12	60
FOR	5	4	6	4	4	15	8	2	7	7	62
IN	9	17	21	11	14	16	20	30	27	9	174
IT	14	13	8	12	6	27	15	13	9	20	137
NO	4	5	2	4	3	4	5	5	3	2	37
NOT	2	4	2	12	7	8	7	7	1	9	59
OF	16	19	13	17	42	15	35	51	57	31	296
ON	9	8	6	9	9	12	7	4	9	9	76
SO	1	2	1	4	6	5	3	–	8	8	38
THAT	6	8	11	18	13	11	7	14	7	12	107
THE	59	55	53	29	48	54	72	64	83	41	558
THIS	5	–	4	4	6	4	3	7	1	1	35
TO	29	18	28	47	35	37	20	18	40	19	291
VERY	–	4	2	4	3	3	1	3	1	4	25
WAS	14	28	8	19	23	23	20	6	13	22	176
NO. of WORDS in SAMPLE	1045	1042	1046	1056	1137	1079	1073	1094	1159	1164	10,855

Table 10.3   The occurrence of some frequent words in preferred positions in English prose

Word	Position of Occurrence	
	First Word in Sentence	Last Word in Sentence
And	*	
At	*	**
But	*	
For	*	*
In	*	**
It	*	**
So	*	
That	*	*

Notes:

*denotes the occurrence as found in most writers

**denotes that it is found in a minority of writers (where the rate of occurrence is low, periodic effects can be expected to appear)

The first author is Sir Walter Scott. To the student of stylometry Scott offers many advantages but for this purpose two are paramount. The first is that he kept a journal,[1] from which the genesis, progress and revision of many of his works can be traced in detail. The journal covers the years from 1825 until his death in 1832. The second feature of Scott's career that is of interest is that he suffered a series of strokes, the first in 1823, the second and third in February and November 1830, the fourth in May 1831 and the fifth in May 1832. He died on 21st September 1832. It is therefore possible to determine what effect these physical disabilities had upon his habits of composition.

The samples available were taken from *The Antiquary*, published in 1816, at a time when he was in full flow, publishing three other books in that year. The comparison samples are from *Castle Dangerous*, a work begun in July 1831 and completed in August of the same year although he had to pay a considerable sum for emendations to the text – 'To Mr. Cadell I already owe with the cancels on these apoplectic books [*Count Robert of Paris* and *Castle Dangerous*] about £200 and must run it up to £500 more at least' *(Journal,* p. 659, note 6).

The examination of *The Antiquary* was conducted with two aims in mind. The first was to establish a norm for Scott by looking at sets of twenty samples for all habits which occurred often enough to supply that number of samples in a length of text which would be of practical interest. Clearly it is of minor importance to examine habits which would need not one but a number of complete works to test. The other aim was

[1] *The Journal of Sir Walter Scott,* ed. by W. E. K. Anderson, Oxford 1972.

Table 10.4   An example of the occurrence of a frequent word in a preferred position: *but* as the first word of sentences in Sir Walter Scott

Text	Occurrences of *but*		
	As First Word in Sentences	In All Positions	
Antiquary			
Chapter 14	7	25	
15	8	29	
16	4	35	
17	5	26	
18	6	20	
19	9	21	
20	10	34	
21	16	39	
22	13	34	
23	3	21	
24	10	31	
25	6	23	
26	9	28	
27	17	33	
14–27	123	399	x^2 21.91, $v = 13.$
Castle Dangerous			
Chapter			
1, 4, 5	14	55	
13, 14	6	35	x^2 0.86, $v = 1.$
Total:	20	90	
Antiquary	123	399	x^2 2.62, $v = 1.$
Castle Dangerous	20	90	
Total:	143	489	

Notes:

There is no statistically significant difference within the works or between the works.

to use these samples to look at possible connections between habits by means of correlation tests.

For purely adventitious reasons connected with the availability of machines, systems and operators, the basic samples were the successive chapters of *The Antiquary* from Chapter 14 to Chapter 33. To enable tests of significance to be applied, a collocation had to occur one hundred times in the twenty samples. If the number of occurrences was little less than this, the number of chapters was extended, the sequence up to Chapter 45 was readily accessible. If the number of occurrences was very much less, then the chapters were aggregated into a small number of large samples. As the sample size increases they become of less practical value for comparisons within the author but not less valuable for comparisons with other authors. For example, in all twenty samples no instance was found of Scott writing *as though*. This alone differentiates him from seven of the ten authors of the first series of samples.

The maximum internal change was examined in two works of Henry James (1843–1916). The samples are from *The Ambassadors* (1903) and *The American* (1877). James was born in New York and was educated in New York, London, Paris and Geneva before entering Harvard Law School in 1862. He settled in Europe in 1875. His works can be conveniently divided into early, middle and late groups and the samples are from the early and late groups. Between writing these books James had settled in England and deliberately changed his cultural background. The feature of James' writing most often commented on is his passion for, and his precision in using, words. 'To his unsleeping artistic curiosity was joined an incomparable skill in the use of words as if they were delicate brush strokes. ... But no English novelist has equalled his power of accumulating delicate shades of distinction in touch after touch of virtuosity that never dazzles, because nothing ever stands out emphatically in the picture.'[1]

The third part of the experiment was an examination of three books written by an author who prides himself on writing in quite different genres and using a style appropriate to each in doing so. The writer is John Fowles and the books are *The Collector*, a hard-boiled crime story, *The French Lieutenant's Woman*, a Victorian pastiche, and *The Magus*, a recreation of the atmosphere of pagan Greece.

In Scott, the collocations and preferred positions of Tables 10.3 and 10.5, 19 words occurred often enough to provide useful samples and information. The 19 words furnished 27 tests. In 11 instances, the number of occurrences allowed each chapter of the book to be used as a sample. In 16 cases the shorter chapters of the book had to be added to the next chapter to raise the expected number of occurrences to the minimum, and so in place of 20 samples there would be 18 or 19. With still lower rates of occurrence, pairs of chapters had to be taken and only long chapters could stand on their own. This meant sets of 9–12 samples. Occasionally 4 chapters were required to supply the minimum number of occurrences but this means that any conclusions based upon such samples would apply to texts of 20,000 words or more and such samples are not often of practical value.

Of the 27 tests, 5 were statistically significant at the 5% level. This is a

[1] Sampson, *The Concise Cambridge History of English Literature*, Cambridge 1943.

Table 10.5   A list of collocations frequently occurring in writers of
English

Key Word	Relation	Collocation
a	FB	*an adjective*
and	FB	*all*
	FB	*the*
	FB	*then*
as	FB	*a*
	FB	*if*
	FB	*the*
	FB	*though*
	FB	*well*
at	FB	*last*
	FB	*the*
been	PB	*have*
for	FB	*a*
	FB	*the*
in	FB	*a*
	FB	*the*
is	FB	*the*
it	FB	*is*
of	FB	*a*
	FB	*course*
	FB	*the*
on	FB	*the*
that	FB	*the*
to	FB	*a*
	FB	*be*
	FB	*the*

Notes:

1. FB denotes *followed by*; PB denotes *preceded by*.
2. In all the data for a word followed by an adjective, the following
   convention has been used:

An occurrence of *and* (or any other word) followed by an adjective
denotes a sequence starting with an occurrence of *and* followed by
one or more adjectives and ending with a noun. Thus 'a glass of
Guinness' is not an occurrence of *of*, FB adjective. 'A glass of Guinness
Stout' is an occurrence of the collocation *of* FB adjective.

(An adjective is defined as a word which specifies a smaller group from
that described by the succeeding noun: thus 'A red hat' is one of the
smaller group of hats, the red ones.)

contrast with the single significant difference to be expected as the result
of chance variation.

The next table, Table 10.6, gives the figures in full for the six sets of
anomalous observations. The first of them is for occurrences of the
definite article followed by an adjective succeeded by a noun. From a

Table 10.6   Sir Walter Scott, *The Antiquary*: the anomalies

	Habit		Habit		Habit		
Chapter	Occs. of *and* as FWS	Total in Sample	Occs. of *and* FB Adj.	Total in Sample	Occs. of *it* FB IS	Total in Sample	Notes
14	2	100	8	100	6	20	1. Total of *and* as FWS:
15	6	100	15	100	—	20	79 in 1691,
16	3	100	21	100	3	20	chi squared 35.18,
17	3	85	—	100	4	20	17 degrees of freedom.
18	1	100	14	100	6	20	
19	3	100	19	100	3	20	
20	2	100	14	100	3	20	
21	9	100	16	100	1	20	
22	8	100	9	100	4	20	2. Total occs. of *and*:
23	—	100	9	100	—	—	FB Adj 250 in 1900,
24	1	100	18	100	—	20	chi squared 23.45,
25	—	100	13	100	3	20	18 degrees of freedom.
26	2	100	18	100	1	17	
27	4	104	9	100	4	20	
30	4	100	15	100	1	14	3. Total Occs. of *it*:
31	—	—	10	100	—	—	FB *is* 44 in 330,
32	9	100	13	100	1	20	chi squared 20.90,
33	6	100	10	100	2	19	16 degrees of freedom.
34	9	100	13	100	—	—	
35	7	100	6	100	2	20	
	(see Note 1.)		(see Note 2.)		(see Note 3.)		

Table 10.6 (continued)

Chapter	Occurrences of *of*			Occurrences of *the*		Occurrences of *to*	
	FB *the*	in sequence	in sample	FB Adj	in sample	FB *the*	in sample
14	17	14	60	36	151	10	100
15	10	9	60	44	250	13	100
16	24	13	60	43	195	8	98
17	27	15	60	71	341	14	100
18	9	7	60	57	231	12	92
19	10	7	60	57	242	12	100
20	10	7	60	45	201	20	100
21	23	15	60	100	430	3	100
22	14	13	60	27	182	9	100
23	14	13	60	31	198	9	100
24	12	9	60	29	218	9	92
25	14	9	60	57	308	19	100
26	—	—	—	54	295	—	—
27	18	14	60	63	255	15	99
30	13	11	60	24	129	9	100
31	18	14	60	37	184	—	—
32	—	—	—	40	244	—	—
33	11	9	60	49	237	—	—
34	11	10	60	41	158	7	100
35	18	11	60	38	206	10	100
36	15	11	60	—	—	10	100
Totals:	278	204	1080	963	4655	192	1681
Chi squared	10.41			23.23		24.10	
Degrees of Freedom	17			19		16	

reading of the text, or the concordance of the text, it is clear that in some chapters of the book there appear one or other, or both, of two characters identified only as 'the old man' and 'the old woman'. These occurrences are really titular rather than descriptive and if they are extracted from the figures, then, as can be seen from the later columns of Table 10.6, the statistically significant differences disappear. This is one example of a fact generally known and often illustrated: that when any word becomes part of the subject matter of a text, anomalies in its rate of occurrence are likely to appear. If, for example, a dual biography of David and Jonathan is written, then it may well be that occurrences of the conjunction *and* between two nouns or names will be high in some sections of the text.

If for any reason this procedure is not acceptable, then the alternative is to look at another form of distribution. It has been so far assumed that these occurrences fit the simplest pattern, the binomial, a pattern appropriate to a mutually exclusive choice for which the rate of occurrence is unchanging from trial to trial. It was earlier discovered that for some of the occurrences, notably the five under examination here, there is a tendency for the observations to occur in sequences rather longer than would be found in an event whose occurrence was due to pure chance. Because of this tendency of occurrences to come together, the minimum sample size had to be increased to allow them to be treated as binomial distributions. In such situations a Poisson distribution will often provide a better fit than the binomial as this allows for some variation of the rate of occurrence from one trial to another. In extreme cases it may be that a negative binomial distribution alone will fit the observations if the variation is still larger. In the present case all the exceptional occurrences are examined as Poisson distributions and in every case the statistically significant differences vanish. As Poisson distributions are much more easily calculated and tested for observations recorded in equal samples, the occurrences are recorded as they are found in the first 100 occurrences of the key-word in each chapter.

The most interesting of the anomalies is in the occurrences of *and* followed by an adjective. In chapters 14, 18 and 28, the three smallest, the average rate of occurrence is 9.5% in samples with an average of 70 occurrences of *and*. In the next group, chapters 15, 16, 20, 23, 29, 30 and 31, there is an average rate of occurrence of 12.0% in samples averaging 107 occurrences of *and*. Chapters 19, 22, 24, 25, 26, 27 and 33 have an average rate of 14.6% of adjectives in samples, averaging 120 occurrences of *and*, and the two largest chapters 17 and 21 have 15.1% of adjectives in 222 occurrences of *and*. It would appear that the rate of occurrence of adjective after *and* depends on sample size. This would not be at all surprising as the length of a chapter will affect the scale of the descriptive passages in it and any elements more likely to occur in such sections will be found more often as a result.

The first general conclusion to be drawn from the data of Table 10.6 is that the pattern of occurrence for words in preferred positions and in frequent collocations is consistent in samples of 1,000 to 4,000 words and samples ten times as large. All the anomalies found in the large samples had been present in the small samples. The second conclusion is that periodic effects, though present, are slight and can be effectively neutralised either by varying the method of counting, for example by recording not the individual observations but the sequences of successive observations, or by a change in the distribution used to describe them, a change from the binomial to the Poisson or negative binomial distributions, or by extending the sample.

The anomalies play a useful part in reminding the researcher that it is literary texts which are being examined. The evidence can only be fully understood and safely interpreted when the nature of the material is kept in mind. The examination starts from a text and it should always end with the text; the statistics are only a useful summary description of what an author is doing.

The other aspect of the occurrence of frequent words in preferred positions or in common collocation that needs to be looked at is the correlations of observations. This is a subject on which there is a good deal of confusion of thought, due to the initial assumptions which are brought to the analysis. Literary men will often argue that they know what correlation is, and they can give a perfectly consistent definition of it but not be able to appreciate that the statistical definition is totally different. To the literary man, correlation generally means either that an author who writes one form of words will not use an alternative, or that the choice of one form of words will make it likely that some other pattern of words will occur nearby. To him, correlation is concerned with the links that exist between the choices continually made in the act of composition. In statistics, correlation addresses itself to answering one simple question: – Does an increase in the number, or proportion, of one observation lead to some change, increase or decrease, in another? Statistical correlation has nothing to say about the nature of such links or their causal pattern. It is easy to give examples of correlations which would be nonsense if any element of causation were introduced. Prosperity leads to people buying diamonds and having smaller families – both are aspects of rising standards of living – but the suggestion that the purchase of diamonds was a form of birth control would be foolish.

The particular issue here is that two tests based on word positions or collocations are to be regarded as independent and correlation tests will show whether or not this is the case. The difficulties in this instance come from two sources. The first is the bulk of the material. Even with this restricted set of samples and this short list of words, there are 27 tests. So if we are to examine pairs of tests, the first member of the pair can be any one of the 27 and the second any one of the remaining 26, 702 tests in all.

Only half this number will be needed, for in such tests the order is not of any consequence and so we need only look at 351 pairs. Naturally with numbers of this magnitude 17 pairs would be likely to show correlation significant at the 5% level and 3 correlation significant at the 1% level.

The second complication is that while it is not difficult with the aid of a computer to display all 351 tests, it is very far from simple to get the human mind to grasp the whole pattern without confusion. It is better to start with a selection of tests and carry on until it is clear either that correlation exists to a significant degree or that it does not exist to any significant degree. The starting point is to take similar tests, for example, the use of word A or word B as the first words of sentences. If these are independent, then a comparison of a test of this type with another of a contrasting type, i.e. the comparison of a test based on a word which often occurs as the first word of sentences with another based on a collocation neither member of which shows any preference for the first position, will take the analysis a stage further. By taking the tests in such groups the mind is much eased in its journey through a mass of data.

The first comparison made was between the occurrence of *the* as the first word of sentences and *but* as the first word of sentences. For the twenty samples from Scott the coefficient of correlation r is +0.304 for eighteen degrees of freedom and so the correlation is not statistically significant. The next type is that in which one word links more than one test, the first element is *and* when followed by *the*; the next *in* followed by *the*, finally *and* followed by an adjective. The comparison of *and* followed by *the* with *in* followed by *the* gives r = —0.057 for 20 samples, *and* followed by an adjective and followed by *the* gives r = +0.220 again for twenty samples. The coefficient between *in* followed by *the* and *and* followed by an adjective is —0.121. None of these shows any statistically significant correlation. Proceeding in this way to check for correlation between tests of the same pattern and then checking the different patterns against each other, it is clear that no statistically significant correlation exists to any greater degree than chance expectation. It is therefore justifiable to take these tests as being independent of each other. This can be demonstrated in a simpler fashion by selecting two authors who closely resemble each other in one habit yet differ widely in another, showing that identity in one habit does not preclude difference in another.

The final step in the examination of Scott is to compare samples from *The Antiquary* with some from one of his last works, *Castle Dangerous*. This was written shortly before he suffered his fifth and fatal stroke. Table 10.4 shows the data for the *Castle Dangerous* samples. Of the nineteen key-words listed and the larger number of tests based upon them, none shows a statistically significant difference when compared with *The Antiquary*. Considering the state of Scott's health and the brain damage suffered in a series of strokes, this is remarkable evidence for the stability of those habits. One sceptic on reading the evidence at once suggested that this must show that, however extensive the damage to Scott's motor system, the cognitive system of his brain must have been spared. A medical opinion was therefore taken which was that, while there is some truth in the statement that different parts of the brain are responsible for different functions, a series of strokes such as those suffered by Scott are always evidence of a general deterioration. Anything unchanged by them must be primitive. The claim that localised damage affects only limited functions applies only to injuries inflicted on an otherwise healthy brain.

In Table 10.7 can be read the results of a comparison of two words of Henry James, one early and the other late. Only two things need be said. Whatever habits James may have altered between the writing of these books, none of his collocations changed to any statistically significant degree. The other point to be made is that some of them occur at very low rates and their consistency was confirmed by recording them in succeeding chapters of the text.

The last stage of the examination was to look at three works of John Fowles. Embraced in the examination were the placing of ten words in eleven preferred positions and in 27 collocations. The preferred positions

Table 10.7   The occurrence of some collocations in the works of Henry James

Collocation		American[1] Occs. of HABIT	American[1] Occs. of KEYWORD	Ambassadors[2] Occs. of HABIT	Ambassadors[2] Occs. of KEYWORD	Chi SQUARED
a	FB Adj.	50	122	58	186	3.11
and	FB *the*	12	132	11	192	1.34
	FB Adj.	6	132	20	192	2.91
as	FB *if*	2	42	18	143	0.11
at	FB *the*	12	47	20	70	0.13
for	FB *the*	4	27	12	98	0.13
in	FB *a*	5	74	14	135	0.76
	FB *the*	25	74	32	135	2.45
of	FB *a*	6	100	16	296	0.06
	FB *the*	15	100	50	296	0.20
on	FB *the*	3	20	16	58	1.28
the	FB Adj.	62	214	93	383	1.57
to	FB *the*	11	130	14	249	1.12
	FB verb	70	130	127	249	0.28
was	FB *a*	5	59	8	118	0.01
	FB *the*	2	59	6	118	—

Notes:

1. *The American*, 1877, Chapters 1, 2.
2. *The Ambassadors*, 1903, Chapters 1, 2.

yielded two highly significant differences, in the occurrence of *and* and of *but* as the first word in sentences. Of these it need only be said that two of the texts, *The French Lieutenant's Woman* and *The Magus*, for the occurrence of *and* as the first word of sentences there are 34 occurrences in 198 sentences for the first text, and 38 occurrences in 198 sentences for the second, the two texts do not differ in the occurrence of *but* as the first word of sentences either. The difference is due to *The Collector* and to the dialogue within this book. The difference between the dialogue and the narrative prose, even though this contains some short passages of direct and indirect speech, is very large. This entirely confirms the previous general conclusion that comparisons within the same literary form are simple but comparisons between contrasting forms are not.

In Table 10.8 can be seen the 27 collocations common to all three of Fowles' works. At first sight one might well conclude that this author was quite successful in changing his habits with the change of genre. Of the 27 habits, 6 occur at low rates and while they would be useful in comparisons with other writers, they would require large samples for any comparisons within this writer. As before, the consistency of these habits was confirmed by further counts in other samples of the books. Of the 21 collocations which occur often enough to be useful for internal comparisons, 5 show statistically significant differences between the three works. This is why it might seem reasonable to claim that Fowles had changed a good proportion of his habits. But of these habits, the first one, the occurrence of *and a* shows a statistically significant difference only for the comparison of the dialogue samples from *The Collector* and these are large enough to affect the comparison with the other works. So the difference is entirely due to the dialogue form of the two central samples in *The Collector*.

In the second collocation, *it is*, the difference is such that either *The French Lieutenant's Woman* or *The Collector* will go with *The Magus* but not both. A reading of the concordance shows why. Fowles writes of times past and uses the past tense to do so, unlike many writers who transport themselves into the period and write of it in the present tense. So in large sections of the samples, *it is* is replaced by *it was*. If these two collocations are taken together, there is no statistically significant difference between the works. It must be kept in mind that the aim is to produce tests of authorship and for these statistically significant differences in habits to be explained only by a difference in authorship, not a change in genre, or of literary form, or of historical perspective. So this habit shows an alternative between two modes of expression for the past and the present; within each mode the habit is consistent but if both modes are included in samples then both collocations must also be taken together.

The third habit to show a statistically significant difference is the collocation *of course*. This shows a large difference within one work, *The Collector*, where it appears in the mouth of one character and is as much

Table 10.8   The collocations common to three of Fowles' works

		Occurrences in Fowles'						
Keyword	Collocation	French Lieutenant's Woman		Magus		Collector		x^2
and	FB *the*	9	198	11	198	20	334	0.50
	FB *a*	7	198	5	198	1	334	7.63
	FB Adj.	17	198	19	198	28	334	0.24
as	FB *the*	1	78	–	59	2	70	–
	FB *if*	15	78	13	59	7	70	3.78
	FB *a*	9	78	8	59	4	70	2.46
at	FB *the*	24	75	13	60	11	52	2.63
	FB *a*	5	75	5	60	2	52	0.02
been	PB *have*	3	21	3	16	12	56	1.77
for	FB *the*	7	56	3	33	6	48	0.05
	FB *a*	8	56	4	33	2	48	1.70
in	FB *the*	34	170	26	122	41	148	2.91
	FB *a*	17	170	14	122	18	148	0.40
it	FB *a*	6	111	2	103	2	192	–
	FB *the*	–	111	2	103	–	192	–
	FB *is*	19	111	2	103	10	192	20.56
not	FB *a*	4	131	4	37	2	32	–
	FB *only*	3	131	–	37	–	42	–
of	FB *a*	2	247	6	177	2	137	–
	FB *the*	52	247	27	177	23	137	2.59
	FB *course*	1	247	–	177	19	137	51.8
the	FB Adj.	–	439	101	325	34	400	P.D.
to	FB *a*	15	278	4	205	1	263	17.3
	FB *be*	28	278	11	205	22	263	3.48
	FB *the*	31	278	14	205	11	263	9.20
was	FB *a*	20	165	12	126	11	212	5.94
	FB *the*	12	165	6	126	11	212	1.06

Notes:

For each entry, the first figure is the total number of occurrences of the collocation, the second figure is the number of occurrences of the key word.

an identifier of the character as was Scott's 'the old man'. This is an illustration of what happens when a comparatively rare combination becomes a catch phrase, a kind of Homeric formula. The habit shows differences within the book as well as between books.

The fifth collocation to show a statistically significant difference is *was a*. In this case Fowles has a tendency to repeat occurrences within a short section of text. Although less than 9% of the occurrences of *was* are immediately followed by *a*, he has two pairs of successive occurrences in *The French Lieutenant's Woman*. The cause of the difference is this periodic effect; if the count is changed to that of one or more occurrences in succession, the statistically significant difference vanishes. A change of distribution or an increase in sample size will also eliminate the significant difference.

Only the fourth collocation to show a statistically significant difference, *to the*, shows a difference which inspection confirms as real and not due to some cause other than chance variation. The level of chi squared, 9.20 for two degrees of freedom, suggests that this amount of variation would appear by chance in one trial in a hundred. As it has appeared in one test in over twenty of this author, and one test in about sixty of this collocation, it is not exceptional in the circumstances.

So in fact, of the 27 tests, 6 occur at low rates which limits their usefulness, 5 show significant differences but of these 4 would not be used for comparisons between books as the pattern of their occurrence shows statistically significant differences within one of the books. The cause of these differences is a periodic element in the occurrence, or a contrast in literary form, or an alteration in historical perspective. Only one habit does show a pure chance variation and this is in line with what would be expected to occur.

It can therefore be argued that what Fowles does is change his habits with his literary form but not within it. So the examination does confirm the starting hypothesis that, for writers in an uninflected language, the placing of words in preferred positions or in collocations offers a range of tests of authorship, the application of which within any literary form is straightforward but the comparison of different forms is complicated. The proportion of tests which are restricted to one literary form or another is not large; it is less than one third of the total, so that in few cases will a paucity of applicable tests hinder an investigation.

What has not been described but has been done and should always be done, is the inspection of the data to confirm the converse proposition, that the absence of any statistically significant result is not due to some periodic effect or other factor. The statistics are meant to be, and should be shown to be, an adequate description of the habits. Being a summary description they cannot be precise nor comprehensive, but they should not mislead by concealing any anomalies which might affect the comparisons made by using them.

It appears that the prima facie case with which the examination started has been borne out by the wider investigation. The placing of words in preferred positions or in collocations is a frequent feature of English writing and, though many of the habits shown in these features are sensitive to a change in literary form and should be used with caution in any comparison of different forms, most are not altered by the influences which impinged upon these works of Scott, James or Fowles. Taken with what has been done in Greek and other languages, this suggests a firm foundation for positional studies.

11 The Occurrence of Proportional Word Pairs

Science begins with observation. A series of observations has been recorded and a hypothesis which seeks to explain it is framed and tested for congruence with further observations. In this kind of discipline the scientist asks the question How? – but rarely asks the question Why? The scientist will tell you how it is that the sky is blue but is unlikely to suggest why the universe was created in such a way that the sensation blue was the chosen colour of the sky. The separation of experience and the reasons for the existence of the experience are customary for the scientist but not for students of literature. It is this difference in background which cases some critical difficulties.

For example, one day the author was watching a line printer turning out parts of a concordance of the orations of Isocrates. It was then printing the entries of the third person pronoun and as they occurred in each oration the printer would set them out. As some orations have 1,500 words and others are over 20,000 words this meant that sometimes the printer would tick out a line or two and at others it would rap out a burst of them. Each line of the index contained an occurrence and its context. What could be seen at a glance was that, however few or many the occurrences of the pronoun might be, the proportion which were genitives looked much the same. So a hypothesis was framed, that the proportion of genitives among the occurrences of the third person pronoun in Greek is a habit of the writer. It was first tested on Isocrates and tested simply by laying a piece of paper down the edge of the print-out and marking off the space occupied by the different classes of occurrence. It was then counted and calculated not only for Isocrates but for a representative selection of Greek authors, and the usual questions of periodic effects and minimum sample size were examined.

The question which then arose is why this might be so. One answer is that in Greek the genitive of the pronoun is the possessive case, *his book* in Greek is the *book of him*. In which case the answer is that, whether the occurrences of the pronoun be rare or plentiful, the proportion which are used in the possessive relationship is much the same. This explanation might be true or it might be totally wrong. If it is wrong, the observations and the hypothesis based upon them remain true, only the reason advanced as to why they should be true is wrong. This is an elementary point but an important one and it keeps being raised by literary critics of the occurrence of proportionate pairs of words. They seem to feel that until some convincing reason is given for the coupling of these words, they are in some sense unreliable as tests of authorship when the truth is that they have been demonstrated to be reliable tests. It is only the reason why they should be so that is in doubt.

The occurrence of proportional word pairs is based upon a number of observations made by different people for different reasons. Some critics, especially whose who are anxious to resist the conclusions that follow from the evidence, will attack the pairings as being nonsensical on grammatical or linguistic grounds. They see no reason why the occurrence of the pair should be linked. But for each pair of words all that is claimed is that their occurrence is proportional, and this is a matter of evidence and not opinion. The reasons why they should be linked are another and quite separate argument. No matter how interesting it may be, it can have no bearing on the validity of the tests. (The kind of reason which the author would advance is one not yet possible to prove, namely that these words share a similar storage and retrieval mechanism in the brain of the person using them.)

Proportional pairs have been discovered in a number of ways; one has just been described. Another came from a study of Greek adjectives, a study which showed that in samples of text of 1,000 to 4,000 words, the number of occurrences of the Greek adjectives for *all* and *many* were so much in preponderance that comparisons of one writer with another came down to comparing the proportion of these two occurrences. The three forms of negative in Greek, *ou*, *ouk* and *oux* were picked out simply by listing all the words which occurred often enough to enable statistical tests to be applied and then testing every one of them as a matter of routine.

Ellegard[1] has noted a number of such pairs and gives a different kind of reason for their discovery. He was trying to match writers with a set of

Table 11.1   Some frequent proportional pairs of words in Greek

First member	Second member
De	D$'$
Te	T$'$
Ou	Ouk, Oux
Pas	Polus
Autos, all cases not genitive	Autos genitives
Definite article, singular forms	Plural forms

References.
S. Michaelson and A. Q. Morton, 'Elision as an Indicator of Authorship', *LASLA Review*, Liege, Vol. 3, 1973;
S. Michaelson and A. Q. Morton, 'The New Stylometry', *Classical Quarterly*, Oxford 2, 1971.

[1] *Who Was Junius?* Stockholm, 1963.

Table 11.2

(a) Proportionate pairs of words in English

	Notes
a and an	There is no necessary connection between
an followed by the various vowels	the members of pairs in any sense other
all and any	than that the rate of occurrence of one
in and into	member is proportionate to the rate of
no and not	occurrence of the pair. In some instances
that and this	one member may be synonymous with
	the other but in most cases this is not so.

(b) Occurrences of proportionate word pairs in

Word Pair	(i) SCOTT			(ii) JAMES			(iii) FOWLES			
	Antiquary	Castle Dangerous	x^2	American	Ambassadors	x^2	French Lieutenant's Woman	Magus	Collector	x^2
$\dfrac{a}{a+an}$	1333 / 1559	511 / 609	0.93	122 / 138	183 / 215	0.69	216 / 357	219 / 246	318 / 349	1.32
$\dfrac{all}{all+any}$	222 / 299	76 / 122	5.94	19 / 26	23 / 31	0.01	28 / 35	32 / 37	78 / 99	1.05
$\dfrac{in}{in+into}$	1120 / 1221	478 / 521	0.01	13 / 83	14 / 149	2.03	170 / 180	122 / 140	148 / 160	5.71
$\dfrac{no}{no+not}$	221 / 522	207 / 490	0.10	13 / 35	16 / 74	2.91	42 / 173	25 / 62	33 / 65	6.75
$\dfrac{that}{that+this}$	777 / 1148	379 / 576	0.88	– / –	– / –	–	154 / 193	91 / 114	106 / 130	0.18

disputed letters, so he noted that there were some pairs of words one member of which was preferred to the other in what appeared a habitual way by the different authors.

Table 11.1 shows a number of word pairs tested in Greek and gives the reference for the published result. Table 11.2(a) shows some proportional pairs in English and Table 11.2(b) demonstrates the occurrence of these in works of Scott, James and Fowles used in the previous chapter.

All that need be said of proportional pairs of words is that while their occurrence in large samples is usually binomial, they tend to occur in anything but random groups and spacings, and the minimum sample size is generally larger than that set by the requirement of having an expected five occurrences. In many instances the distribution is Poisson; both the statistically significant differences in Table 11.2 vanish when the occurrences are recorded in equal intervals and are treated as Poisson distributions.

For tests of such a simple nature, proportional pairs are remarkably effective, as may be judged by looking at the differences between the authors in the table. The number of useful word pairs increases with text length which is why Ellegard, who used very large samples, gives such lists of them.

In any practical application of these tests the evidence of word pairs would be supported by evidence from the other classes, words in preferred positions, collocations and measures related to sentence length. When a text may have been revised, such a synoptic view is essential. How many tests it is desirable to have, or is necessary to have, is a matter discussed in the first part of the next section of the book.

Section III

Applications

12 Introductory

It has long been the author's habit to begin the study of any problem by setting down, on a single sheet of paper, a summary description of its elements. This discipline is to be highly recommended for a number of reasons. One of them, and maybe the most important, is that the summary should show what pattern of problem it is. It may come down to matching a disputed text with specimens from one or more candidates for the authorship of the disputed text; it may be the exclusion from a homogeneous group of an alien member. Not only will the summary reveal the type of problem but it should, in turn, indicate the strategy of testing to be used and specify the crucial elements of the problem. For example, help was sought of the author in an attempt to determine the authorship of a series of anonymous letters. The letters ran to 19,000 words. But what was shown by the first draft of the summary was that there existed the possibility that the anonymous letters were genuine letters altered to suit a particular purpose. Clearly the homogeneity of the letters must be looked at before any attempt could be made to allocate them to an author.

A third useful function of a summary is that it will be a guide to sampling procedure. To continue the example just mentioned, 19,000 words of text will be likely to supply four good samples, possibly eight, but any further sub-division is unlikely to prove worth while. If sections of the letters are disputed, then the emendations might be taken together or the samples could be left as they are but with a note of the proportion of each which was spurious attached to it. If the letters have to be matched to authors, then around 19,000 words would be used and no more than two such samples would be necessary for a straightforward application. There is no point in taking samples of 100,000 words of an author to establish regularities in his writing which cannot be illustrated from the 19,000 words to which the problem is restricted.

The summary will also decide what resources can be allocated to the project. A dispute about the authorship of a piece of Greek prose would start with prior knowledge of Greek prose analysis and could well confine itself to the details of the particular problem. But if an English poem were in dispute and the only comparable material was prose, then the research would have to look at the larger problem of the relation of prose and poetry before any application to the particular problem could be made. If a problem of chronology is undertaken and the disputed work is bracketed by genuine works, then this is a simpler situation and routine of investigation than that in which the disputed work comes at one end of the writer's active career.

The summary of the problem will also make a good part of the introduction to the description of the enquiry. If the summary is well done and the course of analysis is made clear by it, then all that need be added is a summary of the conclusions and the reader will have a useful guide in following the detailed account. No doubt some critics will refuse to read the summary as well as the analysis and will continue to suggest that another book on a different subject would have been more congenial to them, or even remind their readers that no evidence will embarrass their firm stance, but the summary is not for them.

The final advantage of a summary is that it will serve to show how much proof is required. Students of literature habitually express a desire for more evidence. This is not so often said by scientists. If a text has to be allocated to author X or author Y and the odds for X are 10,000,000 : 1 in his favour, not many scientists would feel that going on purely to add to the existing evidence would be worth while. If some new method were to be applied or some other extension of useful knowledge could be gained, they might agree with a proposal to go further but it would not be simply to add to the evidence.

An interesting note about such odds was made by Mosteller and Wallace. In their allocation of authorship they rapidly reached astronomical odds. They felt that these must be reduced; they would have been incredible to most people as no meaning could be attached to them and examples of similar situations would be ludicrous. So they simplified some of their assumptions and applications but still had odds to be measured in millions. This experience accords with common sense. If the odds for or against some event are prodigious, particularly if they support some conclusions uncongenial to us, then they will only appear to be ludicrous. So there are really two problems and not one. The first is what odds are required to settle the dispute? And the other is what odds will convince the scholar that it has been settled? Rather surprisingly it appears that the first odds may be larger than the second.

Mosteller and Wallace made a useful contribution to this debate by employing Bayes' theorem which concerns prior and posterior odds. Suppose I have a firm conviction that Paul wrote the letter to the Hebrews. Asked to put a figure on my conviction, I say the odds in favour of Paul are 100 : 1. If some evidence then appears which is 50 : 1 against the Pauline authorship, I am much reduced in my certainty but it is still 2 : 1 for Paul. But if odds against Pauline authorship reach 64 million to one against, then it hardly matters what prior odds I gave, 10 : 1, 100 : 1 or 1,000 : 1. All are swamped.

If attention is therefore concentrated on the posterior odds and the position is taken that these should be high enough to swamp any practical prior odds, figures of around 10 million to one would be adequate. If these odds were to be reached by taking independent tests which were each significant at the 5% level, then each test would contribute 20 : 1 to the odds, two will give 400 : 1, three will give 8,000 : 1 and seven will give 64 million to one. This would suggest that about seven statistically significant differences would be decisive, always bearing in mind that they do not have to be extracted from 140 tests, a number for which seven tests can be expected to show such differences by the operation of chance alone. The number of tests to be used cannot be stated with any precision; authors do not differ from each other in all respects any more than they differ in all physical details or habits. How many tests will be required depends on the ratio of the variation between authors to the variation within authors and this differs from test to test.

Experience suggests that the number of tests used should not be more than three times the number of significant differences required. If this is not so then the circumstances are exceptional and either the authors resemble each other very closely or the tests used are rather insensitive.

The more common condition is to have material which will supply a limited number of tests. This can mean that a decision has to be made on the narrowest margin, the odds for the hypothesis being true might be 51 : 49. This is not at all satisfactory for anyone looking for a clear-cut decision but it is as well to know that the evidence is as finely balanced.

The most important practical decision which has to be made is whether the texts should be read by a computer or by human beings. The choice is usually simple. If the texts exist in machine-readable form and you have access to them and to a machine, then the computer will do the counting faster, cheaper and more accurately. The difference between the machine and the human being increases with the size of the texts. One of Mosteller and Wallace's early conclusions was that no two human beings asked to count 100,000 words ever came to exactly the same total. On the other hand if the texts do not exist on machine-readable form they must be prepared in that form. The simplest method, that of paying a commercial agency a fee to type out the texts, is reserved for the rich and the well endowed. Preparing a text yourself, if you have access to the equipment, is straightforward but laborious. It is customary for all who prepare such texts to deceive themselves about the time and trouble it involves. It has been said, of the first machine-readable text of the Homeric poems, that the undertaking was best described in the words of the marriage service – not to be undertaken lightly or unadvisedly, but thoughtfully, reverently and in the fear of God. For not only has the text to be typed out in one form or another, punched cards, paper tape or direct access to magnetic tapes, but it has to be proof read and corrected. It is this second stage which consumes the time, the energy and the money. Even with the help of the machine and a flexible editing program for it, a text needs to be revised at least three times to ensure that it is error free. Ideally, and of course expensively, such a text should be kept in an archive and only copies made from the master should be used in any operations. But charges are made for archives and every year or so the system may be changed so that the format of the text has to be altered. Some people cut corners and use the master tape, just once of course; other people are not skilled enough to preserve a text in good condition.

If a large text exists in machine-readable form and is readily available for use, it is because some individual has been responsible for getting it into good condition and keeping it there. The routine facilities of computer installations are rarely adequate for users of literary texts. To say this is not to denigrate the designers and staff of such installations; it is merely to say that it is not economic for them to provide, as a matter of routine, the rather exceptional facilities which literary users would wish to take for granted. For example, reference has just been made to the first machine-readable version of the Homeric corpus. This was made on paper tape and the complete text ran to two miles of paper tape. At that time, in the early 1960s, the average length of paper tape fed to machines was less than twenty feet and the longest piece prepared by any other user was sixty feet. The concordance of these texts ran to 500,000 lines and took a line-printer about sixteen hours to produce. No line-printer could have been monopolised for such a stretch nor could it have run without maintenance or ribbon changing for that time. A micro-film version was made; it was 1200 feet of film and the average length of micro-film was three feet and the previous longest was just over twenty feet. To provide the service required as a matter of routine by the literary user meant that every piece of equipment was operating at the limit of the manufacturer's specification and doing so for long periods. But the priority which would justify such special treatment is usually reserved for urgent scientific investigations or prestige projects. A literary problem which has been awaiting treatment for three centuries or three millennia can wait a little longer without hardship.

In practice the division between the computer set-up and the hand-counting is also the division between the research project and the solution of a single problem by the application of an already established method. For isolated problems, particularly if the solution is to be the starting point of a study, hand-counting will often be faster and entirely adequate. The sole essential is neatness which brings accuracy in its train. Colouring can be done simply and in a variety of contrasting shades. Each word, or feature, is underlined as it is entered in the lists and the revision of the lists is then routine. The second reading of the texts will give some indication of the accuracy of the counting. If 5% of the occurrences of a word were omitted in a first count, this would be a horrifyingly large proportion; then a second reading will account for all but 5% of these and the result would be a text deficient in about 2 or 3 occurrences in every thousand. Admittedly these last few occurrences are the most difficult to detect. Their omission suggests that there is some configuration which leads to them being overlooked, but it is quite simple to reduce the errors and omissions to levels where they cannot affect the conclusions of the analysis. After all, classical scholars have long lived with uncertainties in text approaching one percent in variant readings.

The beginner should try if at all possible to have a chat with someone who has experience of both computing and hand-counting. His advice can be invaluable and it fits in much better right at the beginning. It is easier to plan a good sequence from the start than to amend a poor one in mid-course.

The next stage is to reproduce the initial summary in experimental form, that is to describe the texts, the tests to be applied to them and the conclusions to be drawn from any statistically significant differences which emerge. This can be done while the text is being prepared, for the preparation of the text will normally be by far the longest part of the investigation. An important and useful part of such an operational summary is that it should anticipate critical reaction. When you wish to claim that a statistically significant difference must be explained by one cause, you should exclude other possible causes by suitable cross comparisons of samples. No attention should be paid to the more predictably prejudiced reactions. Most literary men do not like statistics and react strongly against them. It is normal for such critics to attack the imperfections of the printer, or the proof reader, as evidence of carelessness in the author or even evidence of some more sinister motive.

In recent years much has been heard of the unity of the Christian churches, and discussions designed to bring this about have taken place. The participants in these discussions were surprised, if no one else was, to find that the real objections have finally to be labelled non-theological factors. It was not the philosophies of different denominations nor the history which separated them; it was matters of personality, of prejudice and of property. It is in such an atmosphere that most original investigations will have to take place. The problem will have been studied for generations and the opposing armies will be encamped. By mutual toleration they will only snipe at each other and thoughts of battle will long since have subsided. The prospect of action and of decisive action will not be welcome. It took the Americans a long time to realise that a rich nation which is generous to the poor is not welcomed as a benefactor or thanked for its kindness; it is envied for being rich, hated for its condescension and abused for its extravagance. To solve a problem is one thing; to defend the solution, the motives which produced it and the method used to do so, are other problems at least as taxing in time and energy.

The next chapters describe some particular problems but each has been chosen as representing a type of problem as well as an example of it. It is hoped that in each case some evidence bearing on the particular problem will appear and something will be added to the general store of knowledge of the subject as a whole.

13 The Homeric Problem

A visitor to a rural school in Scotland at the present day might well discover a teacher telling a story about the battles fought round the walls of Troy or an adventure which befell Ulysses on his long voyage home from the siege. So continues a tradition which goes back for over 2,500 years; the two great poems of Homer, the *Iliad* and the *Odyssey*, are part of western education. At one time they were almost all the education that a child would receive. The place of the poems and their influence on western culture is quite unique and traces of it are to be found in the most unlikely corners. The popular American novelist, James Michener, writing his novel *Sayonara*, tells how a young boy in an American school makes the bitter discovery that life is unfair and that the battle is not to the strong any more than the race is to the swift. It comes to him when his teacher recites the death of Hector beneath the walls of Troy.

For almost as long as these poems have been read or recited, there has been speculation about the author of them. The name 'Homer' attached to them might be of a person, a place or even a condition, as it might be a reference to being blind. The question is not at all simple. Some critics believe it should be widened to an argument as to whether or not there is one author for each poem, different authors for parts of each poem or even no author at all, the poems being folk productions generated and polished by countless people through generations of use.

Whatever critics may feel to be the questions worth putting to the poems, it may be a simpler procedure to start by considering what it may be possible to prove about them. In literature the Homeric poems are unique, not only in that common sense of the term, a sense in which every poem is unique, but in the deeper sense that there is no really suitable poetry which might be used to make the kind of comparisons which alone would enable some of the questions about the authorship and integrity of the poems to be answered. Homer is unique in three ways. The poems are composed in a different manner from almost all the others; Hesiod might be a comparable case but this is doubtful. The poems are compiled from materials in a way no other poems are. Finally, they are unique in the remoteness and isolation of their origins.

To take this last point first, the poems are generally thought to have assumed their present form in the ninth century BC and no contemporary background has survived which is of any value in identifying the author. It was much later that Homer became a desirable property and the epigram was that seven cities contend for Homer dead, through which the living Homer begged his bread. The earliest information is so general in application that it is of no value in establishing the identity of Homer or the authorship of the poems. The poems are older than the historical records.

The second complication is that both poems are undoubtedly compilations. Each poem contains material of diverse origins and some of the sources were composite even when they came to the person responsible for the poems as we have them. Page[1] traces a detailed example from the blinding of Polyphemus to show how many strands are woven into one small narrative in the peom. So Homer cannot be an author in the modern sense of the word for his role is not that of the composer but, at least in part, that of the compiler. The role of the compiler, as of the modern editor, can range from literally using scissors and paste to make a narrative from fragments of other sources without adding one word of original composition, to the other extreme of taking material and completely digesting it so that even when the source is known and exists separately the version included in the compilation cannot be distinguished from an original composition of the redactor. One example of this was the subject of a joke by Boswell who chided Samuel Johnson with the remark that if he had written the fables of Aesop then all the little fishes had talked like whales. Johnson was indeed a man who digested his reading and reproduced it in his own forms.

Between these extremes of altering nothing or transforming everything, there lies a complete spectrum. The editor can amend, he can supply linking passages, he can delete, he can transpose, he can exercise even more freedom than the author who must compose or leave the page blank. So before anyone can ask the question, Did Homer create the *Iliad* and/or the *Odyssey*? must come a preliminary question – Who do you define Homer to be?

The answer favoured by the author is that Homer is the writer of *Odyssey*, Book 15. The first 300 lines of this book are a linking passage which suggests that if there is a multitude of ingredients but a single cook at work to produce the dish, then here his hand is to be seen. The fact that there are certain ingredients does mean that the question of authorship cannot be taken simply, for many passages in the poems come from other sources than the mind of the writer of *Odyssey* 15. The only questions which can be put with hope of an answer are – Is there anything in either poem which would not fit in with the hypothesis of their having been given their present form by the writer of *Odyssey* 15? In particular, are there any post-Homeric sections in the poems? But the way is not yet clear for testing. Before that can begin we have to find out what are the essential features of these poems.

Asked to name the outstanding feature of the Homeric poems, most scholars would reply that it was the number of repetitions they contain.

[1]Page, D., *The Homeric Odyssey*, Oxford 1955.

These repetitions take two forms. The simpler of them is the repeating of a number of whole lines which are found over and over again in different parts of the texts. The second form of repetition is the pattern of words known as Homeric formulae, a name used to describe a type of repetition which takes up less than a whole line and has a variety of forms. The most striking aspect of a formula is that it contains a descriptive epithet which is often totally irrelevant to the situation being described, like saying that a man is swift-running when he is writing a letter. The reason why these epithets are there is that they fill out the metrical pattern of the line, so making it easier for the composer to frame it, for the reciter to remember it and for the listener to absorb it. This in turn means that the same person will be described by different epithets in different places in the metrical pattern. So glorious Hector, *phaidimos Hektor*, is this in the last two feet of the line but becomes *korythaiolos Hektor*, Hector of the shining helm, if three feet need filling and *megas korythaiolos Hektor*, tall Hector of the shining helm, if three and a half feet are to be supplied.

On the reason for these repetitions there is general agreement. The Homeric poems antedate the widespread use of writing and they were composed for recitation and, for a long time, were publicly recited by specialists. The repetitions were useful to the composer, to the reciter and to the listener. They kept the characters and the story fresh in the recollection because of their familiar pattern. The one difficulty about such a theory is that it is unscientific; there is no comparable material on which any general conclusion can be verified. The other writers of Greek hexameter verse, Hesiod, Aratus and Apollonius Rhodius, belong to the times when oral composition and reproduction were giving way to the paper and pen methods.

The presence of any number of repetitions naturally creates a problem for statistics. It is one thing to find a number of sentences each with seven words but to find a number with the same seven words is a very different proposition. The normal procedure in such situations is to collect all the data and analyse it, first with the repetitions included and then with them excluded. It would be unwise to put forward any hypothesis which was dependent on one or other of these conditions for support. If neither the inclusion nor the exclusion makes any difference, then the hypothesis stands on a firmer footing. But this is not the only consequence of repetition, as will now emerge.

The best advice offered to anyone who is starting a project is that they should begin by repeating what has been done by previous workers in the field – no great burden with a computer to hand – and then go on to extend the study with some original methods. Taking our own advice the place to begin is with the sentence length distributions for the Homeric poems. These are illustrated in Tables 13.1 and 13.2.

The next problem which arises in the study of Homer is that each poem has twenty-four books in it, so for every statistic there are forty-eight sets

Table 13.1   Homer: The sentence length distributions

No. of Words in Sentence	Number of Such Sentences in	
	Iliad	*Odyssey*
1–5	485	720
6–10	1871	2631
11–15	1350	1929
16–20	697	918
21–25	441	559
26–30	241	261
31–35	132	156
36–40	64	74
41–45	39	37
46–50	20	21
51–55	7	9
56–60	5	6
61–65	2	–
66–70	1	2
71–75	1	–
76–80	1	1
81–85	–	–
86–90	–	–
91–95	–	–
96–100	1	1
Total:	5358	7325
Mean	13.80	13.19
St. Error	.08	.09
Median	11.20	11.45
St. Error	.08	.12
1st Quartile	7.28	7.35
St. Error	.27	.07
3rd Quartile	17.29	17.15
St. Error	.72	.21
9th Decile	24.76	30.87
St. Error	.25	.85

Notes:

The distributions are not log-normal, they have too many long sentences. In *Odyssey* 19–24 there are 54 sentences with over 30 words; the number expected in a log-normal distribution is 16.

of figures. Printing all of these would only be justified if useful information was revealed by doing so, otherwise editors take a reasonable objection to the cost. Editorial restraint is fully justified when it is remembered that there are forty-eight sets of sentence length distributions and then the groupings of these, forty-eight positional distributions for each

Table 13.2   The sentence length distributions of *Odyssey* Book 20
in 2 scales

(a) linear scale, grouped data

No. of Words in Sentence	Number of Sentences
1−5	31
6−10	86
11−15	70
16−20	20
21−25	13
26−30	5
31−35	5
36−40	4
Total:	234

(b) metrical line scale

Length of Sentence	Number of Sentences
Less than 1 Line	42
Exactly 1 Line	54
Less than 2 Lines	43
Exactly 2 Lines	48
Less than 3 Lines	14
Exactly 3 Lines	14
Less than 4 Lines	3
Exactly 4 Lines	10
Less than 5 Lines	−
Exactly 5 Lines	3
Less than 6 Lines	2
Exactly 6 Lines	1
Total:	234

of the most frequent words, as many for the particles which occur in preferred positions, as many for the different forms of the negative particles and for all the frequent words with elided forms. When the data was typed for circulation to the experimenters it amounted to more than 200 pages. It is not reproduced here for two good reasons. The first can be seen from Table 13.1 which shows the sentence length distributions of the *Iliad* and *Odyssey*. They are similar but differ in their means and ninth deciles. However most, but not all, of the differences between the two poems disappear if *Iliad* Book 2 is excluded, for in this are the lists of ships and cities which made up the contending forces in the war. These lists are not post-Homeric; they are generally agreed to be pre-Homeric in origin and so the difference might well show the difference in source structure of the poems.

The second reason concerns the form of the sentence length distributions themselves. At a first glance they seem to have a familiar form, being quite like those recorded in simple Greek prose writers, and like some of these having a mean of around 13–14 words per sentence. But a look at the re-grouped data shows that the previous tabulation of the sentence lengths was totally misleading. The most frequent sentence is one of exactly one line; the next most frequent, one of exactly two lines, and so on. This suggests that the distribution might be a series of single peaked distributions added together, each peak being at a number of complete lines. This is not the case since the more components the distributions are broken up into, the more restricted is any conclusion based upon the data.

The end of the line has a predominant effect on these sentence lengths. Just as the foot will slip on an icy pavement until it stops in the gutter, so any line which is likely to end near the finish of the line will be adjusted so that it does. All writers using this form will be subject to this same pressure, and as a result come to resemble each other more than they otherwise would do. So the general similarity of the two poems means much less than it would if the mode of composition were not as dominant.

The constraint which results in so many sentences ending with lines can be used to examine some aspects of the poems. Table 13.3 shows that the proportion of one line sentences which start and end with a line falls continually from Homer to Apollonius Rhodius. An investigation of all lengths of sentences which start and finish with lines (co-terminous is a convenient adjective to apply to them) was undertaken by the author and two of his colleagues.[1]

The investigation showed two things. The first was that there is a series from Homer to Apollonius. As the composition becomes more sophisticated and more literary, the proportion of co-terminous sentences decreases. The sequence can be accepted as some measure of the primitive nature of the composition, but it says nothing about the quality of the verse and not very much about its chronology. Homer and Hesiod are both too uncertain to allow any assumption that primitive in time is primitive in composition. It is easy to frame a testable hypothesis but there is no material on which to carry out the test.

The second fact that emerges from the examination of co-terminous

---

[1] Michaelson, S., Morton, A. Q., Wake, W. C., 'Sentence Length Distributions in Homer and Hexameter Verse', *A.L.L.C. Bulletin*, 1978.

Table 13.3   The proportion of one line, co-terminous sentences
in 4 writers of hexameter verse

Writer	Percentage of all sentences which are exactly one line
Homer (*Iliad*)	26.4
Hesiod	16.1
Aratus	11.3
Apollonius	6.0

sentences is that when a passage generally held to be post-Homeric (such as the description of building a wall round the ships in *Iliad* Book 7, lines 313–482) is removed, then the remainder of the book does seem more primitive, i.e. it has a higher proportion of co-terminous sentences. But does this really argue for a post-Homeric interpolation? It might have been added after the poems took their familiar form or it might have been inserted in an earlier version and accepted by Homer. There is nothing in the statistics which will say which alternative is more likely to be true.

The same problem arises in *Iliad* Book 11. This does show some statistically significant differences from the other books, but do these differences mean anything when it is one book selected from a set of forty-eight? The seat of the differences is the scene which describes Nestor's cup (lines 624–641) and his discourse (lines 664–762). But immediately we face the same problem as before. The difference may be due to a later addition to the poem or to an undigested source. Nothing in the statistics will decide which it is.

It may seem a very negative attitude to take, to say that the problem of authorship and integrity in Homer is unique and so a scientific answer to either question is unlikely to emerge, but this is the case. The poems are composed in a manner quite different from any others which have survived, and without comparable material the differences which are detectable cannot be separated into those due to the mode of composition and those due to a difference in authorship or of origin. The best service which an investigation of this kind may do is to show that many scholars have been too simple-minded in their approach to Homer. The poems contain many more problems than some people have supposed.

It may well be that one of the oldest arguments, one with some scientific basis, is the best. No one knows what the population of 'Greece' in Homer's day was, but that the country should nourish two geniuses of such stature at much the same time is a coincidence beyond acceptance. Against this can be set the view that the poems have no author, but are the result of generations of accretion and adaptation. Of this hypothesis it can be said that it is a scholar's dream. It can be endlessly argued but never resolved.

14 The Authorship of the Pauline Epistles

One of the best known literary problems concerns the uncertain author-ship of the fourteen letters from Romans to Hebrews, which in the various translations of the Bible, at one time or another for one reason or another, have been attributed to the Apostle Paul. To the student of stylometry the Pauline epistles present a nice problem. Within the compass of 50,000 words are a variety of texts and problems, and any positive solutions require some precision of analysis. The Pauline epistles can be correctly described as a challenging problem.

But the Pauline epistles present another and quite different problem which has nothing to do with the origins of a set of letters written during the century which began around AD 35. The Pauline epistles are widely accepted as sacred and the reaction which follows any attempt to analyse a sacred text is violent. It may be that one element in religion is a search for certainty and assurance; it is counted by many religious people as a virtue to believe, and one thing commonly believed by such people is that the Bible is an inerrant record and that traditions about its origin and authorship are similarly immune from human frailty. As a result, any research into Biblical origins will meet with quite a different reception than would a paper on Homer or Isocrates. In the author's experience only Plato and Shakespeare among secular writers have acquired some-thing of sanctity. Write on Sir Walter Scott, on Henry James, on Samuel Johnson and criticism will follow its usual course. Write on Shakespeare or Plato and angry letters begin to arrive. Write on Paul or Jesus and abusive and anonymous letters will surely flood in.

Biblical scholarship is also constrained by a sophisticated view of its own unique role. It has just been argued that the poems of Homer are unique and three senses in which this is true have been defined. The poems are the oldest poems in the language and antedate the historical records of their origins; they stand at the start of a series, so there is no pair of poems which can bracket the Homeric poems. The second sense in which one can say Homer is unique is that the mode of composition and of reproduction used to create them and keep them alive are unparalleled in Greek. The third claim to uniqueness in Homer is that it has always been accepted that these poems incorporate a number of earlier sources and any argument about authorship becomes an argument about compilation and the blending of sources into the poems.

Parallel claims are often made for the uniqueness of the Pauline epistles. It is difficult to see how it can have a foundation in fact. There are numbers of letters from the same period, from earlier and later periods too. The mode of composition and of reproduction is unremarkable. Any claim that the letters might have been based on other sources is stoutly contested. The letters of the Pauline corpus are just letters. When it became clear that there were large differences within the corpus, a special case was made that Paul had used an amanuensis to write down what he wished to say and that this was the cause of the differences. This argument has two fatal defects. The first is the question – If an amanuensis gives us something quite unlike Paul, what right has anyone to call it Paul's? The second objection is that though amanuenses were commonly employed, only in this case has it to be argued that the use made any difference to the text. It can be added that Paul's name alone appears on a letter he did not write and it is coupled with the name of another person on one which he did write.

The Pauline letters are Greek prose and every feature of them can be paralleled in Greek prose writing. There is no reason why they should not be treated as a particular example of a general problem, the authorship of Greek prose. Yet this is just what many scholars cannot bring themselves to accept. Their resentment is clear, but it is seldom clear which object it is directed against; it may be that mere human agency and intelligence presumes to measure the word of God, or that the results of such enquiries do not support their own published views; perhaps the very idea that views on the Bible can change is repugnant to them even with the irrefutable evidence of history before them. Whatever the source of the animus, the consequences are the same; hypotheses are ridiculed rather than tested, the normal imperfections of publication, printer's errors and omissions, are blamed on the author, challenges are thrown down but refused when the gauntlet is picked up. In 1965 the Bishop of London wrote a letter to *The Times* saying he would believe this kind of science only when it was shown that Henry James had stable habits in his range of writings. Evidence of this having been available for more than two years, the Bishop has not been heard from.

The Pauline epistles have played a unique role in the history of stylometry. The oldest surviving reference to the creation of a scientific stylometry is in a letter written in 1851 by Augustus de Morgan, then professor of mathematics in London, to a friend at Cambridge. De Morgan suggests that the measurement of word length, using the letter as a unit, might well enable the authorship of the Pauline corpus to be decided. De Morgan's letter is noteworthy for containing so many of the basic principles of stylometry, the use and description of samples, the disregarding of the meaning of words and the concentration on their occurrences. The letter had further consequences, a copy of it started Thomas Corwin Mendenhall on the Shakespearian research described in the next chapter.

The first successful test of authorship, sentence length distributions in

Greek prose, devised by Dr. W. C. Wake, used the Pauline epistles as a prime example and his findings on the epistles were published separately. They were ignored. Pauline studies had long been polarised. At the one extreme were those who accepted as the word of God the text of the epistles and the later headings and also the subscriptions added by various editors. For such students all fourteen letters came from Paul. At the other end of the spectrum were the radicals, principally the Germans of the nineteenth century and for them the only Pauline letters were the big four, Romans, Galatians, I and II Corinthians – they did not much care about Philemon – and so they settled for four or five. In the middle were the moderates, the Anglicans leading. They accepted anything from seven letters to thirteen with most settling for ten, Hebrews being given up as a lost cause and letters of Timothy and Titus being regarded as having some Pauline elements rather than being his compositions. Dr. Wake's paper was published just after the Revised Standard Version of the Bible appeared in which Paul's name was for the first time left off Hebrews. Wake now produced some evidence which seemed to suggest that the nineteenth century radicals might have been right after all and, if they had been right about the authorship, what else might they have been right about? Little wonder that Wake's work was denied its due recognition.

Dr. Wake's paper could be criticised on two grounds. The text he used was out of date. While a more modern text would have been better, it was unlikely to change his conclusions; but this had to be demonstrated. The second reason for criticism was that C. B. Williams had published a paper[1] on sentence length distributions in English writers and in it suggested that log scales might be more appropriate to the measurement of a sentence length distribution.

What Wake did not have to defend was his investigation into the definition of a sentence by punctuation and the establishing of minimum sample size, yet on both counts he was often challenged by critics who seemed not to understand what he had done and took no pains to find out.

If New Testament studies had really been a free enquiry and a fearless search for truth, then the publication of Wake's paper would have been followed by a burst of activity. His work would have been repeated on various texts, it would have been extended and, when it stood up to the investigation, it would have become the starting point of a search for other comparable tests of authorship. Nothing happened and for some time it became even more difficult than it had been to persuade a New Testament journal to publish any technical papers.

The Pauline corpus – the name is used without prejudice as the lawyers would say, to cover all fourteen letters from Romans to Hebrews –

[1] Williams, C. B., 'A note on the statistical analysis of sentence length', *Biometrika* 31, 356–361.

presents two problems. The first is to establish the authorship of the epistles taken as individual units and allocate them to Paul or to some other author. The second problem is to establish the integrity of the individual epistles. Some of them, e.g. Romans and II Corinthians, are regarded as Pauline but having sections of the text which are open to question.

This means that the logical sequence of testing is to start with the sentence length distributions, go on to tests shown to be independent of sentence length and then use positional distributions to isolate anomalies within epistles. However, as one aim of this book is to show the reader how to carry out fundamental tests so that the method is clear and can be adapted to other problems, it will start with an exposition of the methods of establishing minimum sample size and then look at the choice of linear or log scales. Wake had noticed, as had every other person who recorded sentence length in Greek or English, that writing at some places will march in stately sentences and at others hurry in a succession of short sentences. Wake had also noted that the opening of Greek texts differs markedly from what comes after, almost as if the writer had one round up the spout of his rifle and his weapon would not fire automatically until this round had been fired by hand. This particular problem Wake largely avoided by cutting off from the text of the epistles the first and last paragraphs. He did this for the good reason that it is in these that emendations are most often and most easily made and so these sections are most open to question.

Wake established the minimum sample size by continually dividing and comparing two sets of figures. The first had been taken from the actual sentences in the text, recorded in the order in which they stood in the text. The second set was the same numbers but now written on cards and shuffled and dealt out as required to make up a sample. One set is in text order, the other in random sequence.

An alternative is to divide the text in a way that ensures that sentences from all parts of the text, beginning, middle and end, occur in equal proportion. One way of doing so is to make, for example, three samples by taking sentences 1, 4, 7, 10 . . . ; a second sample from sentences 2, 5, 8, 11 . . . and a third set of sentences 3, 6, 9, 12 and so on. Table 14.1 shows the results of following this routine in the epistle to the Galatians.

In Table 14.1 the epistle is divided into three successive block samples each of 55 sentences. The inspection of both sets of samples might seem to support the view that the minimum sample to represent the Apostle Paul is one of 55 sentences. The standard errors quoted at the end of the table are for the whole epistle and so are less than those for any sub-sample and all six samples lie well within the range of two standard errors. But how misleading this is can be seen from Figure 14.1 which is a cusum chart of the first hundred sentences of I Corinthians. The chart shows how the epistle starts with a group of sentences much longer than

Table 14.1   The sentence length distribution of the epistle to the Galatians examined

No. of words in Sentence	Number of such sentences in							
	S1	S2	S3	S4	S5	S6	Epistle	
1–5	5	3	13	9	7	4	21	
6–10	21	19	13	13	17	24	54	
11–15	15	16	15	17	14	15	46	
16–20	7	8	9	5	11	8	24	
21–25	1	4	2	3	1	3	7	
26–30	3	1	1	2	3	—	5	
31–35	1	1	—	1	1	—	2	
36–40	1	—	—	1	—	—	1	
41–45	—	2	1	1	1	1	3	
46–50	1	—	—	1	—	—	1	
51–55	—	1	—	1	—	—	1	
71–75	—	—	1	1	—	—	1	
Totals:	55	55	55	55	55	55	166	
Median	10.50	11.72	10.50	11.83	11.25	9.90	10.87	St. Error 0.70
1st Quartile	7.08	7.83	5.29	6.83	6.99	7.03	6.90	St. Error 0.52
3rd Quartile	15.21	17.19	17.28	17.50	16.59	14.50	15.73	St. Error 1.16
Log Mean	1.018	1.066	0.996	1.052	1.040	1.000	1.025	
St. Error of log mean	0.033	0.034	0.051	0.041	0.037	0.031	0.021	

Notes:

S1, S2, S3 are sentences 1, 4, 7 . . . . and 2, 5, 8 etc.; S4, S5, S6 are sentences 1–55, 56–110, 111–165.

Figure 14.1   A cusum chart of the first 100 sentences of I Corinthians.

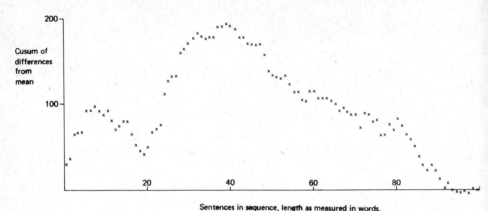

Notes:
The chart shows very clearly that the first thirty sentences are much longer than the average, and the later sentences are shorter.

the mean, follows with some slightly below the mean, then a sequence well below the mean and then, from sentence twenty to sentence forty, has a sequence well above the mean. The consequences of this variation are shown in Table 14.2 which shows that the mean length of the first ten sentences is 22.30 words and then falls continually as more and more sentences are included in the sample until at sentence 100 the mean is 14.30. Carrying out *t* tests shows that it is at sentence 92 that there ceases to be a statistically significant difference between a sequential sample starting from the first sentence and another sample which is the

Table 14.2   Variations in the mean length of sentences in I Corinthians, measured from the start of the Epistle

Sequence of sentences from 1st sentence to sentence no.	Mean length of sentence in sequence, in number of words
10	22.30
20	16.15
30	19.83
40	19.05
50	17.10
60	16.17
70	15.46
80	15.13
90	14.49
100	14.30

remainder of the epistle. This might suggest that the minimum sample to represent Paul is one of 92 sentences. But if a similar cusum chart is made of the first sixty sentences of Galatians, then the first 35 sentences have a mean of 19.14 words against a mean for the remainder of the epistle of 13.45 words; this difference is statistically significant, t is 3.93 and the minimum sample required to show no such difference is the first 49 sentences.

These differences in the first sentences of these epistle are readily paralleled. In the majority of writers of Greek, the text begins with a group of long sentences which are longer than any other group within the text. The start of composition appears to be anomalous and there is a difference between the starting condition and the free-running condition. This effect is so widespread that it is readily illustrated. For example, in Aristotle's *Nicomachean Ethics*, the numbers of words in groups of twenty sentences from the start of Book I are 407, 373, 306; in Demosthenes' first oration the numbers of words in successive groups of twenty-five sentences are 669, 500 and 401; in Plato's *Republic* the numbers of words in groups of twenty-five sentences are 358, 228 and 223. This effect is so widespread that it is not easy to find a text to which it does not apply. Another feature of the opening is that the anomalous group varies in size with the size of the work which it introduces. There are quite long groups in the opening of Hesiod's *Theogonia*, at the start of Diodorus Siculus and of Strabo; in each case the introduction is formal and comparatively elaborate.

In almost every Greek text there are groups of sentences which are significantly longer or shorter than the mean length of sentence for the whole text. The longer the sequence, the rarer it is to find a statistically significant difference between the sequence and the rest of the text. The minimum sample is the number of sentences needed to ensure that there will be no statistically significant difference between any sequence above the minimum length and the remainder of the text. In Galatians the longest and most distinctive sequence is the first 35 sentences and the minimum sample is of 49 sentences from the start. In I Corinthians the most prominent anomaly is the first 40 sentences, and this requires a sample of 92 sentences to reduce the difference to below the level of statistical significance. In both epistles later samples can be smaller; a sample starting from sentence seven of I Corinthians need only be of 60 sentences. So if sequential samples are taken, the minimum sample size for Paul ranges from just under 50 sentences in his short letters like Galatians to just over 90 sentences in long letters like I Corinthians. The point is not one of much importance, for, as Table 14.3 shows, only Hebrews is long enough to permit sub-division into more than one sample and if it is taken in four parts only the first would be affected by an initial anomaly if it existed in that epistle. Table 14.3 shows the sentence length distributions on linear scales for all the epistles in the

Table 14.3

(a) The sentence length distributions of the Pauline epistles

No. of words in sentence	Number of sentences in													
	Romans	Cor. I	Cor. II	Galatians	Ephesians	Philippians	Colossians	Thess. I	Thess. II	Tim. I	Tim. II	Titus	Philemon	Hebrews
1–5	78	99	40	21	3	9	5	4	3	14	14	5	1	13
6–10	160	190	70	54	5	20	14	15	7	22	13	5	7	47
11–15	101	126	44	46	24	19	10	7	9	19	22	7	3	73
16–20	52	73	43	24	10	13	7	11	5	20	10	3	2	39
21–25	51	32	31	7	8	3	6	7	—	10	5	3	—	29
26–30	14	15	19	5	4	5	8	4	3	4	4	2	1	22
31–35	12	7	9	2	4	5	2	6	1	5	5	—	1	12
36–40	7	5	7	1	5	4	2	4	2	—	—	1	—	9
41–45	9	1	5	3	2	5	2	—	1	1	1	1	1	7
46–50	8	4	—	—	2	1	1	3	2	1	1	1	—	6
51–55	2	2	1	1	2	3	—	—	—	—	—	1	1	2
56–60	3	1	2	—	4	1	1	1	1	1	—	—	—	1
61–65	—	—	—	—	—	—	—	—	—	—	—	—	—	1
66–70	—	—	1	—	1	1	1	1	—	1	—	—	—	—
71–75	—	—	—	1	—	—	—	—	—	—	1	—	—	—
76–80	1	—	1	—	1	1	1	1	—	—	—	—	—	—
81–85	—	—	—	—	1	—	2	—	—	—	—	—	—	—
86–90	—	—	—	—	1	1	1	1	—	—	—	—	—	—
					106			158	158					95
					124									
					130									
					141									
No. of sentences in epistle	498	555	273	166	80	86	66	66	35	99	77	33	17	262

Statistic and standard error of statistic

Epistle	Mean	S.E.	Median	S.E.	1st Q.	S.E.	3rd Q.	S.E.	9th Dec.	S.E.
Romans	14.33	0.50	10.55	0.55	6.45	0.30	18.32	0.93	27.21	2.39
Cor. I	12.23	0.34	9.70	0.31	6.05	0.27	15.09	0.71	21.89	1.07
Cor. II	15.99	0.71	13.01	0.94	7.02	0.51	21.25	1.15	29.66	1.30
Galatians	13.78	0.77	10.87	0.70	6.90	0.52	15.73	1.16	23.14	2.76
Ephesians	30.31	3.21	19.00	2.22	10.50	0.81	37.00	3.87	58.75	3.33
Philippians	13.59	1.60	13.68	1.22	8.13	1.00	25.50	6.69	36.13	4.64
Colossians	23.98	2.41	17.89	2.90	9.11	1.26	29.69	2.21	50.00	12.18
Thess. I	22.77	2.06	18.18	1.85	9.67	1.17	31.25	2.93	46.67	4.06
Tim. I	16.03	1.19	13.55	1.31	7.44	0.98	19.81	1.13	31.00	2.99
Tim. II	16.05	1.52	12.61	1.00	7.02	1.46	19.38	3.79	32.00	13.17

(c) The comparison of the statistics of the sentence length distributions of the epistles of the Pauline Corpus

(i) Linear scale

The limits set by adding two standard errors to the statistics of Galatians

	Mean	Median	1st Quartile	3rd Quartile	9th Decile
Upper limit	15.32	12.27	7.95	18.05	28.66
Lower limit	12.24	9.47	5.86	13.41	17.62

Notes:

Statistically significant differences appear in the statistics of Eph., Col., Thess. I and Hebrews in the mean; Eph., Thess. I and Hebrews for the median, Eph. and Hebrews for the 1st quartile, Cor. II, Eph., Col., Thess. I and Hebrews for the 3rd quartile, Eph., Thess. I and Hebrews for the 9th decile.

(ii) Log scale

The upper and lower limits for the mean of Galatians are 1.067 and 0.983. Statistically significant differences appear between the means of Galatians and the means of Eph., Phil., Col., Thess. I and Hebrews.

Pauline corpus which have at least 50 sentences. It requires from 30 to 50 sentences to fit the observations to a distribution, and the standard errors of smaller samples are so large that they are not separable from almost any other piece of Greek prose, so that in practice only 11 of the 14 epistles can be compared by sentence length distribution.

Before any comment is made on the data of the linear sentence length distributions, the second question which was posed earlier must be looked at, the question as to which scale, linear or log, is more appropriate for this series of sentence length distributions. The starting point is to look at two series of numbers: the first, 2, 4, 6, 8, 10, the second, 2, 4, 8, 16 and 32. The first series is linear for the difference between each pair of successive terms is the same; one is always 2 more than the other. The second series is called logarithmic, for the difference between successive terms is not a constant quantity but a constant ratio; each term is twice its predecessor. Such series are called log series because substituting the logs for each number converts the series into a linear one.

If the logarithms of these numbers are taken from a set of tables they are, 0.301, 0.602, 0.903, 1.204 and 1.505. This makes a linear series. To multiply two numbers together their logs are added, and the step of multiplying by two is equivalent to adding 0.301 to the log of the preceding number. The mean of the series of logs is 0.903 and the antilog of this is 8, which is the central value of the original series and is the log mean, for the mean of the series is not the sum of all the numbers divided by five but the product of all the numbers with the fifth root extracted, i.e. the mean is the number which multiplied together five times will give the same result as $2 \times 4 \times 8 \times 16 \times 32 = 32{,}768 = 8 \times 8 \times 8 \times 8 \times 8$.

To relate the issue to the sentence length distributions, suppose that two writers wrote sentences of 10, 20, 30 and 40 words in the following proportions:—

No. of Words in Sentences	10	20	30	40
No. of Sentences Writer A	40	30	20	10
Writer B	40	20	14	10

Writer A is writing on an arithmetic scale; for every increase of ten words in length of sentence there are ten sentences fewer. Writer B is not writing on an arithmetic (i.e. linear) scale, since equal increases in length bring about reductions of 20, 6 and 4 in the number of sentences. B is writing on a log scale since every doubling of length brings about a reduction to half the number of sentences. This can be seen in the number of 20 word sentences; for writer A the number would be estimated by taking the sum of the two adjacent values and dividing this by two, $40 + 20/2 = 30$, the actual value and the correct one for a linear scale. For a log scale the two values would have to be multiplied together and the square root taken. For writer A this would give 28 – nearly but not quite the right value. For writer B this procedure does give the number of 20 word sentences, the number of 10 word sentences multiplied by the number of 40 word sentences is 400, the square root of which is 20, the actual number of 20 word sentences.

In practice no writer will write such tidy linear or log distributions, and the practical question comes down to whether or not the sentence length distributions can be regarded as log normal or not. If the distributions can be fitted to a log normal pattern then they can be completely represented by only two statistics, the log mean and log standard deviation.

The method of discovering whether or not data can be fitted to a log normal distribution is straightforward and is done in two stages. The first step is to calculate whether or not the data roughly conforms to a log scale. The data is recorded in the usual way and the mean, median, 1st and 3rd quartiles are calculated. In a log normal distribution the mean and the median coincide and the quartiles are equidistant from the mean.

For no distribution yet recorded in a Greek text has this been true, but in a number of cases the distribution can be adjusted to conform to these requirements. Some adjustment would have to be made to the data in any case for the log of 1 is 0 and, unless some adjustment was made, all the one word sentences would simply vanish from the distribution. This difficulty can be avoided by adding 1 to the number of words in all the sentences – calling 1 word sentences 2 word sentences, 2 word sentences 3 word sentences – and at the end of the calculation subtracting the added word to restore the original form of the data.

The addition of a constant, such as the one word just described, has a different effect on the different parts of a log scale. For example, if we take sentences of 1, 10, 20, 30 and 40 words and add 1 to make them sentences of 2, 11, 21, 31, and 41 words, then the logs change from 0.00, 1.00, 1.30, 1.48 and 1.60, to 0.30, 1.04, 1.32, 1.49, and 1.61.

The effect of adding a constant to every value diminishes as the scale extends to the higher values. This means that by adding a suitable correction constant to every value, then the tails of the log sentence length distribution can be moved relative to each other. Naturally the range of movement is restricted but it is the freedom conferred by the constant which makes it possible to fit many sentence length distributions to the log normal form.

The first step is to calculate the Davies coefficient of skewness for the data. If this coefficient is less than +0.20, then the data is likely to fit a log scale. The Davies coefficient[1] is given by:

$$D = \frac{(\log Q_3 + \log Q_1) - 2(\log M)}{\log Q_3 - \log Q_1}$$

If this coefficient is less than $+0.20$, the data may well be logarithmic; if the coefficient is more than $+0.20$, a linear scale is more likely to be applicable. There are three conditions which must be met for the correct use of this coefficient:

1. The data should have one peak and be asymmetrical.
2. The high frequencies should come over the lower values.
3. There should be not less than 50 observations.

The Davies coefficient applies to all the New Testament epistles with 50 sentences or more, and for all of them the coefficient is less than $+0.20$. The distribution may well be log normal.

The seond stage in the fitting routine is to calculate the expected values for a log normal distribution based on the statistics of the sentence length distribution. Table 14.4(a) is a specimen calculation of this type and is based on the sentence length distribution of I Corinthians. The table has nine columns and the first and last columns give the frequency distribution, that is they record the number of words in sentences and the number of sentences in the epistle having the number of words specified.

For the first twenty entries there are more than five occurrences in cells of one word but after that the data must be grouped to keep above this minimum number. The second column of the table repeats the figures of the first column when the correction c has been added to them. In this example:

$$c = \frac{M^2 - Q_1 Q_3}{Q_1 + Q_3 - 2M} = \frac{(9.70)^2 - (6.05 \times 15.09)}{6.05 + 15.09 - 2 \times 9.70} =$$

$$= \frac{94.09 - 91.30}{21.15 - 19.40} = \frac{2.79}{1.75} = 1.59$$

Thus the entries in column two are the entries of column one plus 1.59.

The third column contains the logs, to the base ten, of the numbers in column two. A sufficient degree of accuracy is obtained by using three place log tables such as are commonly supplied for school examinations, though it is simple to omit the last figure from the more usual four figure log tables.

The fourth column is derived from the third column by first calculating $\log (M + c) = \log (9.70 + 1.59) = \log 11.29 = 1.053$. The entries in column

[1] Davies, G. R., 'The analysis of Frequency Distributions', *Journal of the American Statistical Association*, vol. 24, 1929, pp. 349–368.

Table 14.4

(a) The sentence length distribution of I Corinthians fitted to a log normal distribution

1	2	3	4	5	6	7	8	9
L	L + c	Log (L + c)	dM	t	A	dA	E	O
1	2.59	0.413	0.640	2.55	0.005			
2	3.59	0.551	0.502	2.00	0.023	0.028	15.5	16
3	4.59	0.662	0.391	1.56	0.059	0.036	20.0	24
4	5.59	0.747	0.306	1.22	0.111	0.052	28.8	28
5	6.59	0.819	0.234	0.93	0.176	0.065	36.1	31
6	7.59	0.880	0.173	0.69	0.245	0.069	38.3	36
7	8.59	0.934	0.119	0.47	0.323	0.078	43.3	36
8	9.59	0.982	0.071	0.28	0.390	0.067	37.2	42
9	10.59	1.025	−0.028	0.11	0.456	0.066	36.6	39
10	11.59	1.064	+0.011	0.04	0.516	0.060	33.3	37
11	12.59	1.100	0.047	0.19	0.575	0.059	32.8	29
12	13.59	1.133	0.080	0.32	0.629	0.054	30.0	14
13	14.59	1.164	0.111	0.44	0.670	0.041	22.8	27
14	15.59	1.193	0.140	0.56	0.712	0.042	23.3	26
15	16.59	1.220	0.167	0.67	0.749	0.037	20.5	30
16	17.59	1.245	0.192	0.77	0.779	0.030	16.7	18
17	18.59	1.269	0.216	0.86	0.805	0.026	14.4	8
18	19.59	1.292	0.239	0.95	0.829	0.024	13.3	18
19	20.59	1.314	0.261	1.04	0.851	0.022	12.2	16
20	21.59	1.334	0.281	1.12	0.869	0.018	10.0	12
21−25	26.59	1.425	0.372	1.48	0.931	0.062	34.4	33
26−30	31.59	1.500	0.447	1.78	0.962	0.031	17.2	15
31−35	36.59	1.563	0.510	2.03	0.979	0.017	9.4	7
36−40	41.59	1.619	0.566	2.25	0.988	0.009	5.0	5
41+					0.012	0.012	6.7	8
						Totals:	557.8	555

Notes:

For the comparison of the observed and expected values chi squared is 21.74 for 21 degrees of freedom and for this p = 0.45. I Corinthians has 555 sentences. The median is 9.70, the first quartile is 6.05 and the third quartile 15.09.

The required correction is:

c is equal to $\dfrac{M^2 - Q_1 Q_3}{Q_1 + Q_3 - 2M}$ and it is 1.59 for this epistle.

The log mean of the distribution is: $\dfrac{\log Q_1 + \log Q_3 + 1.255 \log M}{3.255}$.

The log standard deviation is 0.741 $(\log Q_3 - \log Q_1)$.

Table 14.4 (continued)

(b) The expected values for the sentence length distributions of the Pauline epistles fitted to log normal distributions

No. of words in sentence	Number of sentences in			
	Romans	I Corinthians	II Corinthians	Galatians
1–5	70.7	97.7	45.9	24.4
6–10	164.3	188.7	55.7	49.3
11–15	98.6	129.3	55.4	46.2
16–20	55.8	66.6	40.1	26.4
21–25	34.4	34.4	27.8	12.1
26–30	20.9	17.2	16.9	
31–35	14.4	21.1	11.7	
36–40	10.0		} 19.4	
41–45	6.5			
46 or more	22.5			
No of sentences in epistle:	498.1	555.0	272.9	158.4
Chi squared	14.60	0.84	7.60	7.17
Degrees of freedom	7	4	5	3

Notes:

In all cases the last cell contains all the sentences longer than the upper limit of the penultimate cell, e.g. in Galatians the expectation is that there will be 12.1 sentences with 21 words or more.

No. of words in Sentence	No. of sentences in						
	Eph.	Phil.	Col.	I Thess.	I Tim.	II Tim.	Hebrews
1–5			9.1		17.2	14.2	
6–10	15.8	29.9	9.0	17.2	19.1	15.7	58.7
11–15	16.0	16.9	9.7		17.9	16.7	74.4
16–20	9.8	10.2		18.9	18.6	13.3	41.4
21–25	7.5		16.2	12.1	14.5		25.7
26–30		11.8				17.3	15.7
31–35	9.4		10.2				11.3
36–40				7.3			7.1
41–45	5.8	9.4	5.7		11.7		–
46–50	15.6						10.0
51 or more		7.7	6.1	10.4			17.8
Total No. of Sentences:	79.9	85.9	66.0	65.9	99.0	77.2	262.1
Chi squared	3.85	2.69	4.26	1.07	2.17	2.28	12.22

Table 14.4 (continued)

Degrees of Freedom	4	3	4	2	3	2	6

Notes:

The omission of an entry means that a cell has been amalgamated with the next to preserve the minimum number of occurrences in each cell.
Hebrews shows a statistically significant difference from a log normal distribution but the Davies coefficient suggests the use of log scales.

---

four are the differences between the entries in column three and this figure of 1.053. Up to the tenth cell the differences are the amount by which log $(M + c)$ exceeds the entry in column three, after that they are of the amount by which the figure in column three exceeds 1.053. This should be borne in mind, and perhaps marked on the table, for reference at the next stage.

A useful check can be made at this point for if the correction c is right then log $(Q_1 + c) + \log (Q_3 + c) = 2 \log (M + c)$. The values from the sentence length distributions are $Q_1 = 6.05$, $Q_3 = 15.09$ and M is 9.70, when c is added these become 7.64, 16.68 and 11.29. Taking logs we have $0.883 + 1.222 = 2.105$ which should be equal to $2 \times 1.053 = 2.106$, which is as it should be when allowance is made for the rounding off of the last figure. The log standard deviation is given by the equation log standev $= 0.741$ (log Q_3 — log Q_1). For I Corinthians the log standard deviation is $0.741 \times 0.339 = 0.251$.

The fifth column is obtained from the fourth column by dividing each value in the fourth column by the log standard deviation, in this case dividing by 0.251.

The sixth column is of entries read off from a statistical table. The table, to be found in almost any book of statistical methods and in all sets of statistical tables, is of the area of a normal distribution; it is given in units of the standard deviation and is most often labelled 't'. The last column was a conversion of differences into units of the standard deviation of the observations and so this column is in the desired units of t. The tables of t run from 0.00 to 3.00 or to 3.99 in the larger sets. Corresponding to 2.55 for t we read 0.49461. This has to be subtracted from 0.5000. The reason for the subtraction is that the tables are of half a normal distribution; the distribution is completely symmetrical and it would be a waste to print two identical sets of entries in a table, but when $\log(L + c)$ is less than $\log(M + c)$ then the figures from the tables are subtracted from 0.5000, when $\log(L + c)$ is greater than $\log(M + c)$ then the figures are added to 0.5000. That is why it was earlier suggested that some indication of the changeover point might usefully be made in the column. Thus the first entry in the column is 0.005 (0.5000 — 0.495) and the last entry is 0.988 (0.500 + 0.488).

The seventh column is obtained from the sixth column by successive subtraction of the entries. The area up to $t = 2.59$ is 0.005, the area up to $t = 3.59$ is 0.023, so the area equivalent to the cell 3.63 is $0.023 - 0.005 = 0.018$, the third cell has an area of $0.059 - 0.023 = 0.036$, and so on.

The seventh column contains the expected values of the log sentence length distribution which are obtained from the sixth column by multiplying each entry by 555, the number of sentences in the whole distribution. As the first entry is 0.005, the number of sentences in the first cell would be less than five and so it has to be taken with the next cell as sentence of one or two words.

The final column is a record of the observed numbers of sentences in I Corinthians, and the final stage of the calculation is to carry out a chi squared test between the last two columns. The result is that chi squared is 21.74. The number of degrees of freedom is three fewer than the number of rows, for two extra degrees of freedom have been used in fitting the data to a new mean and standard deviation. The result is that chi squared is 21.74 for 21 degrees of freedom and so p is near to 0.45. The sentence length distribution of I Corinthians can be fitted to a log normal distribution.

Table 14.4(b) shows the expected values for the sentence length distributions of the epistles calculated for log normal distribution. Only one of the New Testament epistles, Hebrews, cannot be so fitted; the epistle has too few long sentences for a log normal distribution. As log normal distributions are defined by their mean and standard deviation, Table 14.5 gives the log mean and log standard error of the log mean for all the epistles. In this table Hebrews is included though it is anomalous. The answer to the second question posed at the beginning of this chapter is that all the Pauline epistles can be fitted to a log scale. The statistics are set out in Table 14.5.

The comparison of the data for linear and log scales shows how little depends on the choice of scale in the Pauline epistles. Romans, I and II Corinthians and Galatians form one group and the others are separate from it. In the linear scale there is an anomaly in the third quartile of II Corinthians and this might be due to chance. The table has five statistics for five epistles and one 5% difference is likely to appear in it, for it might turn out to be some indicator of the emendation of this text. Wake has erected a firm foundation. It has been his misfortune to endorse an unpopular view of the origins of these epistles.

Further testing takes two divergent paths. The first step is to look at some frequent words in preferred positions, Table 14.6, for these are independent of sentence length but not of punctuation. The first column of Table 14.6 shows how many sentences in each epistle have the

Table 14.5   The statistics of the sentence length distributions of the Pauline epistles on a log scale

Epistle	Log Mean	Standard error of Log Mean
Romans	1.031	0.015
I Corinthians	0.984	0.012
II Corinthians	1.097	0.022
Galatians	1.025	0.021
Ephesians	1.288	0.045
Philippians	1.150	0.040
Colossians	1.230	0.047
I Thessalonians	1.248	0.047
I Timothy	1.103	0.038
II Timothy	1.080	0.037
Hebrews	1.187	0.017

conjunction *kai* as their first word. Again, the four major epistles are a consistent group, chi squared is 5.45 for 3 degrees of freedom, but when this group is compared with all the others taken as another group chi squared is 12.5 for 1 degree of freedom and so p is less than 0.001. Similar

Table 14.6   The occurrence of some frequent words in preferred positions in the epistles of the Pauline corpus

Epistle	No. of Sentences in epistle	K1	D2	G2	E1
Romans	498	22	85–147	116–144	32–48
I Corinthians	555	28	122–210	74–103	42–64
II Corinthians	273	18	49–73	57–76	49–73
Galatians	166	3	46–59	28–35	14–21
Ephesians	80	11	9–11	5–19	0–4
Philippians	86	8	15–27	8–12	3–13
Colossians	66	8	1–5	5–6	4–4
I Thessalonians	66	5	14–15	19–23	1–1
II Thessalonians	35	3	10–11	6–6	0–2
I Timothy	77	3	12–24	7–14	4–4
Hebrews	262	36	40–70	61–91	8–19

Notes:

K1 denotes an occurrence of *kai* as the first word of a sentence,
D2 an occurrence of *de* as the second word,
G2 an occurrence of *gar* as the second word and
E1 an occurrence of *ei* as the first word.

In the later columns of the table the first figure is the number of occurrences in the preferred position, the second the number of occurrences in all positions.

results follow from each comparison within the table, except that the forming of one group of all but the major epistles means that the occurrence of the particle *de* as the second word of sentences is the same for both groups, but within the remainder group there are differences which are highly significant.

It can reasonably be argued that it is illogical to count the occurrences of *kai* as a first word or *de* as a second word in sentences which have only one word, or that the word *amen* is not really a sentence. Such adjustments will not affect the results, nor does counting the proportion of occurrences in the preferred position to the occurrences in all positions, leaving out of all consideration the number of sentences in which they appear. The data supplied by these tests takes the odds which sentence length distributions left as odds for Pauline authorship of around a hundred to one against up to over a million to one against.

The second step is to show that none of these results depends on punctuation. The author and a colleague have published a paper[1] in which the occurrence of the most frequent words is recorded, using other words as markers; for example the occurrence of *de* is counted between successive occurrences of *kai*. These occurrences were examined over a wide range of Greek authors before being applied to the Pauline epistles and they reinforce the earlier results. The odds against Pauline authorship are astronomical. Paul can be accepted as the author of the group of four which the Germans gave him, Romans, I and II Corinthians and Galatians. Philemon is too short to permit any useful testing but there is no reason to deny it to Paul. The other epistles are either isolated (Ephesians, Philippians and Colossians) or are in pairs (I and II Thessalonians, I and II Timothy). Titus is so short that any conclusion about it must be tentative. With a long letter like I Corinthians, it is easy to test for minimum sample size and confirm that any statistically significant difference corresponds to some feature of the text. But when an anomaly appears in an epistle like Philippians, it is rarely possible to test one part of the text against another, so that while one can say with precision that the epistle is not by Paul, assumptions must be made about the unknown author which stand on a much less secure footing than those about Paul, simply because material exists on which one hypothesis can be confirmed but does not exist for the other.

Romans and II Corinthians present another kind of problem, indeed two kinds of problem. It has long been suggested that Romans has been altered by revision of its first and its last two chapters. There is textual evidence of copies in which the ending came not only where it now does but after chapter fourteen and also after chapter fifteen. Testing these parts against the whole does support the view that the start and finish of the epistle are not Pauline. If all the positional distributions, nearly forty

[1] S. Michaelson and A. Q. Morton, 'The Spaces in Between', *L.A.S.L.A. Revue*, 3, 1971.

of them, are compiled for all words which occur thirty times or more in Romans, and these are compared with the similar distributions of I Corinthians, then the differences accumulate in chapter one and again a little later in chapter three. It would seem that Romans is a genuine Pauline letter adapted from one addressed to another party, at a time when the possession of a letter by Paul would bolster the Roman claim to primacy after the fall of Jerusalem.

II Corinthians is a different matter, a letter compiled from parts of at least two other Pauline letters. There are some very slight traces of emendation, mostly in chapter one, but the important question is whether or not chapters one to nine and chapters ten to thirteen are from two separate letters. If these latter chapters are taken as a sample they appear Pauline, but if a cusum chart is made of the sentence lengths of II Corinthians and of Romans, a neat demonstration can be made with them. The superimposition of II Corinthians and I Corinthians shows that the last four chapters of II Corinthians are a Pauline letter which has lost about 8 – 10 sentences from its start. If that number of sentences is transferred from I Corinthians, the two charts are very similar. Romans on the other hand looks like a Pauline epistle which has acquired some 6 – 8 sentences in its first chapter.

The weight of evidence accumulated about the authorship of the Pauline epistles is impressive. So far, attempts to counter it have involved special pleading, but each piece of such pleading further complicates the simplicity which alone would commend the traditional position. If you assume all fourteen letters are by Paul and any difference must have an explanation which shows that special circumstances applied to modify the pure Paul, then you are really in the same position as the Ptolemaic astronomers who argued that all the planets followed the sun round the earth. Every discrepancy needed another complication to be added to the theory, until it collapsed under its own weight and it was at last conceded that the sun was the centre of the system and not the earth. The defence of Paul as the author of more than four major letters has already produced some fine examples – an assertion that Paul's writings alone cannot be measured in a unit of sentences, another that his experience on the road to Damascus can be proved to have been an epileptic fit by the different styles in which he wrote. The most salutary experience for the advocates of such refinements is to look at the historical records and see what has been attributed to Paul and why. They might well begin with the museum in Tarsus which showed the boots in which Paul walked the Mediterranean world or the Italian village which had on display both skulls of the Apostle, one as a man and the other as a boy. Many traditions last a long time for reasons other than verity.

15 The Shakespeare Problems

The last chapter began with a note on the special problems of dealing with sacred texts. Usually some theory of the origin of these texts is presented in a form which is almost impossible to test, and any evidence which might seem to make such a theory unlikely is at once turned into further proof that it is true. Some people believe that the Bible is true in the sense that, when the version authorised by King James seems to say that Moses wrote a book which described conditions which existed some centuries after his death and even describes his own funeral, all this shows is that among his other gifts Moses numbered prophecy.

The text of Shakespeare is taken as sacred by many people. Not because the author is inerrant or prophetic, simply because he was evidently a genius and so cannot have been a common playwright but must have belonged to a social group more given to genius than playhouse people, and so the name is but the pseudonym of a member of the aristocracy from whom such works can be more reasonably expected. The attraction of the theory is that it puts the student on a level with Shakespeare himself. As much as you want to unravel the mystery, and reveal the true identity of the man, by the same measure did he wish to conceal his identity, leaving clues only for those as percipient as he was. So have been generated the silly Shakespeare controversies, the attempts to prove that the works were by Bacon, Oxford, Marlowe or some other suitable person. The most interesting aspect of the silly Shakespeare problem is that twice at least it has led to fundamental contributions to knowledge. The first is fully described by C. B. Williams in his book, *Style and Vocabulary*.[1] Williams actually recovered the work of T. C. Mendenhall who had in 1887 and 1901 written two papers on the subject of stylometry. Although lacking modern statistical methods, Mendenhall had grasped some fundamental principles and counted the number of letters in the words of large portions of Shakespeare and of Bacon. This showed that while Shakespeare has a peak usage among the four letter words, Bacon had a peak usage among the three letter words. Mendenhall's second paper looked at a number of writers and showed that J. S. Mill had a peak at two letter words, most writers had a peak in the three letter words but Marlowe as well as Shakespeare was a four letter word man. To some it seemed as if Mendenhall had laid the ghost of Bacon but raised the spectre of Marlowe. But this is hardly so; the proponents of Bacon merely asserted that in adopting the manner of Shakespeare he naturally adopted a

[1] Griffin, London 1970.

184

different set of habits. Every difference between Shakespeare and Bacon will only demonstrate the skill he used to assume another identity.

The next development is surely one of history's finest examples of serendipity. In the United States a prominent Baconian took on some assistants to unravel the ciphers which concealed in the text of Shakespeare the identity of Bacon. He took on a Russian immigrant, William Frederick Friedman. In the work he was commissioned to do, Friedman hardly succeeded; he finally published a demolition of all such ciphers[1] in a witty exposition of their inadequacy, but he continued his interest in ciphers, went on to publish some very important papers in decipherment and enabled the United States to read the Japanese codes in use during World War II. Few people can rival the claim to have had such a decisive effect on the outcome of the war than the eccentric who started Friedman on this fateful journey.

It is therefore not proposed to show that someone else wrote Shakespeare, partly because the claimants are literally endless but mainly for the reason already given, the more evidence that is produced,

Table 15.1   An examination of *Pericles*

(a) Some frequent words in preferred positions

Word and Position		Occurrences in *Pericles*				Chi squared
		Acts I, II		Acts III, IV, V		
a	FWS	29	150	32	199	0.01
and	FWS	66	217	100	305	0.33
as	FWS	18	67	13	66	0.96
but	FWS	25	63	38	99	0.01
for	FWS	25	88	20	92	1.07
if	FWS	13	37	26	50	1.69
in	FWS	8	104	13	117	0.73
it	FWS	8	81	8	74	0.01
	LWS	15	81	9	74	1.19
no	FWS	3	24	13	42	2.74
of	FWS	9	140	18	172	1.60
that	FWS	23	98	40	171	0.01
the	FWS	17	260	24	375	0.01

Notes:

FWS denotes an occurrence as the first word of a sentence.
LWS denotes an occurrence as the last word of a sentence.

In Acts I and II there are 29 occurrences of *a* as the first word of a sentence, 131 which are in other positions.

[1] W. F. and S. Friedman: *The Shakespeare Ciphers Examined*, Cambridge University Press 1957.

Table 15.1 (continued)

(b) Some frequent collocations

Collocation	Occurrences in *Pericles*		Chi squared
	Acts I, II	Acts III, IV, V	
and	217	305	
fb *a*	1	6	—
fb *the*	7	6	0.82
as	67	66	
fb *the*	2	2	—
by	41	34	
fb *the*	12	6	1.38
in	104	117	
fb *a*	3	5	—
fb *the*	20	16	1.25
it	81	74	
fb *is*	5	5	0.01
of	140	172	
fb *a*	4	8	0.65
fb *all*	9	6	1.46
fb *the*	11	9	0.88
the	260	375	
fb adjective	39	65	0.46
to	200	200	(Sample of
fb verb	121	84	200 occur-rences, Poisson distribution, no significant difference.)

(c) Proportionate pairs of words

a/(a + an)	17 150	14 199	1.95
all/(all + any)	47 54	41 53	1.57
no/(no + not)	24 96	42 125	1.92

the more it will be asserted that it proves the opposite of what it normally would be construed as doing.

The serious problems in Shakespeare concern the unity of some of the early and late plays. It has been argued that some of these are either based on sources which have been imperfectly digested, or that a collaborator had a hand in their composition. The simplest of these problems is *Pericles* (1609). Whatever the reason for the difference, scholars seem to

Table 15.2   A simple comparison of Shakespeare, Bacon and Marlowe

(a) Some frequent words in preferred positions

Word and Position	Occurrences of words in samples from		
	Shakespeare	Bacon	Marlowe
a	349	113	92
fws	71	3	2
and	522	193	359
fws	166	21	20
but	162	48	66
fws	53	13	20
of	312	197	207
fws	27	–	–

(b) Some frequent collocations

Collocation	Occurrences in samples[1] from		
	Shakespeare	Bacon	Marlowe
and	522	193	359
fb *a*	7	3	2
fb *the*	13	3	8
of	312	197	207
fb *a*	12	16	6
fb *the*	20	29	33

Notes:

1. Samples are:– Shakespeare: *Pericles*; Bacon: Essays 1, 2, 22, 23, 40, 41;
Marlowe: Acts I and II of *Tamburlaine*, 1587; *Faustus*, 1590; *Jew of Malta*, 1590.
(There is no statistically significant difference within samples of each author.)

be agreed that it depends on the contrast between Acts I and II on one hand against Acts III, IV and V on the other. Another reason for looking at *Pericles* is that, to judge from the introduction to the New Cambridge *Pericles* edited by J. C. Maxwell, the arguments have a distinctly theological cast; they depend on an unprovable hypothesis. 'Shakespeare's hand is present and predominant in Acts III-V, but scarcely if at all detectable in Acts I and II.' This type of assertion bears the hallmark of the theologian. It nowhere states its initial assumptions; it asserts there are large differences between parts of the play but does not say what they are or where they can be found; the scale of measurement runs from a hand present and predominant down to its being scarcely if at all detectable. However the hypothesis has one testable aspect; if it is correct, there should be some obvious differences between Acts I and II and Acts III, IV and V. The appearance of such differences will not prove the hypothesis but it will confirm that it has some foundation and further comparisons with other plays will soon show its validity.

In testing a play written in English, sentence length distributions are unlikely to be helpful. In the first place sentence length in English is very variable. In the second place there are stretches of rapid dialogue exchange and narrative within the text which will further complicate comparisons based upon sentence length. In the third place the metrical patterns of parts of the text will affect the sentence length distributions, not as prominently as was the case in Homer but perhaps enough to make comparisons with the material in *Pericles* rather unenlightening. If no other resources existed, these handicaps would be overcome or avoided by a suitable choice of words and the examination of their positional distributions. But there is no reason to choose this more complicated comparison when material exists to enable preferred positions, collocations and proportionate pairs to be looked at. The data for *Pericles* is set out in Table 15.1.

It can be quickly summarised; in all of the comparisons there is no statistically significant difference. Some part of this may be due to the literary form suppressing differences between authors who use it but it is very simple to show that both Bacon and Marlowe show very large differences from *Pericles* in the same comparisons. (See Table 15.2.)

This evidence does not prove that *Pericles* is by Shakespeare, but it does suggest that a hypothesis which predicted that large differences would appear is facing a challenge. If the differences do exist and so show a difference of authorship, these scholars would do us all a service by saying what they are and testing them on a range of samples and authors.

16 The Inimitable Jane

A first encounter with stylometry tends to produce a reaction which reveals the character of the critic as much as the nature of the science. To one type of critic it seems that stylometry is saying that we are all slaves to our habits. To another it says that we are all different from each other, that no two of us share precisely the same habits of speech and writing.

Those who resent stylometry as an intrusion or complication in life tend to follow predictable paths even in their objections. Stylometry is nonsense, they will assert, because they know that they are quite different from what they used to be and they speak and write quite differently on different occasions. In reply, one points out that some things no doubt change but other things do not, and the foundations of stylometry are habits shown not to change under the circumstances of the particular problem being investigated.

A rather more serious and sophisticated objection is that a person who tries hard to imitate another will at once succeed in being unlike himself and also like the other. This might be so; in the absence of evidence speculation can range unhindered. That is why this chapter looks at a case of such an imitation, an example which can hardly be bettered – the completion of an unfinished work by the inimitable Jane Austen of the complex style and biting wit. The artefact is *Sanditon*, a novel Jane Austen began on 27th January 1817 and left off on 18th March. She died on 18th July of that year. She left part of the novel complete and part in summary. As the publisher says of the imitation, 'A long time admirer of Jane Austen's novels, fascinated by the mystery of *Sanditon* decided to try her hand at completing it – following the clues laid down by the author and writing in a style modelled on her. The result is a romantic novel imbued with the delicate satirical humour for which the original author is famous.'[1]

A comparison of this kind raises a number of questions, but not all of them can be resolved in the compass of one set of comparisons and a single chapter. Attention is limited to two main questions. The first is the relation of Jane Austen's writing to the counterfeit: is it easily detectable by stylometry or not? This question involves an assessment of the relation of traditional literary analyses of style to the science of stylometry. Jane Austen has been the subject of a number of stylistic studies, notably in the introduction to the Oxford edition of the novels by R. W. Chambers and a chapter in *Jane Austen and Her Art* by Mary

[1] *Sanditon, a novel by Jane Austen and Another Lady*, Peter Davies, London 1975.

Table 16.1   A comparison of Jane Austen and The Other Lady

| Habit | Occurrences of the Habit in | | | | Chi squared | |
	Sense and Sensibility	Emma	Sanditon (Jane Austen)	Sanditon (The Other Lady)	(a)	(b)
_an_	25	26	11	29		
_a + an_	172	212	112	112	1.40	12.85
_a_	147	186	101	83		
P.B. _such_	14	16	8	2	0.20	3.92
and	253	299	151	154		
F.B. _I._	12	14	12	1	2.45	6.84
the	270	271	229	221		
P.B. _on_	11	6	8	17	1.58	8.45
F.W.S.	22	26	19	8	0.43	6.34
this	32	39	15	15		
this + that	126	144	52	37	0.25	3.64
with	59	74	28	43		
with + without	77	84	38	47	5.02	3.71
very	37	68	26	27		
P.B. _the_	4	2	3	7	—	12.7

Notes:

1.) The samples are:

Sense and Sensibility	— Chapters 1, 3.
Emma	— Chapters 1, 2, 3.
Sanditon, Jane Austen	— Chapters 1, 6.
Sanditon, The Other Lady	— Chapters 12, 24.

2.) The figures for chi squared are for the comparison of the three genuine samples, (a), and then for the comparison of these samples taken together for the comparison with The Other Lady, (b).

Lascelles.[2] A reading of these studies shows that no single element of the stylometric analysis is mentioned as a characteristic of Jane Austen. This is natural in critics who wish to discuss what is personal to her, and not what she has in common with all other writers of English prose, but in doing this they completely overlook the characteristics which will select Jane Austen from the others.

The primary question is settled by Table 16.1 which shows a simple

[2] Oxford 1966.

comparison of samples from *Sense and Sensibility* (1811), *Emma* (1815) and the genuine portions of *Sanditon* (1817) with the imitation *Sanditon* (1975).

In one sense The Other Lady is to be congratulated. In many features of the author she wished to copy she has made an excellent imitation. The one which strikes a pupil of Scottish schools is that Jane Austen did what they are warned to avoid, the use of *and* following commas, semi-colons and colons. This habit has been reproduced with some precision. But even with the deliberate limiting of the samples to small sections of the text, it is easy to see that the imitation is not Jane Austen. To argue that Table 16.1 shows an accurate imitation which differed from the model only by chance variation is to endorse a proposition for which the probability is less than one in one thousand million.

It would be nice to be able to follow up this investigation with the complementary one, by finding the identity of The Other Lady and looking to see if the imitation differs in any respect from her normal composition in a stylometric analysis. But without some clues to limit the search to a number which can be examined with the resources available, nothing can be done. Any readers who consider that they know the answer to this problem should first carry out some comparisons on the basis of Table 16.1 and then send the results to the author.

To judge from experience in legal cases and with police officers, the comparison of original composition with what is produced when the writer is trying to imitate another person is not likely to be simple. Officers in this situation tend to produce something which is by no means a free composition in a new style but rather a pastiche of phrases copied from the model and others supplied by themselves. In the limited number of cases where it has been possible to investigate the relation of an imitation to the person who created it, about all that can be said is that usually the result resembles its creator much more than it does the model, at least in stylometric details.

If a highly literate lady is so unsuccessful in hiding herself in Jane Austen, it does suggest that police officers are unlikely to succeed in their attempts to fabricate and that critics who assert, on no better grounds than their feelings, that they can alter their habits beyond recognition are not likely to be correct when speaking of the complex set of habits which stylometry uncovers. To change spots is difficult for more than the leopard.

17 A Word from Baker Street

The applications so far described have all been serious, at least in the scholastic connotation of the word. But not all of life is earnest and there is no reason why the techniques described should not be used for enjoyment as well as enlightenment, for fun as well as lending weight to a thesis.

The most famous solver of problems was Mr Sherlock Holmes. Like all great men he has his detractors and his imitators. Stylometry would have been a subject to meet with his warm approval, and it might be that among the papers which Dr Watson threw aside was an outline of the principles of stylometry, an outline which that medical man would have been in no position to appreciate.

A tribute to the memory of Holmes is the band of disciples who still practise his art, who still investigate the circumstances of his life and work. Two such students of Holmes are Austin Mitchelson and Nicholas Utechin. Nicholas Utechin has been for some time connected with the journal dedicated to the cult of Sherlock Holmes. He is recognised as a skilled imitator of the style of Holmes as preserved in the reports of Dr Watson. When the two collaborated in some further adventures of Holmes, *The Earthquake Machine*[1] and *Hellbirds*[2], it seemed to offer a challenge which could not be resisted. If two recognised authorities on the style and matter of Sherlock Holmes combine to produce an adventure to be issued as coming from him, is it possible to tell one from the other and both from Holmes? As Nicholas Utechin has written other things, can it be shown either that he can be replace his natural habits with those of Holmes or that, in spite of every effort to conceal his own habits and replace them with those of Holmes, he has failed to do so?

In fact two experiments were made. One was a full-scale detailed examination of the habits shown by all three sources.[3] The other was a simple study designed to show that the principles of stylometry are such as to enable a useful decision to be made in the best Holmes manner using a few sentences based upon a few words.

The most frequent word in English is the definite article *the*. Is it possible to tell the two collaborators from each other and from Holmes simply by looking at some aspects of the occurrence of *the* even in samples of a few thousand words? The experimenters had been told that

---

[1] Belmont Tower Books, New York 1976.

[2] Belmont Tower Books, 1977.

[3] To be published as a research paper, by the author and some colleagues including Nicholas Utechin.

Table 17.1   The Case of *The Earthquake Machine*

Habit	A	B	Holmes	Utechin
Occs. of *the*	210	180	350	316
1. p.b. *of*	38	11	36	48
%	18.1	6.1	10.3	15.2
2. p.b. *on*	4	17	14	6
%	1.9	9.4	4.0	1.9
Occs. of *to*	62	55	188	101
3. f.b. *the*	17	4	21	32
%	27.4	7.3	11.1	31.7

Notes:

The samples used were as follows:

A *The Earthquake Machine* pp 9–13; 166–171; 202–206.
B *The Earthquake Machine* pp 63–68; 108–112.
Holmes: *A Case of Identity* by A. Conan Doyle.
Utechin N.: 'The Villages Perche', *Blackwood's* magazine (March 1977, pp 251–257).

one of the authors, A, had written some sections of the book and so the remainder of *The Earthquake Machine* had necessarily been written by the other. To represent Holmes the story, *A Case of Identity*, was used. Finally a paper written by Nicholas Utechin for *Blackwood's* magazine,[1] 'The Villages Perche', was used to represent him.

In Table 17.1 are set out the three habits used in the examination. A differs from B in all three habits, A differs from Holmes in numbers one and three, B differs from Holmes in the second habit. Utechin shows no difference from A but differs from B as from Holmes. A must therefore be Utechin, although the lack of any difference between him and A is no positive proof, he must be either A or B and B does differ from Utechin.

This light-hearted demonstration would not be acceptable in any situation in which a rigorous proof was required but it is interesting to note that a full-scale investigation, taking into account all the factors of sample size and periodic effects, comes to exactly the same conclusion, that when perpetrating a counterfeit which a number of people well qualified in literary criticism regard as being very like Holmes, neither imitator can reproduce the habits of Holmes which are of value to the stylometrist nor can he apparently suppress his own habits.

Another useful aspect of this experiment is to ask people to decide the identity of A or B by the inspection of a list of words. In the list are all the

[1] *Blackwood's*, March 1977.

words which occur five times or more in one author but not at all in the other. The suggestion made as the lists were shown was that, as these words had appeared at least five times in one author but not at all in the other, it seems reasonable to suppose they are more frequent in one than the other. So if we take a third sample from one or other author, then we should have a clear indication of authorship because the words in one list were much more frequent than the words in the other. The lists were

(1)	(2)
Certainly	*Almost*
Every	*Away*
Extraordinary	*Because*
Few	*Either*
Through	*Yes*
Together	
Too	

Shown the lists, the majority of those who knew Utechin personally chose him as the author of list (1), which is correct, but when his *Blackwood's* article was listed it had 15 occurrences of words in list (1) and 13 of those in the second list. This shows how totally misleading vocabulary studies can be. It is not what we do not know that causes us to remain ignorant, it is what we assume that we know when we do not know. In the resolution of cases of disputed authorship a feeling for literature is not without value but it comes a long way after a few well chosen experiments.

18 Let Justice Be Done

In all applications of stylometry so far described nothing much has been at stake except the interest and judgement of the few people who are concerned about the problems. It is possible to conceive some situation in which academic advancement and reward depend on a correct decision made upon stylometric grounds, but it is only in such exceptional circumstances and by such indirect influences that historical applications of stylometry affect the lives and property of ordinary human beings.

This is not the case with the application of stylometry to legal problems and legal statements. Upon the resolution of such things depends the liberty, the fortune – even the life – of individuals. This lays upon the practitioner of stylometry grave responsibility, considerable financial pressures and an additional burden which comes from trying to import into a legal system, built upon challenge and confrontation, some of the calm and reservation of scientific knowledge. It is soon found that all parties to the disputes want you to say much more or much less than the evidence suggests and it is wise for you to say. However, the practical difficulties of operating in the legal system are no reason for refusing to help where so much depends on help being available.

The first surprise which the stylometrist receives in entering the world of trials is that many cases are decided on the bitterly contested evidence of two or more police officers who assert that the accused said something which he denies ever having said. According to a practising solicitor, half the cases in the London Crown Courts come down to such simple confrontations. This is possible only in England or in countries such as the United States or Canada which have followed the English system. Under such circumstances the course of a police investigation is to question a suspect and keep a record of his replies until he is charged. Then a more formal procedure is followed. It may be that the accused writes out his own statement or that he asks an officer to write it for him. In either of these cases, the accused will sign each page of the statement and it becomes the record of the conversation and will be almost impossible to challenge at a later stage in the proceedings.

Statements of this type rarely cause difficulties but, when they do arise, they are quite extreme. In the case of Timothy Evans, an illiterate labourer who made two such statements, it is difficult to see how he could have verified a record which he could not read without trusting that the police were reading out to him precisely what they had written down. And this record was to hang him by reason of a series of damaging admissions which he always denied having made. His later exoneration was an official repudiation of the statements but came rather late to benefit Evans.

But the common cause of trouble is the statement signed by one or more police officers, as a record of what was said, and which the accused has refused to sign. When this comes to court the accused will argue that he did not sign it because it was misleading or untrue, and the officers will contend that it was neither.

Before going on to say anything about the creation and use of statements, it may be helpful to give some idea of the scale of the problem. It is quite unsafe to use as a measure the number of instances in which a statement is disputed in court. People do tell the truth and come to regret having done so. But in a twenty-year period, the English Home Office released 70 people who had been wrongfully convicted. The society, 'Justice', which offers help and advice to accused and convicted people, had in its files rather more cases, 93, which were closely parallel to those conceded by the Home Office to be mistaken but in these other instances no miraculous concatenation of circumstances had brought the injustice to light. These figures are a small proportion of the cases which go through the courts but if the cases are classified then a rather more disquieting picture emerges.

Most cases have some physical, circumstantial or other kind of evidence to convict the accused. In the marginal cases wher either identification alone or an admission by statement alone, constitutes the whole case against the accused, the possibility of error is so large that the Court of Criminal Appeal has recently issued instructions than no one should be convicted on uncorroborated evidence of identity. Those who have been so convicted are having their cases reviewed and most have been released. It seems reasonable to suggest that by a parallel argument no one should be convicted on the sole evidence of an uncorroborated confession. This has long been the case in Scotland, where confessions have always been treated with great reserve. If you say to a Scottish officer that you have murdered your wife and thrown the gun into the canal, this will be admissible as evidence that you knew she had been shot and where the gun was hidden. But confession in Scotland is taken in itself to be evidence only of your state of mind at the time you confessed. There is good psychological reason for being sceptical of confessions.

To be admitted in England a statement has to be voluntary, in the sense that it has not been made in fear of some prejudice or hope of advantage, and it must comply with the Judges' Rules. The relevant part of these Rules for the stylometrist is the one which says that what is to be recorded is the actual words of the accused, not some tidy version of them. The actual wording is, 'In writing down a statement, the words used should not be translated into "official" vocabulary; this may give a misleading impression of the genuineness of the statement.'[1]

[1] Rule I (c).

To this rule it is not difficult to find some notable exceptions. From almost every statement the hesitations, repetitions, allusions, digressions, oaths and all other signs of speech are absent. In fact a statement is an edited summary of what took place. Material judged to be irrelevant is omitted. The Judges' Rules specify the method to be used in editing, namely the words attributed to the accused shall be his as he spoke them. It is not enough to record that the accused strongly denied the suggestion when what he said was, 'I did not f...ing, b...ing do it.' This means that it is quite simple to compile a totally misleading statement which conforms to the Judges' Rules in every respect. It can be done either by asking questions, recording the answers with complete precision and then changing the questions so as to alter the meaning of the answers given, or by putting both question and answer into a framework which completely changes their significance. In this connection it is interesting to note that the average police statement in England contains between three-quarters and nine-tenths of the words of the officer recording the statement, yet is entitled 'a statement by John Smith' whose contribution to the statement may be very small indeed. When the statement is read out in court, the jury must be greatly influenced by the matter which is supplied by the officer and which will be used to interpret the admission.

The pattern of police statements raises some primary questions. Officers keep a record in a notebook; they use it to type up their versions of the interview and so one finds 4128 words in one statement and 4127 words in another, the difference is that where one officer typed 'don't' the other had 'do not'. Yet these two statements are taken to be independent accounts of the interview. In any historical enquiry such an assumption would be so simple minded that it would disqualify the historian from serious consideration. Not only historians will object to this method; experimental psychologists have long since shown its fallacious nature. A number of experiments, carried out in circumstances much more favourable to accuracy than the routine of a police station, have shown that agreed versions of what was said in an interview are much rarer, and vary much more, than the regular productions of the police. It cannot be argued that it is their training and experience which produces this desirable result, for in Scotland any number of police officers giving evidence about the same thing is regarded as one officer. It was a Scottish judge who said that it would be unsafe to convict on the uncorroborated evidence of six policemen. All police statements are adjusted to agree. So in Scotland statements are only admitted when corroborated. If this rule was extended to England the rate of conviction would drop, the courts would become even more overtaxed than they now are but fewer people would be wrongfully imprisoned.

Another point made by the psychologists is that it is not possible for one person to make an accurate record of what another has said in the convention outlined in the Judges' Rules. There is between the two parties to the statement a conflict of interest. By the time incriminating statements are taken the atmosphere is hostile, the officers are applying all the pressures they can to induce a confession; they will be pretending to knowledge they do not have; they will be suggesting troubles and complications which might arise if cooperation is not forthcoming. In this situation mutual misunderstanding is almost certain, and some deliberate misunderstanding will be a weapon of the interrogator; these misunderstandings will be recorded and can be almost impossible for the accused to remove from the record. Even at best, the two parties have different viewpoints and interests and so a series of questions and answers, for example, will have different connotations for both and the record will be interpreted quite differently by them.

It might seem that little can be proved about any police statement. The possible causes of distortion are so many and so powerful that there might seem little prospect of any test of the validity of a police statement. But this one rule, 'use the words of the accused', is the key which turns the lock. The hinges on which the door then swings are that the foundation of stylometry is the occurrence of trivial habits which no police officer thinks is having any significance. So if he is honest, and most of them are, he writes down what the accused said and this can be shown to have been the case, or he writes down something else and this can be shown not to be the words which the prisoner would have used. The one surprise in all this is that the distortion which looms so large for the psychologist is of little consequence for the stylometrist. Presumably, because the distortions concern meanings and associations, they do not penetrate to the deeper levels of habit and it is these which produce the habits on which stylometric tests are based.

Turning to the treatment of a statement, or a set of statements, the first essential is to obtain from the accused, preferably through his solicitor, a summary of what his allegations are. This is not as easy as it sounds; few prisoners are of high intelligence and most of them are disturbed characters who tend to incoherence in thought and speech as well as action. In most cases the accused seems to feel that stylometry is a kind of magic by which words wrongfully attributed to an accused will leap out of the page. He needs to have the principles of stylometry explained to him so that he can appreciate that it is only when he has underlined all the words wrongfully attributed to him, that testing can begin. The next complication is that most prisoners and lawyers have little conception of scientific method; they not only assume that a large enough fee will produce the advocacy they require; they will even include, in the category of rejected text, genuine words spoken by the accused in some mis-apprehension that this extension of the sample will help their case. Even when it has been explained to them that they must underline only words which they are sure they did not speak, and you have told them that there is not enough evidence to support any conclusions, they will suggest that words spoken on another occasion to a different officer should be added to the sample and that a fee commensurate with the added complexities will compensate. Offers and payments are very different things when dealing with the accused persons.

It is soon borne upon anyone dealing with criminals that they are basically untruthful, unreliable and very poor credit risks. If the author's experience is any basis for generalisations, then five out of six accused persons are completely irresponsible and totally reckless in making charges against other people when they think it will be in their own interest to do so. The kind of experience which enlightened the author was the receiving of a set of statements with a request to read them over and then get in touch with a Queen's Counsel. On doing so he was told that this was a case in which his assistance was essential. Some years before a man had been accused of murder; he had been tried, convicted and sentenced to life imprisonment. A couple of years later an informer told the police that they had sentenced the wrong man. They arrested, tried and convicted the right man and when the first accused went to the court of appeal, the judges decided that the officer who recorded the confession which was the sole evidence against the accused, might not have realised that the accused had been a little drunk at the time and had, as a consequence, misunderstood what the accused had been trying to say. The officer concerned had a record of bullying people into confessions which most of them later tried to retract. Now another man was being charged with murder and the only evidence was an incriminating statement made to this officer.

In vew of the importance of the case, and the adequate resources available, statements were obtained which had been made by this officer over a period of six years in a number of different cases. The results of the testing would have been immediately fatal to the defence. The police officer was consistent in all his habits throughout the period, he was clearly to be distinguished from all the accused and the present accused was, in his confession, completely himself. The news was greeted with a shrug of the shoulders by both accused and counsel. It had apparently been worth trying as a defence.

Another case was of a West Indian who was convicted although the confession which implicated him contained only 200 words allegedly spoken by him. Nothing in it could have reached any level of statistical significance, yet all that it contained of the West Indies was a phrase or two which was about as genuine as the cry of 'gay Paree' in the mouth of the music-hall Frenchman.

So one begins with a hypothesis but attaches no weight to it until some evidence comes to support it. The first step is to get photo-copies of all the statements with all the disputed passages clearly underlined. One typical trouble with statements is that they have page numbers and these differ in the copies used by defence, prosecution, records office and clerks of the court. This confusion is fertile ground for an aggressive counsel. It is easy to feel that a violent quarrel about page numbers is a childish matter but the counsel sees his duty as to destroy your evidence and authority and to confuse the jury. A muddle about page numbers is a good place for him to begin. The author used the letters written to him by an accused man as evidence but abandoned the practice after waiting a whole day for the correspondence register of a prison to be brought to court. The fact that the letters were written on prison notepaper and signed by a warder was not enough. The letters are now used only as supplementary test material.

The provision of authentic material to represent the accused usually takes one of two forms. A statement made by him in another matter, or best of all, another statement made by him to the same officers, will eliminate problems of literary form. If evidence of this type cannot be produced without complications, then the accused is asked to write an essay on any neutral subject – 'What I would do if I won a fortune on the football pools' or 'My Schooldays'. Any subject but the law, the trial or the relation of the accused to the examiner.

The next step is to size the material. If you have two thousand words or more of the accused which he rejects, then the omens are favourable but this will not happen often as it would require the complete fabrication of the accused's contribution to a statement of anything from six to ten thousand words. In many cases a sample of one thousand words will be adequate but with less than that complications are to be expected. In samples of around one thousand words of English, there should be 10–15 habits which occur often enough to test. If the two samples are from different people, then about one third of these habits will differ by a statistically significant amount. But the number of tests, and of those likely to show statistically significant differences, will fall as the square root of the sample size. This means that samples of 500 words will have only half-a-dozen habits which are testable and only one or two can be expected to differ by a statistically significant amount.

With small samples, samples of less than one thousand words of running text, there arises the other complication due to the adversative form of the law courts. In a court of law it is not possible to put forward any sensible qualification of an argument; it must be black or white. With large samples and a correspondingly large number of statistically significant differences, you can assert that there is a difference in author-ship. But in the situation where little evidence is likely to appear and that little does appear and it favours the accused, a situation in which it is reasonable to say that you have before you the officer and the accused, and some evidence which suggests that the statement is not completely representative of the accused, look at the parties with some caution. It is simply not possible to say this in a court of law; atmosphere and convention are against you.

All evidence in court is open to challenge but the challenge is so mechanical as to be meaningless. If your qualifications are recent, you are inexperienced; if they are long standing, you will be out of date. If you command a high fee, you are in it for the money; if your fee is reasonable, you are not worth much; if you don't know what you will be paid, you must be unbusinesslike.

In theory, the expert witness in England is the servant of the court. He is supposed to be exempt from the conditioned reflexes of opposition and the questions are designed to bring out the nature of his evidence and the explanations which might be advanced to account for it. In any actual trial, he will be accused of all kinds of intellectual incompetence and misdemeanours, have motives of greed and conceit attributed to him and come away rather consoled by the knowledge that to earn his living he need not behave like counsel in court. It must be said in the plainest language that giving evidence in court is an ordeal that no one should go forward to without weighing the likely consequences. It seems hard that any person wrongfully accused must rely for his deliverance on people who are prepared to sacrifice themselves and undergo an ordeal which at best can only be mildly unpleasant and at worst be degrading, but that is the convention in which the courts operate.

Naturally all preparations must be meticulous, the originals of all papers preserved, numbered and indexed. It is a first duty to ensure that valuable evidence is not buried under a barrage of questions about titles, dates, or page numbers.

But there are cases in which the stylometric evidence is decisive. One such case is set out in Table 18.1. In this table T2 is the set of genuine utterances of the accused. Included in it are a statement made to a police officer and written down as it was made, another written by the officer after some days, and personal letters written by the accused and a very large statement made to the same officers in connection with another part of the case and accepted by all parties as completely accurate. T1 is the confession which the accused made.

In the first examination 40 tests were made; 25 of them showed statistically significant differences between T1 and T2 after having been shown to be entirely consistent in all parts of T2. The list was reduced to 25 tests of which 11 were statistically significant simply to rule out any word-class which would allow counsel to confuse the issue by raising irrelevancies. For example, if a preposition is defined to be a word on a given list of prepositions and all of them function as prepositions, then counsel can do little. But if the list contains *after* as a preposition and there comes an occurrence of 'he looked like the morning *after*', the question arises, as we saw earlier, as to whether this occurrence of *after* is to be counted as a preposition. It does not matter in the least in any instance, for such occurrences are very rare and will not affect the results. But counsel will use the possible difference (he would not count this as a

Table 18.1   Some habits of an accused in accepted texts (T2) compared with those texts which he rejects (T1)

Habit	Occurrences of the habit in		
	T1	T2	
1. *a*	42	273	
pb preposition	8	115	
%	19.0	42.1	
2. *have*	31	69	
fb verb	7	37	
%	22.6	34.3	
3. *I*	155	658	
fb *have*	18	12	(T1 has 2 *haven't*, T2, 2 *I've*)
%	11.6	1.8	
4. *it*	54	125	
pb *that*	1	18	
%	1.9	14.4	
5. *me*	34	149	
pb *to*	2	31	
%	5.9	20.8	
6. *me* pb *that*	—	33	
%	—	22.1	
7. *my*	32	91	
pb preposition	4	47	
%	12.5	51.7	
8. *that*	40	415	
fb *is*	8	6	(*That's*: 1 in T1, 3 in T2)
%	20.0	1.4	
9. fb personal			
pronoun	11	196	
%	27.5	47.2	
10. *the*	74	713	
FWS	10	22	
%	13.5	3.1	
11. 2LW	11	41	
%	14.9	5.8	

Notes:

pb denotes preceded by, fb followed by, FWS denotes an occurrence as the first word of a sentence, 2LW an occurrence as the second last word of a sentence. All the differences are statistically significant.

preposition for the rest of the phrase has been suppressed) to convey the impression that the whole subject is full of disputatious definitions and personal prejudice. So it is better to avoid any test in which any possible ambiguity arises, if there is evidence to spare.

Stating that T1 is not the work of the writer of T2 is fairly simple; the differences between them are such that they would arise by chance variation in rather less than one sample in one million times one million times one million times one million times. But this raises two other questions. As we have seen, it is common in stylometry to raise these astronomical odds. It is not easy to convey much meaning for these figures. If the accused wrote ten thousand words a day, for $333^1/_3$ days per year, in three years he would have written $10,000 \times 1,000$ words – 10 million words. If he had written like this for one hundred thousand years he would still have been unlikely to have written a sample with such differences in the measure of being still one million times one million times. These figures and comparisons are almost meaningless.

The other form of illustration, the use of diagrams, is worth consideration and one method of this is shown in the Appendix.

On the subject of trials and legal statements, only two things remain to be said and both come under the head of preparing for the worst while hoping for the best. In preparing data, imagine yourself to be a cheat, think how you would falsify the data and then adopt some preventive precaution. Have all your calculations checked by another person. Then when you are accused of cheating, a matter of simple routine to many counsel, you will be ready to explain how your procedure differs from that which the cheat would adopt.

The main assault on your evidence will not be directed at the data or its interpretation. You will be accused of destroying the career of a police officer who has a wife and children to support and destroying the confidence of the body of men who stand alone against the tide of barbarism. All you can do is keep pointing out that you have not fabricated any statements, that most officers are honest and it is important that those who are not should be shown to be so. You must also point out that you are not making any accusation against an officer; psychologically the more frequent distortion is not the deliberate fabrication but that human hunger to hear what we want to hear. This distortion is unconscious, and the more dangerous for being so.

How much good has been done by the knowledge that fabrication is now detectable we can only guess, but one police station in London has completely changed its practice and brought it into conformity with the Judges' Rules.

The innovator of forensic stylometry faces one great problem; his best material – both in the sense of being the most interesting to read and the most useful for research – is confidential. As a scientist he would like to make the evidence available for all to see, but as an expert witness he must not do so. Nothing must be published from which the source can be identified unless permission has been given. For example, the important demonstration that one senior police officer had been entirely consistent in his habits over a number of years and a variety of cases is of primary scientific value but it cannot be made public.

The English Home Office will not recruit outside experts; what cannot be done by their staff is not done. Apparently a problem which confronts them is that of anonymous letters in serious crimes. It took the author some time to credit the claim that when a gruesome murder has been committed people will write letters of twenty pages, letters which betray guilty knowledge but which are not of any use as they cannot be matched to the statements which the police have taken but written out in their own hand. It seems that an application to examine a classic case in which all the protagonists are long since dead would not be looked on with sympathy by the Home Office.

It is perhaps as well that no details of most of the criminal cases can be published, for the recital of the bare facts and the repetition of the statements made would strain the credulity of the most willing reader. The case which established the legal precedent in England came to the author at the end of 1974 when a letter asking for help arrived from Steven Raymond who was, as he put it, confined in a prison of stone by a tissue of lies. My reply was that although willing to help anyone in distress it did not seem possible that I could do so. A statement was surely an edited summary of what had been said and its validity does not depend on how it has been phrased. This reply received a sharp answer; all such statements were, by the Judges' Rules, made in nothing but the accused's own words.

To show that the words attributed to him were unlikely to have come from him would destroy the prosecution's case. In Raymond's case there were 11 police statements containing words attributed to him. Seven of these statements he accepted as genuine, four he rejected as fabricated. The genuine material ran to 2,200 words; what he rejected amounted to 1,100 words. He had heard that it was possible to prove the authorship of texts and had written to a number of people prominent in different disciplines seeking help. He had secured a professor of mathematics who was willing to say that he could not consider the accepted and rejected texts to have come from a single source. He had then been told that he would need some kind of expert to authenticate his expert. Applying to the Association for Literary and Linguistic Computing he had been given the author's name. The stylometrist's view of a case is very odd. He gets copies of a few selected statements and some parts of others.

He must not discuss the case with any witness or interested party. So, when he reads that a police officer says that an accused will be charged with some offence, he has no way of knowing if he was so charged, or if this was one gambit in the exchange between the officer and the accused.

This problem was a simple one in outline. Steve Raymond admitted speaking or writing 2,200 words and denied having written or spoken another 1,100. By one of the happy coincidences which seem so sinister to the legal mind, the two letters he had written asking for help contained 2,200 and 1,100 words, or totals within five words of these figures. So there were five samples of 1,100 words which were genuine and a sixth sample of 1,100 words which was claimed to be spurious. At that time neither the author nor any colleague knew of any techniques in English studies which could prove this. Their recourse was to convert for use in English the techniques which they had been using for many years on Greek texts. Some features would convert quite simply. In all languages sentences come in three parts, according to Aristotle's principle that all works of art have a beginning, a middle and an end. The beginning of a sentence is a highly conventional structure which warns the listener or reader that something is about to be uttered and the relationship of the new material to the old material is of a certain kind. Then follows a free construction which is the middle of the sentence. Finally, preparation is made to round off the sentence and this is another conventional structure. So at the start and finish of sentences you will find some words which occur very frequently in a narrow range of positions, first words or second words, last words or last-but-one words. A number of tests of authorship can be based upon the occurrence of these frequent words in their preferred positions. The main complication is that the proportion of occurrences in such positions changes with literary form, particularly the change from continuous prose to dialogue. Also common to both the inflected and uninflected languages are pairs of words which have no other common feature than the link between them.

The difference between Greek and English is that in Greek word order is very free and words can occupy a wide range of positions within a sentence; in English word order is much more restricted. So the range of movement is important in Greek and gives a sound base for positional stylometry, but in English the most characteristic feature is immediate context which is most easily measured by recording the next word.

So the evidence in Raymond's case was a set of preferred positions, some collocations and some proportionate pairs. There were eleven habits which occurred often enough in the samples to be tested and by one of these happy coincidences not only were all eleven consistent within the accepted texts, and differed by a statistically significant amount in the rejected texts, but many of them were simply illustrated for a jury. The layman could see that Raymond only used the word *no* as a measure of quantity, e.g. '*no* time' or '*no* money'. But in the disputed statements this word always stood first in the sentence and introduced a damaging admission. Criminals and politicians have a special language and neither of them replies to a question with a simple admission, both start with non-committal introductions and only say anything specific when they have become quite sure of their ground. On this evidence the accused was found not guilty of all charges in which the disputed statements were cited. The legal precedent had been established with some success. But some aspects of the case are less than satisfactory. The evidence was laid before the prosecuting counsel in court and the proceedings were adjourned for ten minutes to allow him to absorb the opinion and the evidence on which it was based. This could only be fair to a counsel who was highly numerate. That it was unfair to the advantage of the accused is some consolation, but there are circumstances in which it could be very much against the interests of justice.

Raymond got a short sentence for other offences. Some weeks after the trial he wrote a letter of thanks and asked if any payment was due. The reply was that just over twenty pounds had been spent on his behalf and if he was in any position to repay this amount it would be acceptable. Raymond then dropped out of sight. In April 1976 the BBC were running some interviews on aspects of the law which seemed to require emendation and, when they came to statements, it was suggested that he might usefully appear. He could not be traced. A few weeks later the reason became obvious. According to the report in the *Daily Telegraph* of 22nd April 1977 Raymond, who was alleged to have been involved in the famous Heathrow Airport strongroom theft in June 1976, was in custody in Zurich.

One aspect of this case which has turned out to be quite typical is that the accused is a person with some criminal record and some criminal acquaintances. There is no case known to the author of an innocent bystander being framed by the police. The difficult cases all involve people with at least guilty knowledge. Some of them appear to have been charged in the hope that they will establish their own innocence at the expense of another party. But if this bluff fails then the police are in the unpleasant position of either proceeding with a slender case, dropping it, or improving it as best they can. To sharpen up a statement is one way of improving evidence without leaving too many traces of the action.

A forensic stylometry could be very useful. But it may be that the existence of the science will be enough to prevent abuse of the confession and the statement. It has been a standing temptation to the officer whose case is not quite complete to adjust it a little, but as soon as he comes to realise that such alterations can be detected he will find the attendant risks too great to run. This is as well for two reasons. The first is that while the adversary system of justice, under which all evidence is first examined for its virtues by one side and then probed for its weaknesses by the other, is probably the best system available, it does not really work with expert witnesses. They are called because they have knowledge beyond the skills and experience of the court. This means that they cannot really explain why they have reached their conclusions unless the jury happen to be highly intelligent. They may disagree with other experts on issues which do not really affect the value of their evidence but only another expert will fully understand that this is the case. So cross-examination of expert witnesses is not very well done in the majority of trials. The whole value of scientific evidence, that it is independent of the observer, is lost in the contention which seeks to make of the expert a wise man or a fool. Success for an expert witness is to carry conviction, not to solve a real problem in a scientifically elegant and efficient way.

The second reason is the difficulty in creating a scale of fees which would be necessary if the use of stylometry were to become frequent. Most expert witnesses are professionals who have acquired their useful knowledge in the practice of their profession and so charge a fee which reflects only the time and trouble taken by the isolated examination. A doctor whose education has cost a great deal of money and who uses expensive instruments can charge a fee which ignores these things, and reflects only the day or two of his time which he might have had to devote to his work on the case. But stylometry is not yet taught, it has only very recently become teachable. So the stylometrist must create his own qualifications. Then he must guess at a fee which is some balance between his expenditure of time and effort and the resources of the client. He must face the great difficulty that his examination will be almost complete before he can make even a useful guess at the outcome of his investigations. So if he were asking for fees, it would only be on the basis that he could offer no advice until the money was spent. As the great majority of claims are spurious and made with no sense of responsibility, he would then have to try to collect his fee from a client who has been told that his expert opinion is not going to help him, indeed whose opinion may be quite fatal to the claim.

It is not a promising situation in which to work. But it seems rather defeatist to say that in no circumstances will any action be taken until a conviction has been made and evidence appears that it was wrongfully made. To act only as a consultant on appeals is hardly satisfactory. The real answer is to change the conventions of offering statements in evidence. Forensic stylometry would then be a branch of historical studies and all the better for that.

Conclusion

Looking back, the development of stylometry is easy to see. De Morgan was the first to point out the pattern of argument which should be used in stylometry, statistics would describe samples and sampling differences would become the measure of similarity or difference. But to suggest that something might well be true and to show that it is true are two different propositions and it was a long time before anyone actually developed a statistical test of authorship. It should have been done by Udny Yule in his book, *The Statistical Study of Literary Vocabulary*,[1] but he made an unfortunate error in calculating the standard errors of sentence length distributions with the result that it was not until W. C. Wake corrected the error and continued his study of sentence length distributions of Greek authors in 1946 and 1957 that a reliable test was established.

With the pattern of argument confirmed, attention then turned to what should be counted and analysed. Like all his colleagues, the author spent some time looking at those features of style which literary critics had noted and used as the basis for their judgements. This was making stylometry the conversion of stylistic description into quantitative terms; it was using the accumulated experience of scholars as it had been expressed in traditional forms. This proved to be an unexciting quest. In some cases, for example the suggestion of Sir Kenneth Dover that the number of finite verbs used by a writer of Greek prose might be an indicator of authorship, it turned out to be valid but required samples impracticably large for any New Testament application, and in others it soon became clear that the observations had no firm foundation in any objective data. It was the realisation that in Greek writing position was of prime importance that gave stylometry its first general theory. That such a theory was justified was confirmed when a dramatic plea for help with a police statement written in modern English posed a problem which was rapidly solved by an adaptation of positional methods to the constraints of an uninflected language. In Greek where word movement is free, look at word movement and position; in English where word movement is restricted, look at immediate context.

There is so much material available that routine applications of stylometry will present few problems. What remain intractable are problems of mixed tests where one writer has been revised by another or other situations in which the homogeneity of the text is in doubt.

[1] Cambridge 1944.

Immediate progress seems likely to be made in two directions. Both concern the efficiency of methods rather than the further development of methods. A simple way to increase the separation of two authors is to combine a number of tests in multi-variate statistics. Properly done this will generate figures which show vast differences where such exist, although the differences are diffused throughout a number of statistics and are nowhere to be seen as clearly as the measure of their combined effect.

The difficulty is that multi-variate statistics can conceal the underlying features and in some instances lead to confusion or misapprehension. One such set of statistics showed the differences between brands of cigarettes and showed very large differences. But a study of the statistics which were combined in the analysis revealed that the largest differences concerned the packing and the printing on the packets. While this might be useful for anyone designing a machine to select brands and sort them automatically, it was much less useful for any smoker who wanted to know about the quality of the cigarette.

The other development which is easy to forecast is the formation of profiles of individual writers so that quick reference and resolution of problems will be possible. One way of doing this is to start with a set of collocations. It might be that after *and* a writer is very fond of using *the* and hardly ever uses *so*. This can be made a test of how often *the* after *and* occurs compared to *so* after *and*. The combination of a few such tests based upon the personal maxima and minima of an author will soon provide a measure by which he can be detected in a large number of candidates.

The ultimate aim has been set by the information theory experts who, many years ago, calculated that in any 200 words, written or spoken, there was enough information to enable their author to be picked out of the human race. This is like saying that every cubic mile of sea water contains twenty tons of gold; it may be there but getting it out is not easy. But the aim must be to be able to say of any couple of hundred words, it is or is not the sole production of the person who produced this other sample. It may seem that we are a long way from being able to do so, but how much nearer we have come in the last twenty years. Who will say that the next twenty years will not produce the desired result?

Appendix
The Illustration of Statistical Data

It has often been said that one picture is worth a thousand words – many people would go on to add that it is worth ten thousand figures. People much prefer a picture to a table of figures. This is so obviously true that there must be good reasons why statistics are so rarely illustrated. There are. The two main reasons are that the scale of any diagram can be so manipulated that from the same figures quite different pictures can be drawn. One is familiar with the astounding growth of the share prices selected by some person willing to share his knowledge for a fee and how it shrinks if the scale is made more realistic. The second reason is that for the comparison of statistics the standard errors of the statistics or some comparable indication of the amount of chance variation to be expected in the statistics must be included. This brings with it the complication that for low rates of occurrence standard errors become useless. The standard error of a mean of zero is zero.

Having entered these two caveats, it is only fair to say that a diagram can illustrate a set of statistics in a way which no table can do. The form favoured by the author is modelled on a clock face. The reason for this is that the history of the clock suggests that this is congenial to humanity. Suppose we decide to illustrate Table 16.1. In the rejected texts (T2) 19.0% of the occurrences of a are preceded by a preposition; in the accepted texts (T2), 42.1%. Before much use can be made of this information it is necessary to calculate the standard errors of these two statistics. As they are binomial in form this presents no difficulty, and for T1 it is 6%, for T2 5%. The definition of a standard error reminds you that nineteen samples out of twenty will lie within a range of two standard errors of the sample mean, so that for T1 they will lie between 31.2% and 6.8%. For T2 they will lie between 47.1% and 37.1%. If a line is drawn (see Figure A) which has a scale marked on it, a scale running from zero to 100%, then on one side of the line, say the left side for T1, marks can be made at the two limits. Similar marks can be made for T2 and it will be clear that the two samples do not overlap as they would do if they belonged to a single population. The line which they are drawn to straddle can be thought of as the hand of a clock. This means that anything from four to twelve pairs of statistics can be put on the one diagram and a synoptic view of the whole pattern seen at a glance. This is one reason why eleven statistics were chosen, with one position for the scale; the radial lines were exactly as the hours of a clock face. In court there were two other similar sets of statistics. The diagrams were drawn on

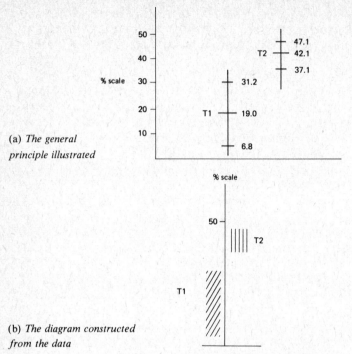

(a) *The general principle illustrated*

(b) *The diagram constructed from the data*

Figure A   The illustration of statistical data

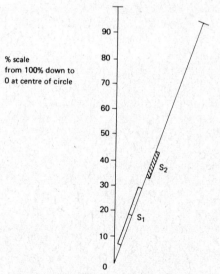

Figure B   How the comparison of two sets of a statistic is made by putting the sample statistics along a set of radial lines

transparent sheets and in colour. By simply laying one diagram on top of another the situation was dramatically illustrated. The accused was quite unlike his confession but the officer who recorded the confession resembled it closely.

The principle is shown left in Figure B. In the figure, S1 and S2 are the same statistic for two samples as above. S1 ranges from 31.2% to 6.8%, S2 from 47.1% to 37.1%.

Glossary

The following terms are used in describing the application of stylometry. They are fully described in earlier chapters of the book, but it may be useful to have them listed together.

The terms are grouped into the three main divisions of the subject: descriptive measures, such as averages; the selection and use of samples; the distributions to which observations conform.

The glossary covers the following terms:

Arithmetic mean	Minimum sample size
Average	Mode
Binomial distribution	Negative binomial distribution
Block sampling	Negative exponential distribution
Decile	Ninth decile
Distribution	Normal distribution
First quartile	Percentile
Frequency distribution	Poisson distribution
Geometric mean	Population
Heterogeneous	Random sampling
Homogeneous	Range
Log distribution	Sample
Log mean	Sequential sampling
Log normal distribution	Serial correlation
Mean	Spread sampling
Median	Standard error
	Third quartile

1 AVERAGES

The word **average** comes from the Latin word *havaria* which was the compensation paid out after a shipwreck. Money was paid on the number of jars or boxes in the cargo, not on the value of their contents. You got money calculated by taking the number of boxes or jars you owned and dividing this by the total number of boxes or jars in the cargo. Averages are now more complex but retain the basic idea of giving a simple figure to represent, in some useful sense, a whole set of objects or observations.

There are a number of different types of average. The usual one is the **arithmetic mean**, often simply called the **mean**, calculated by adding all

215

the values and dividing the total by the number of values (e.g. the average height of three people, one five ft., one six ft. and one seven ft. tall, is $5+6+7=18$ divided by 3 to give a mean of 6 ft.).

The **geometric mean** is used for things such as sheets of paper or houses which go up not in equal steps but in equal proportions. If the areas of three sheets of paper are 'a', 'b' and 'c', then the geometric mean is 'b'

$$= \sqrt{(a \times c)} \text{ for } \frac{a}{b} = \frac{b}{c} \quad \text{so } b \times b = a \times c$$

(e.g. if the three sheets were 4, 8 and 16 square feet, the geometric mean would be 8 square feet).

The **log mean** is used for a set of values which are proportional, but not in the simple regular steps of paper sizes or floor areas. In sentence lengths some writers write long sentences which increase in proportion, and for that reason the number of words in each sentence is replaced by the logarithm of the number. All the logs added together and then divided by the number of observations gives the log mean.

Averages are measures of central tendencies. They are useful because they describe data and do so in a way independent of the quantity of data. The average height of ten men should be much the same as the average height of ten thousand men.

There are other measures which have similar characteristics. One is the **median**, the value which divides the observations into two equal groups. If the observations are divided into quarters, then the first division comes at the **first quartile**, the second at the median and the third at the **third quartile**. As with the mean there should be no change in these measures brought about by increasing, or decreasing, the number of observations.

If the observations are divided into ten equal parts, these would be called **deciles**, if into one hundred equal parts, **percentiles**. The only such division in common use in stylometry is the **ninth decile**, the point below which lie nine-tenths of the observations and above which lies one tenth of the observations. The ninth decile is a useful measure of the proportion of large or long items without having the complications brought about by isolated extreme values. For example, a writer may produce sentences with more than two hundred words in them but do so very rarely. The ninth decile of his sentence length distribution will give a better measure of his long sentences than the **range**, which is the difference between the largest and smallest values among the observations, for the range will be greatly affected by the presence or absence of a single giant sentence.

Averages are often misunderstood and completely unrepresentative. An average is useful when it describes a feature of all the observations and this usually means that it complies with three conditions:

1. Some observations are average.
2. Many observations are near to the average.
3. Few observations are far from the average.

The arithmetic mean applied to human height meets all three conditions; applied to salaries or bank balances it would meet none. In such circumstances another form of average should be used.

One other useful measure of central tendency is the **mode**, the value which is found most often in the observations.

Averages are often completely misrepresented. 'This teacher is a poor one; half the children in her class have marks that are below average.' If the average is the arithmetic mean, then half the children are almost certain to be below average and half above it. 'If expenses claims exceed the average, they will be rejected.' This turned out not to mean that half the claims were rejected, but that less than ten percent of the claims, which were very much above the average, were to be questioned. 'In my opinion an intelligence quotient of 100 is very low.' But intelligence is measured on a scale of which 100 is the average. Is this a claim that the human race is not intelligent enough? These are examples of the common confusions which surround averages when the term is used without regard to its statistical meaning.

The **standard error** of a statistic is a measure of the uncertainty attached to the value given for the statistic. For example, the standard error of the mean gives a figure of which it can be said that nineteen samples out of twenty from the sample population will have means lying within a range of two standard errors above and below the sample mean. Standard errors are large in small samples, small in large samples.

2 SAMPLES AND SAMPLING

A **sample** is a small group selected from a larger group, called a population, according to a set of rules. The rules constitute the sampling method.

A **population** is a large group from which samples are taken to provide information about the population.

a) *Sampling methods*

The basic sampling method is **random sampling** in which every observation in the population has an equal chance of being selected for the sample.

Spread sampling is used to give a picture of a large set of observations by taking, for example, the first sentence on every left-hand page. Spread sampling provides equal numbers of observations from equal sections of a text.

Block sampling is used when a sample starts at any given point and continues until the sample is larger than the minimum sample size.

Sequential sampling is a method for looking continuously at the whole of a text and testing it for consistency as the inspection proceeds.

Homogeneous means that all the parts are consistent with the whole. In statistical tests it means that all the samples differ only by random sampling differences.

Heterogeneous means that the samples differ by more than random sampling differences and must be regarded as belonging to different populations.

b) *Minimum sample size*

To yield any useful information, samples must have a **minimum sample size** – a minimum number of observations in them. The actual number varies and is fixed by three factors.

The minimum sample size depends on there being enough occurrences to enable statistical tests to be carried out. For many tests a minimum of five occurrences or an expectation that five occurrences should have been recorded is needed.

If any comparison is being made of samples from two populations, then there must be enough observations to enable the samples to be separated. If two writers employ the same habit, the difference between the levels at which they use the habit must be sufficient to demonstrate a statistically significant difference between them. In other words, writers who resemble each other need larger samples to separate them than would be required if they were quite different.

The third factor is the periodic nature of many events associated with words and their use. In most writers' work long sentences tend to come together, as do short sentences. The minimum sample must include enough of all types to be representative of the writer.

Serial correlation is the measurement of the influence of one observation on the succeeding observation. If a Greek prose writer is likely to follow a long sentence with another, positive correlation is at work. If he is writing hexameter verse he is likely to follow a long sentence with a short one to complete the line. If he does this he is showing negative serial correlation.

3 *DISTRIBUTIONS*

A **frequency distribution**, often abbreviated to **distribution**, is a record of how often observations having specified characteristics occur or can be expected to occur. These are certain distributions which result from specified situations.

The **binomial distribution** arises when two exclusive alternative events can take place, for example when a coin is tossed and the result must be heads or tails.

A **Poisson distribution** is to be expected when a random event is recorded in equal intervals of space or time. If you count the number of phone calls made in one minute, or the number of proof readers' errors on pages, Poisson distributions should be found.

If the occurrence of a random event is recorded in variable intervals, or if it is recorded in equal intervals but the expectation varies from trial to trial, the result may well be a **negative binomial distribution**.

A **negative exponential distribution** is to be expected when random events are recorded not in equal intervals, but are used to mark off the spaces which separate the occurrences. If you count the number of seconds between telephone calls, the results should form a negative exponential distribution.

The **normal distribution** is a familiar bell-shaped curve which fits the occurrence of an event for which the central value is the most common and variations above and below it are equally likely. The heights of human beings, the measurement of intelligence, these result in normal distributions. The importance of the normal distribution lies in the fact that statistics, e.g. means, quartiles and such measures, are normally distributed.

Log distributions

When the observations are proportional, for example when sentences are recorded not in groups ending at 10, 20, 30, 40 and 50 words, but in groups which end at 10, 20, 40, 80 and 160 words, then replacing the values with the logarithms of the values will convert the series into one with equal steps. This is called converting to a **log distribution**.

The most usual one is that used in this book, the conversion into **log normal** form, i.e. the making of a normal distribution by using the logs of the values in place of the values.

Bibliography

Anderson, W. E. K. *The Journal of Sir Walter Scott*, Oxford, 1972.
Bailey, N. T. J. *Statistical Methods in Biology*, English Univ. Press, London, 1975.
Dover, K. J. *Greek Word Order*, Cambridge, 1960.
Ellegard, A. *A Statistical Method for Determining Authorship*, Gothenburg, 1962.
Ellegard, A. *Who Was Junius?*, Stockholm, 1963.
Goodman, R. *Teach Yourself Statistics*, English Univ. Press, London, 1966.
Hoel, P. G. *Introduction to Mathematical Statistics*, New York, 1963.
ICI Research Monograph, *Cumulative Sum Techniques*, Oliver and Boyd, Edinburgh, 1964.
Moroney, M. J. *Facts from Figures*, Harmondsworth, 1956.
Mosteller, F. W. and Wallace D. *Inference and Disputed Authorship*, The Federalist Papers, Reading, Mass., 1964.
Page, D. *The Homeric Odyssey*, Oxford, 1955.
Williams, C. B. *Style and Vocabulary*, London, 1970.
Yule, G. U. *The Statistical Study of Literary Vocabulary*, Cambridge, 1944.

Index

POLICE
STAFF
COLLEGE
LIBRARY
BRAMSHILL